Sole Mates

The True Story Of One Couple's Walk Across America

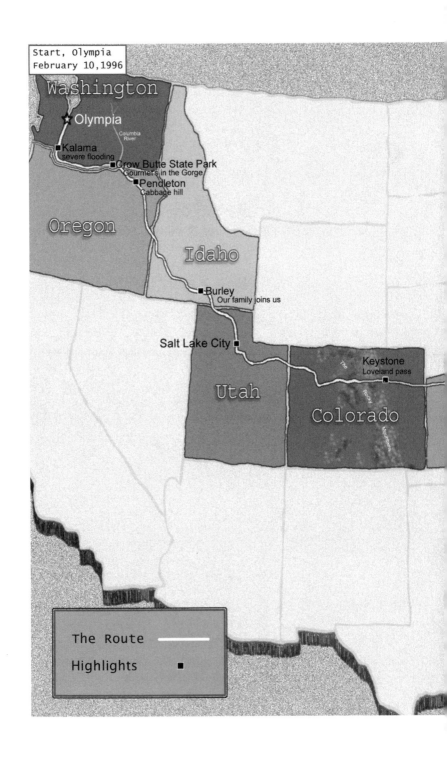

Start, Olympia
February 10, 1996

Washington

☆ Olympia

Columbia
River

■Kalama
severe flooding

■Crow Butte State Park
Gourmets in the Gorge

■Pendleton
Cabbage hill

Oregon

Idaho

■Burley
Our family joins us

Salt Lake City ■

The
Rocky
Mountains

Keystone
Loveland pass ■

Utah

Colorado

The Route ———

Highlights ■

Habitrek For Humanity 1996

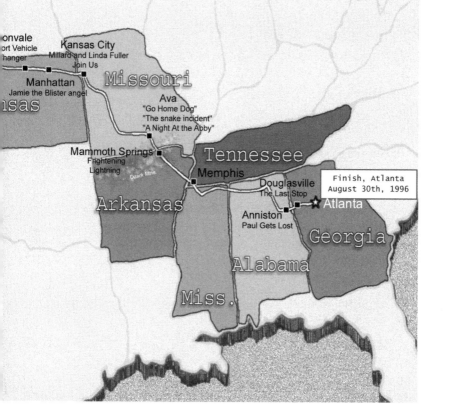

onvale
ort Vehicle
hanger

Kansas City
Millard and Linda Fuller
Join Us

Missouri

Manhattan
Jamie the Blister angel

Ava
"Go Home Dog"
"The snake incident"
"A Night At the Abby"

Isas

Mammoth Springs
Frightening
Lightning

Ozark Mtns

Tennessee

Memphis

Douglasville
The Last Stop

Finish, Atlanta
August 30th, 1996

Atlanta

Arkansas

Anniston
Paul Gets Lost

Georgia

Alabama

Miss.

Sole Mates:
The True Story Of One Couple's Walk Across America
Copyright © 2003 by Jerry and Cindy Schultz

Shiny Penny Press
1435 65th Ave. SE
Olympia, Washington 98501

Book design by:
The Floating Gallery
244 Madison Avenue, #254
New York, NY 10016-2819
(1-877) 822-2500

PRINTED IN CANADA

Sole Mates-
The True Story Of One Couple's Walk Across America
Jerry and Cindy Schultz
1. Author 2. Title

Library of Congress Control Number 2002115150
ISBN 0-9726783-0-1 Softcover

Sole Mates . . . is dedicated to
our large and lovable
family. Without their
devotion, this dream would
have been much more arduous
and not nearly as much fun!

Contents

Acknowledgements

It has taken a village to write *Sole Mates*. You see, we never intended to write a book about our *little* trek. The plan was to document it in journals and with a microcassette recorder, which we did. We planned to describe the passion and the pain as the drama unfolded. When the walk was over, we would put the documents in a safe place and that would be it. We visualized our great grandchildren dog-earring the pages and maybe even feeling inspired to follow in our footsteps. That would be the end. At least that is what we planned.

Soon after we began walking, though, interviews and conversations often led to the same question.

"Are you planning to write a book about your adventure?" Our response was always the same.

"No, that is definitely not something we have considered."

Then on July 19, as we were walking through the Missouri Ozarks, Jerry decided to count the number of steps in a mile. This would distract him from the effects of old sol beating down on him. Cindy would pass the time in silence and prayer. In that prayer, she asked the same question she had asked for months.

"Lord, what should we do, once the walk is over? We have failed to make a plan."

In the silence and beauty of that day, the answer was so loud it seemed to echo right off those green Ozark hills.

"SPREAD THE GOOD NEWS!"

Spread the good news? Cindy was confused. Had she really heard those divine words or was she suffering from heat stroke?

It took 2,640 steps to walk that mile. It took five days to tell Jerry what she had heard. It took much longer for the two of us to decipher that message. We wondered–were we being called to spread the good news about America and her people? Could two ordinary people like us release these folks from the message of mostly hopelessness coming from the evening news? We suddenly got a tiny glimpse of how Noah must have felt. We wanted nothing to do with it. We would just blow this whole thing off real fast!

It wasn't that easy. People continued to ask us about a book. We continued to answer negatively. We couldn't possibly take on such a project. Then we met a messenger whose words we could not ignore.

Virginia Clay volunteered to be our support driver on the last walk day before family would join us to finish the walk. Virginia asked the same question everyone else had asked about us writing a book. For some reason we heard her response differently than the others. Perhaps it was God's last-ditch effort to get through to us?

Virginia explained, "It's been an amazing experience for you. You have a story to tell. I believe the message you heard that day could best be accomplished in a book. You should write it."

That afternoon, an overwhelmed but historically obedient Cindy said a new prayer.

"OK, if this is truly how you want us to spread the good news, please send us the people who can help make this book a reality. We cannot do it alone."

Lucile Torgerson started the ball rolling with her insistence that we create an outline for the eventual book. We did that at Suzie and Jim Bryan's donated condo in Sun River, Oregon soon after we got home. Lucile never gave up on the book or us.

Our friends, Dorothy Johnson and Judy Alford, offered their expertise as English professors. Our words began to spill onto paper. We met Marjorie Skafte at Holden Village Retreat Center when she heard us speak about the walk. She began her own crusade to see our words in print. We were invited to join Bayview Writers

Group a few months later. We bought books on the subject. Publishers' proposals began to take shape.

We contacted Habitat volunteer, Don Compton. He began encouraging us. As a small publisher, he had a lot of good ideas. Then our lives took a few twists and turns and we were stalled for over a year. We were ready to consider the book a misguided idea until we met Bob and Judy McDaniel. Writers themselves, they donated their time and kept nudging us until every chapter was finally written. Bob did the first edit.

There was still work to do, though, and McDaniel's jobs were making their lives crazy right then. That's when we met Marilyn Fallis. She was on fire for this project and donated her time for the second edit, completing it in record time.

Our son, Mark, used his artistic talents to create the cover and maps. All three of our adult children and their spouses gave valuable feedback after reading the first manuscript. So did Kay Chubbuck, Pam and Denny Hardesty and Lucile Torgerson.

With textbooks and journals nearby, the details of the walk have slowly poured out of our hearts and memories. And always these special people and many more have prodded and pried. They've edited and encouraged. We have all prayed. They never gave up on our ability to finish *Sole Mates*, even when we did. They have helped us discover a joy in writing. We cannot thank our "village" enough.

Our hope is that you will be inspired to follow your dreams and risk taking the steps necessary to make those dreams a reality. For it is in the risk-taking that true discovery becomes possible. And there's enough good news in that discovery to last a lifetime!

Foreword

Millard and I first met Jerry and Cindy Schultz when they joined in a 1,200-mile "House Raising Walk" down the east coast of the United States in 1988. We shared sleeping on the same gym floors at night and talking as we trekked along the highways with hundreds of other walkers. That following year, the Schultzes founded South Puget Sound Habitat for Humanity in their hometown of Olympia, Washington. Then, in 1991, we worked together on the same house at the annual Jimmy Carter Work Project in Washington, D.C. Jerry made me laugh with his dry sense of humor and "let me do it" attitude and I came to appreciate Cindy as a "tell me what you need" kind of person.

Soon afterwards, Jerry and Cindy began planning their retirement and came up with an exciting idea…to walk 3,000 miles across the United States from Olympia, Washington to Atlanta, Georgia starting seven months prior to Habitat's 20th Anniversary Celebration. From living with Millard, I was familiar with how seemingly impossible ideas can somehow become reality if we allow ourselves to "think big." Jerry and Cindy were thinking big and had caught the vision of eliminating poverty housing from the face of the earth.

I remember sitting in the back seat of their Suburban as Jerry drove Cindy, Millard and me to some Habitat speaking engagements. We had maps spread all over the place as we helped them plan their ambitious walk and brainstormed a name for it. We decided on Habitrek '96. Also, on that trip, we set the schedule for them to make their arrival in Atlanta at the same time as Millard and I were arriving from Americus with a band of walkers who were walking the 140 miles from our international headquarters in that city. Simultaneously, a hundred bikers would be rolling in from the north. All of us, joined by several thousand others from around the world would celebrate Habitat's 20th Anniversary beginning on August 30, 1996.

In June, Millard and I made time to join Jerry and Cindy for a day of walking through Kansas City, Missouri. This was especially meaningful since it was there that the 10th anniversary of HFHI was held following our 1,000-mile walk from Americus, Georgia in the summer of 1986.

Being back in Kansas City, this time walking with Jerry and Cindy, was great. Members of local Habitat affiliates and the press joined us along the way. A house dedication was an appropriate blessing to end that phenomenal, memory-packed day. On the following morning, we waved good-bye to Jerry and Cindy as these fellow "sole mates" continued their journey.

Sole Mates is a story of ordinary people accomplishing extraordinary things through common day-to-day struggles, dependent on each other and trusting in God to provide strength and basic needs.

As of this writing, in late 2002, Habitat for Humanity has completed more than 130,000 homes in 87 countries around the world for people who otherwise would still be living in substandard conditions. Jerry and Cindy Schultz are two of the multitudes of Habitat for Humanity volunteers who have made this accomplishment possible.

Linda C. Fuller
Co-Founder, Habitat For Humanity® International

The Journey Begins

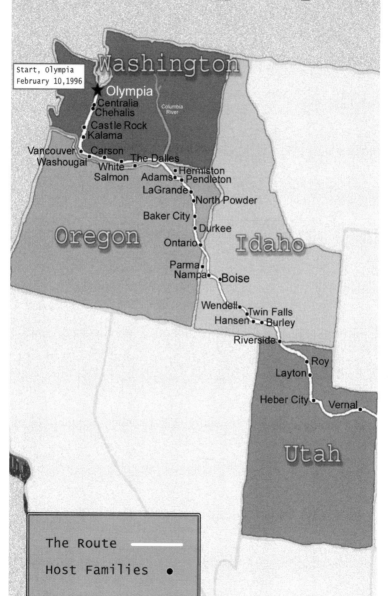

Start, Olympia
February 10, 1996

Washington

Olympia
Centralia
Chehalis
Columbia River
Castle Rock
Kalama
Vancouver
Washougal
Carson
White
Salmon
The Dalles
Hermiston
Adams
Pendleton
LaGrande
North Powder
Baker City
Durkee
Ontario
Oregon
Idaho
Parma
Nampa
Boise
Wendell
Twin Falls
Hansen
Burley
Riverside
Roy
Layton
Heber City
Vernal
Utah

The Route

Host Families

1

It's Not Hard to Go, It's Hard to Leave

Friday, February 9, 1996

Cindy

My nerves are as jangled as our incessantly ringing telephone. I hustle around the house like a Chihuahua on a double shot of espresso. Our departure date has been set for over a year. It seems like all I have done is plan and prepare. I am still in an all-out panic. How can I possibly complete the many tasks that remain? I tell myself to take a chill pill. I choose diversion instead. I pop my favorite Rod Stewart tape into the boom box and finally get a grip. I reach for my very long to-do list and review it. Then I get to work. Slowly, I begin to make progress, checking off each task with a celebratory "YESSSS!"

Jerry, my husband of nearly 32 years, is in our basement garage, making room to store our Suburban and some extra furniture. Our daughter and her husband, Katie and Curtis Bryan, and their five-month-old son Logan, will live here while we are gone.

It is still raining outside. It has not stopped since February 2. Over seven inches of precipitation have fallen since then and now floodwaters have closed Interstate 5 near Centralia, 20 miles south of here. Homes and businesses from Centralia to Salem, Oregon, a stretch of more than 100 miles, have been damaged or destroyed by Mother Nature's wrath. I find myself constantly looking out our picture window toward Lake Susan. I will miss the view. I will not see the first green buds of spring popping out on all the trees that surround our little one-acre lot. The ducks will hatch their young without me to cheer them on this year. The raccoons will bring their nursing offspring onto our deck without my camera flashing in their eyes. I feel guilty enjoying the lake at its highest water level in years while so many people are suffering at the hands of this extra rain.

The phone has been ringing since 8 a.m. Harlan and Betty Bayer, Jimmy Carter Work Project friends, call from Florida to wish us well. Elmer Kellner calls twice from St. Francis, Kansas. He is making plans for our Memorial Day arrival in his town. Jack Wolters calls from North Carolina. He's making sure our support vehicles are in order. Sheilla Snell calls from Habitat for Humanity headquarters in Americus, Georgia. We have worked with her since July, and her support throughout has been strong and appreciated. DeAnn Peterson calls from Birkenstock, Inc. in California to see if we received our prepaid FedEx mailers that we will use to ship our sandals to them for repair. Wayne Hagen calls from KJOY radio in Atlanta. He's making final plans for our weekly live interviews with him.

Interspersed are calls from local friends. Some have concerns for our leaving in light of the flooding.

"How can you possibly leave as scheduled?" some ask.

I patiently explain that we must leave on the tenth. The date of our arrival in Atlanta, August 30, cannot be changed. Habitat for Humanity's 20th Anniversary Celebration will begin that day. We must be there.

We continue to pray for a break in the weather.

Day 1

February 10, 1996

The alarm jars me from a short night's sleep. I listen for the sound of rain even before I open my eyes. I hear birds chirping instead! Hastily opening my eyes, I rejoice at the sunshine filtering through our pleated shades. Many prayers have been answered. We will leave as scheduled!

I snuggle deep down into the familiar flannel sheets, the ones with the blue snowflakes on a field of white. Our long anticipated dream is about to begin. How on earth have I gotten to this day? There were many times during my last 50 years when the thought of walking 3,000 miles across America would have seemed preposterous. When I was 18, my feet would swell so badly that I could not walk across the room. When I was 37 and recovering from a quadruple discectomy, walking one mile was an accomplishment. I steal a few more moments under the covers to remember my childhood, our early marriage, our three children and the wonderful life that has brought me to this moment.

Then the reality of this day jars me back to the present. My sleep-deprived body has no time for additional contemplation. In three hours, Suzie and Jim Bryan will be here to load our luggage. Behind them, our oldest son Patrick, and his wife Kim and our two grandsons Drew and Conner will be here to pick us up.

As I emerge from the bedroom, Jerry is standing over the erupting mountain of luggage overflowing near our front door.

"Is this pillow bag absolutely necessary?" he grumps.

"Yes, it is" I reply defensively. "Absolutely."

We are at a standoff as we stare at the pile before us. There are two large soft-sided suitcases, a huge wheeled duffel bag, my blue canvas briefcase, Jerry's laptop computer case, a medium size suitcase, a small duffel bag, two Treknology Loadmonster suspender packs and the all-important pillow bag. They are all packed as tightly as Bratwurst, ready to burst their casings. "The pillow bag will be mine to carry. Where else could we cut back?" I ask.

It doesn't take us long to realize that our necessities for seven months requires this many pieces of luggage. It will all go into the back of Jim and Suzie's car. We will follow.

Walking out of the comfort and familiarity of our home, we realize the next seven months hold many possibilities for discomfort and no sure promise of success. We anticipate times of great challenge. We pray for times of exhilaration as well. Jerry takes my hand and we walk out the front door toward the unknown. Together, as we have throughout our marriage, we will pursue our dream.

As we step out of the car, the frosty grass crunches under our

Taking our first official steps of Habitrek'96.

new Birkenstocks. We strap on our daypacks. An enthusiastic crowd of family, friends and Habitat volunteers cheers our arrival at Tumwater City Hall. "Good Luck Jerry" and "Good Luck Cindy" helium balloons are tied to our packs as we first stop for group warm-up exercises and then make our way to the podium for the send-off ceremony. Rob Hofstad, pastor and friend for 16 years, is the master of ceremonies. He reads a letter of encouragement from Millard Fuller, president and co-founder of Habitat for Humanity International.

After we say a few words, Rob imparts a meaningful blessing upon us.

Someone hands us the new Habitrek '96 banner and we each take an end. We then take our first steps in what we hope will be a seven-month odyssey. It is a surreal moment that requires no words between us. After years of planning, dreaming and training, we are really on our way to Atlanta.

About 80 friends and family walk with us for the first mile, 40 of those stay with us for the first five miles and 17 hearty souls walk the entire first 20 miles of Habitrek '96 with us. Most of the important people in our lives are either driving one of the four support vehicles or walking with us today. We feel their love through this act. We know most walking days from now on will be spent alone.

Surrounded by family at the February 10, 1996 send-off event.

We appreciate our friends and family who are willing to spend this momentous day with us. It is a day of pure pleasure.

When our victorious group finally walks into Centralia at 4 p.m., we all become silent at the sight of the flood devastation surrounding us. We walk gingerly through muddy streets littered with debris; streets that are not yet open to vehicles.

Finally, our hushed tones are interrupted by the enthusiastic voices of our grandsons.

"Faster, Poppa! Faster!" Drew and Conner beg.

Jerry's face breaks into a grin as he runs with the twin running stroller into George Washington Park. This is his birth and growing-up place. It is fitting that this be the place from which we launch ourselves into an adventure he would never have dreamed of when he was peddling his bike around this town 40 years ago. As it should be, Jerry's childhood friend, Kay Harris, is here at the park with her husband Dale, to welcome us to Centralia. They will be our first host family of the walk.

Now we must say goodbye to the friends who have given up their Saturday on our behalf. Our family, however, is not yet ready to leave us. Kay and Dale recognize how difficult this will be and spontaneously invite everyone over to their house for pizza.

With the smell of pepperoni pizza wafting through the house and amidst enthusiastic chatter about the day's events, a solemn realization slowly emerges. We must begin saying goodbye. Kim quickly suggests that all the "kids" meet up with us next Wednesday. They will drive the 60 miles south of Olympia, retrieve us from our host family's home and go to Dairy Queen in Kelso, Washington for a Valentine's Day treat. These ice cream shops have long been the places we go to celebrate all things important in the Schultz family. We have missed our son, Mark, today, who lives in Los Angeles, and will miss him again on Valentines Day. We are relieved that final farewells to the others will be postponed until February 14.

We will see my brother Paul in Memphis, Tennessee when he joins us for a three-week support vehicle stint in August so we hug without tears. It is my "little" sister Kay Chubbuck I will have the hardest time parting from. We are very close. I will not see her until we return mid-September. Tears of uncertainty dampen our hugs as her stooped shoulders carry her message of concern.

For many months now, there has been uneasiness among friends and family about our undertaking this walk. Their concerns have swirled around us like flakes of snow, sometimes blurring our vision, sometimes coating our plans with a little doubt.

"Are you sure you wouldn't rather ride your bikes?" some would ask.

"What will you do if one of you gets sick or injured?" others inquired.

Loved ones assured us that there would be no disgrace in abandoning the entire venture.

"No one would think the less of either of you," they assured us.

This wasn't true. Someone would be let down. Someone would be very disappointed.

It would be us.

The Face in the Tree

On their last day of warm weather training in Palm Springs, California, in January 1996, Cindy and Jerry complete an 18-mile trek, then relax and luxuriate in Casa Cody Inn's Jacuzzi spa. They discuss their imminent return to the rainy northwest while musing over all that needs to be done in the month before their February 10 departure. The discussion turns to address the struggle Jerry has been going through for the past few months. It's not so much being away from home that bugs him, it's leaving the family that bothers him–being away so long. What if they need him? What about holidays? From time to time these thoughts have caused him to feel melancholy.

Suddenly the conversing stops, and Jerry sits with a fixed stare.

"Do you see anything in that tree?" he asks in a serious, hushed tone.

"No, I don't see anything. What are you talking about? A bird or something?" Cindy replies.

"No," he says. "I see something that looks to be a rustic likeness of Christ in the branches. Come over here and place your eyes near mine. See! Right there! Can't you see the likeness?"

He is pointing into a large leafless tree in front of them.

Cindy sees nothing but branches.

A small turtledove lands on a branch near the spot where Jerry sees the image. It sits for a few seconds and then flies off toward the San Jacinto Mountains. The image soon fades from Jerry's view, and with it, his apprehension about leaving.

2

Hand Grenades in the Day Pack?

Day 2
Monday, February 12
Chehalis, Washington

Cindy

I push open the glass door and enter Trodahl's Market. The floor creaks like it did in the days of my youth. There is a middle-aged man standing behind the counter.

"Mind if I use your restroom?" I inquire with the urgency of a woman who has just walked 10 miles. The man's fixed stare bears no resemblance to the kind-faced Mr. Trodahl I remember. This guy's reply is gruff and more than a little hesitant.

"It's my personal restroom, and I don't usually let the public use it."

He pauses and I roll my eyes. I'm waiting for his quick approval.

"Oh, I s'pose you can use it, but don't be tellin' no one else."

"Well, my husband will need to use it also."

I point between the cigarette posters and the neon beer signs hanging on the window.

"That's him in the blue warm-up suit."

Mr. Sourpuss doesn't care who it is and presses on.

"What's he got in that backpack. . .hand grenades?" he snorts.

"Heavens no, he would never carry hand grenades. Does that Robin Williams look-alike seem like a terrorist to you?"

I'm desperate and he knows it, but the interrogation continues.

"Can't be too careful these days–there's a lot of crazies out there."

His attitude is not entirely surprising. This is conservative, rural Lewis County where just about everybody who has not lived around here in the last 20 or so years is often viewed with suspicion. We have lost our status as locals, and I am afraid I will have to tell him the truth of why we're here begging to use his precious bathroom. It doesn't look like I'll ever get past him otherwise.

"Well, we're about to find out how many 'crazies' are out there because we're walking across America. Twenty miles a day, five days a week. We hope to be in Atlanta on August 30th for the 20th anniversary of Habitat for Humanity. You may not know that Habitat is a non-profit house-building ministry, the one Jimmy Carter's associated with."

I continue my babbling.

"This is only our second day of the walk and so far, blisters are a bigger threat than people. You wanted to know what is in Jerry's Treknology Loadmonster? Well, it's filled with everything he deems necessary to make it through each day, and that's a lot of stuff. Our support vehicle drivers transport the rest of our luggage to a new host family each evening. That is the stuff we use during the day. Now, if you'll excuse me, I really need that restroom."

Finally relieved, I trade places with Jerry after warning him about the chilly reception that he's likely to receive.

"He thinks you have hand grenades in your pack," I whisper.

Jerry

The guy behind the counter puts me in memory of a certain type of rural individual I encountered frequently in my youth that I have struggled to forget. I don't have to like this person. He is treating me like he has more intelligence than me, because he doesn't know me. Well, I am not thinking he is too bright, either.

My memories flit back. He has that rural suspicion that I sensed in the country folk when I was young. City was city and country was country and never the twain–well, something like that.

"Am I carrying hand grenades?"

He had actually asked my wife if I was carrying hand grenades! What a stupid question. If only he knew, of course I am! I want to make sure my daypack is heavy enough to make the walk really challenging and nuclear missiles are not nearly as easy to come by. Asking to use restrooms is one of my pet peeves about places like this. They say their restrooms are not open to the public, or they label them "out of order." Normally, I would have some caustic comment like, "What do you do, hold it all day?" That usually warms them right up. They'll be glad to sell you expensive gas, take your money for their high-priced snacks, sell you coffee or soda, but allow you to use their restroom–no way.

Sorry to digress, but now I have to humbly ask this guy if I can use the bathroom that is not open to the public. I do ask if it is okay, and he grunts something and points the way. He has had no customers the whole time we have been here, yet it seems that we are inconveniencing him. Intuitively, I know we must pay a price for interrupting him.

As I attempt to exit his domain, he nabs me. He comments on how I look and says he finds it hard to believe that I'll be able to walk all the way to Atlanta as worn out as I look already. (Where's one of those hand grenades?) I am not tired. I am not worn out mentally or physically. I am simply stopping for a picnic lunch with friends and needing to use the restroom. This is the second 20-mile day of our walk. We have trained by walking a thousand miles. How can I be worn out at noon on the second day? What am I doing? Why am I even asking myself these questions?

He tells me I am going to have a really rough time because it is uphill all the way to Denver. I waste some words I should have saved for someone with a verifiable I.Q. Where did he get a license to question and throw cold water on my parade? I am mixing my metaphors.

Does he think I am some poor little kid from a large family that might have stopped by his blasted store 40 years ago? I am a mature adult with a wife and a family and a dream. Where is he going with his life? He hasn't moved any further than from one end of the counter to the other the whole time I've been here and he only did that once. His smugness is irritating me. Why am I reacting this way? Why do I react at all? Perhaps it is about the whole trip ahead of us. What can we expect of the people we are going to meet? Will it be like this each time we venture into someone else's territory? Will we be accepted? Not? Labeled? We have progressed one percent of the way. Maybe this guy was a plant. Would there be more?

The best thing I can do is eat the lunch our friends Annie and Larry Wilson have kindly brought for us, elevate my blood sugar and go on with my life.

It is surprising how quickly I put him out of my mind. He was actually right about one thing, though. There was a hand grenade in my backpack and it was pointed directly at me. It was a holdover from my days growing up poor in an area that still can reincarnate a lot of bad memories and reveal more than a few scars.

Cindy

An hour passes quickly with Larry doing Yo-yo stunts and Annie and I making plans for the rest of the day and evening. As I "repackage" my feet, I reflect on how good it has felt to be with longtime friends during the last three days, first with Kay and Dale and now Annie and Larry. Annie and I were best friends when we were in high school and I've known Larry since we were both little kids. I find myself thinking of the old saying about making new friends but keeping the old. Some really are silver and the others gold.

The "repackaging" continues. I dunk one foot at a time into a Ziploc storage bag full of Dr. Scholl's foot powder. Then I wrap lamb's wool strips around each toe, check to see that the molefoam covering the blister is in place. Then I replace this morning's sweat-soaked socks with clean ones.

Rising from the old wooden bench, I poke my head inside to thank the resident grouch before we head down the road. Our word sparring ends when he attempts the knockout punch.

Eating lunch at the "hand grenade" mini mart outside Chehalis, Washington.

"You know that walk yer doin'? Sounds crazy to me. I really doubt you'll make it. You already look winded to me." Pivoting his rotund body, he then disappears into the back room.

Annie and Larry drive two miles ahead to wait. We are walking south on the Old Jackson Highway, heading for Toledo. We are both absorbed in our own thoughts. Jerry breaks the silence.

"What's bugging you, Mar? You've got that clenched-jaw, determined body language thing going."

"Yeah, that guy's parting shot really bugs me. You know how I react when someone doubts my ability to complete something."

"Yep, it makes you all the more determined," Jerry muses.

"Jer, what if he is right? What if we do fail?" I interrupt.

Deep down, I know he could be right. That's what's bugging me.

Shortly, we walk past a very old farmhouse that has been in my memory for as long as I can remember. Standing in the pasture to the south of the house is a lamb. There are probably 50 other sheep in this pasture, but he is closest to the fence that separates us from him. He seems cleaner and whiter than the other sheep. He alone has a red nylon collar around his neck, the kind you normally see on a dog. Being a former 4-H member I comment on him to Jerry.

"That lamb is so clean and calm. He must be someone's 4-H project."

"You are probably correct, but I have to say he's sending me a message and it's one of peace."

Jerry's reply confirms what I am feeling and pushes the storeowner's comment out of my mind.

"The longest part of the journey is said to be the passing of the gate."

Marcus Varro

3

Flooded with Images

Day 4
Tuesday, February 13
Kalama, Washington

It has been four days since we walked into the flood-strewn streets of Centralia. During our weekend in the twin cities we had stared in awe at plastic bags, normally litter on roadways, dangling from trees 20 feet above our heads. We had tiptoed through slimy mud and stepped over logs that littered streets not yet open to traffic. On Sunday, while attending church, the pastor spoke of parishioners whose homes were devastated by the flood and needed the help of anyone who could help. We had pulled our New England overshoes on over our new Birkenstock sandals, borrowed work clothes from Kay and Dale and sloshed into 12 inches of sewer-tainted water to help salvage items from our friend Jan's house. Alongside many other volunteers, we had hesitantly tossed many of her most precious belongings into a huge blue dumpster. On top of carpeting that could be replaced we found baby pictures and antiques that could not. On that day, Jan's appreciation and determination overrode her overwhelmed, yet determined spirit to make the best of a very bad situation. She inspired us to remember these attributes during the next seven months before us.

Once we walked out of Centralia, we walked on higher ground

for a day. Now we are walking through the most flood-devastated area of the Northwest. President Clinton visited this area, 60 miles south of Centralia, yesterday. He had swooped in aboard an Air National Guard helicopter because roads were not open to traffic. He had tromped through the mud wearing knee boots and a plaid flannel shirt. He had come to give hope to the discouraged residents of Kalama and Woodland, Washington as they began the massive cleanup efforts from the worst floods to hit the area in over 100 years.

We have walked past unforgettable images today. A fence intended to keep a white-faced heifer from harm contributed to her execution when the floodwaters propelled her headlong into the barbed wire, leaving her body trapped long after the floodwaters receded. We cannot get the horrible sight out of our minds.

We are able to walk where few can drive, observing up close the fury of Mother Nature's wrath. We briefly stop to watch muddied workers desperately trying to save the Kalama River Bridge from a massive logjam that threatens to destroy it. A few miles later, we see the gigantic mudslides covering the northbound lanes of Interstate 5, evidence of rain-soaked soils on the hill above. Along our route, we see carpets hanging over fences and dripping furniture set out to dry in driveways. We celebrate the sunshine that is allowing folks to dry out their belongings and us to walk in shirtsleeves.

There is heavy traffic on Pacific Highway, where we walk, because of the Interstate 5 closure. We are holding out orange flags to warn motorists that we are sharing the same tight curves they are today. We recognize the danger we face and wonder if we will be able to continue walking, safely and unimpeded, on the back roads Jerry has so carefully mapped out for us.

Our support vehicle driver today is Ray Johnson. This is the first day Ray has accompanied us. Because many of the roads are not open to vehicles, he cannot drive along with us part of the time. He is able to meet us at access points along the way. His kind and caring nature encourages us at the top of steep hills and he offers water and snacks before we realize that we need them. He treats us to lunch at Burgerville in Woodland and drives us to a nearby drugstore for blister repair supplies. The tailgate of his

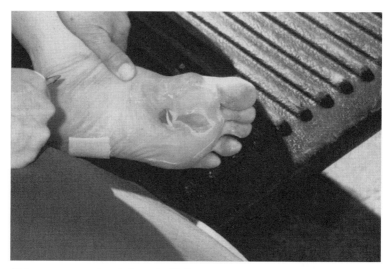

Blisters were an ongoing challenge for Cindy.

blue pickup serves as a bench while Cindy covers her road-worn blisters with "New Skin."

It is normally used for burns, but we are hoping it will make the raw skin on Cindy's feet comfortable enough to get her through the rest of this week. We ask Ray to take an oath of secrecy about the blisters when we go for a newspaper interview tonight. He agrees, not because he is willing to be dishonest, but because he knows that we do not want to give reporters fodder for negative stories so early in the walk.

Ray leaves to see if we can make it over the washed-out road ahead while we walk to our agreed-upon meeting point. Finally, Ray returns with good news.

"Okay, I've checked it out. It's a mess up there, but I think you can make it across. The mud is oozing across the road like melting chocolate so you'll have to watch your step. I can meet you on the other side."

Ray's warm smile is encouraging, although we know he will have to drive an 18-mile detour to meet us at the end of our half-mile walk. His years of working for The Portland *Oregonian* newspaper in rural areas give him extensive knowledge of the back roads he guides us through. We are grateful for this and so much more about this big-hearted man with the gentle and generous spirit.

Each mile we walk takes us further away from the devastation.

There is a certain amount of guilt associated with this. We can walk out of this muddy mess in pursuit of our dream. The hard working residents of this quiet river valley do not have that luxury.

We found $3.25 this week.

The Kalama River Bridge and a post-flood logjam.

Walking through more flood damage near Kalama.

Walking through flooded areas not yet open to cars.

The flooded Cowlitz River took out half of this highway.

Sliding through the muck on a closed road outside Woodland, Washington.

Ray Johnson waits to be sure we made it through the detour okay.

Cindy

Mary Cynthia Marshall was born in the small northwestern town of Chehalis, Washington in April of 1945. She was named after her two grandmothers, but Aunt Jane quickly nicknamed her Cindy. Jerry prefers her given name, usually shortening it to Mar.

Cindy's parents moved around a bit until she was two. Then they moved seven miles south of Chehalis to Napavine, population 332. Located on the tiny main street of this rural community was the most memorable business in Napavine, Mamie's Variety Store. The owner was a little redheaded dynamo named Mamie Shattuck. She knew every child who pushed open the old creaky door and stepped onto the uneven wooden floors. The entire store was no larger than a two-car garage, but it was gigantic in the eyes of Cindy and the other children in town.

Mamie's sold Lik-em-Ade, Double Bubble gum, Red Chief pencil tablets and eight-count Crayola crayons that smelled strongly of wax. With each purchase a child received free words of encouragement and a smile from Mamie. Those words helped build self-esteem and inspired Cindy to dream big dreams.

Cindy's world was small and safe. It revolved around three siblings and a loving mom and dad who always encouraged her. On neighboring acreage lived her maternal grandparents, an aunt and uncle, great aunt and uncle and cousins enough for endless days of climbing trees, building fern forts and making mud pies and miniature farms under the big fir tree. Cindy's life was all country, so when she got older, her outdoor interests were replaced by the importance of her local 4-H club which was led by her mom. She won purple ribbons and traveled to fairs. She began to realize she could accomplish anything she set her mind to.

Once a week her hardworking family drove to Chehalis for groceries and other necessities. Vacations were spent expanding the size of the family's hand-built house or digging a well so that the outhouse could be abandoned. One week each year they went to the beach, about 100 miles away.

When Cindy was 15, the family moved to Chehalis, which would be closer to her Dad's job and had a larger high school. With a population of 5,500, Chehalis was big by Cindy's standards. Her view of the world was broadened, too.

She first worked for a weekly newspaper where she began to appreciate the printed word. Later she worked at Saint Helen's Hospital after school and weekends. Washing dishes and serving patients their meals meant long hours on her feet. This caused severe swelling of her ankles and legs. Added to that was a sudden decline of thyroid production. She was hardly the athletic type of person one would envision for cross-country trekking. Years later the thyroid disorder was corrected and a vascular specialist would correctly identify the swelling problem as primary lymphodema of the ankles. She had been born without the mechanism necessary to pump water out of her legs. Regular exercise would help the condition.

In 1978, Cindy was happily married and the mother of three active children when she injured her back in a fall. Her doctor performed a quadruple discectomy of the lower back and suggested walking as the best form of physical therapy. She started with one very painful mile. It is hard to imagine that 18 years later she would be walking 20 miles most days for so many months.

4

Tunnel Vision

Since leaving the I-5 corridor last week, we turned near Vancouver, Washington and headed east through the lush, green forests of the Washougal River valley onto Highway 14 along the Columbia River.

It was also during this time, while guests at Ray and Harriet Johnson's, that Cindy made a moneybag for Jerry's growing road-find coins. Each day, Jerry would toss the coins he had found on the road into the bag. At the end of each walk week, he would write the total amount of money found during that week.

Day 12
Wednesday, February 21
White Salmon, Washington

Jerry

The day broke gray and stark, with persistent rain and cloud-laden skies muting the scenic beauty along the Columbia River. The sting of cold spreads from toenails to fingernails making walking a struggle. As we plod along, clothing damp but spirits not, I reflect on the reasoning I used to justify the route we are taking and remind myself that choosing to walk Washington Highway 14 along the Columbia River was not a mindless decision.

Our other option would have meant walking across the Cascade Mountains, which are subject to frequent snowstorms during mid-February. Stopping our walk to wait out a storm would throw off our schedule and affect plans for local events to coincide with our arrival in each town with a Habitat affiliate. For me, that left only one practical choice, this route.

As we had plotted our journey, we wanted to stay as close as possible to the diagonal red line we had drawn connecting Olympia, Washington, with Atlanta, Georgia on our map of the United States. Choosing to travel the lower elevations of the Columbia Gorge rather than through the high Cascades did not guarantee us relief from intense winter storms, but we felt it improved our chances of maintaining our schedule.

Now, clad in layers of clothing topped by my forest green and Cindy's red rain jackets, we keep our heads down, feebly attempting to fend off the blowing rain. We tell ourselves this route was the right decision, saying it again and again.

The rain surges in intensity, occasionally giving us a mild reprieve, but never giving up. It is just the two of us walking today. Our routine, now tested by the first 140 miles, calls for Linda Boca-Roberts, our support vehicle driver, to drive a couple of miles ahead and then wait for us to catch up. If she notices trouble or senses that we have taken too long, she drives back to us.

As my thoughts turn to Linda, I realize that perhaps it is better to be walking in the rain and wind than to be in her car. When Linda came to pick us up this morning, she excitedly explained that she had a mouse in her car. As we headed for our starting point for the day, the mouse erred in his choice of a route through the car and entangled himself with the heater fan. There was a disturbing noise, followed a short time later by the unpleasant aroma of a cooking mouse. In spite of the weather, we were glad to get out of the car before the scent overwhelmed us. Linda, eight months pregnant, unfortunately had no other choice but to drive on. Our rain hoods and the wind make hearing each other difficult. Conversation has become a chore, and we say little without first making eye contact to signal that words are about to come forth. Other than traffic and the rain, the only other sounds we hear come from the metal guardrail beams on our left. Their harmonic struggle with the wind entertains us as the wind tries to wrest it from its posts. Bolts and nuts, once torqued to highway department specifications, are slowly giving in to the extremes in temperature and to the thrusting and twisting of the relentless winds.

Our toil on this lonely morning is interrupted by the arrival of four women in a red Toyota 4-Runner. Waving and smiling, they drive by us, and then pull into a turnout up ahead. It is a welcome surprise visit from our friends, staff from the Habitat Northwest Regional Center in Bend, Oregon. They have come to walk with us for part of the day. Although they have been cooped up in the car for hours, they spill enthusiastically from their vehicle. We are glad for their companionship and excited that they have come to share this time with us.

Their plan calls for one of them to drive the vehicle while three walk with us. Their chatter soon lightens our mood. There is a friendly critique of my walking style. I'm told that if I swing my hips correctly, my walking will be more efficient. My attempts to comply are fruitless as my hips go willy-nilly to the frustration of my self-appointed mentor. Recognizing that the concept is beyond my comprehension, she finally gives up with a good-natured laugh.

At lunchtime we retreat to a small, flat, low area near a waterfall off the north side of the road. Though we are still cold, by being up against the hills we are slightly protected from the wind as we visit and eat. The rain has taken a lunch break too, but just as we prepare to move on, it returns to rejoin the cold. The once spry steps of our companions have begun to falter, and we sense the slowing of their pace. We slow our pace to accommodate them and to encourage them to stay with us longer, for we know they will need to leave soon for the four-hour drive back to Bend.

Distracted by conversation with our comrades, we do not notice that Ray and Harriet Johnson have arrived from Vancouver. It is the same Ray Johnson that drove support vehicle for much of our walk through the Vancouver area and his wife Harriet, our "hostess with the mostest" last weekend. Once again, our spirits are renewed. It seems whenever the cold and wind start to get us down, someone has come along and recharged us.

When we prepared for this walk, we trained in a variety of climate conditions that simulated what we might encounter along the way. Ahead of us looms a challenge we couldn't include in our training, the first of five highway tunnels. We had contacted the State Patrol regarding the legality of walking through these tunnels, but we had received no reply. Now, as we approach the first tunnel we do not know if we can legally walk through it, or the following four. We want to believe that the State Patrol's failure to comment about the tunnels was intentional. We speculate that they may have that realized that we had no choice except to go through the tunnels when walking this route.

As we approach the first tunnel, our friends seem reluctant to leave us without knowing that we are safely through. We, too, are hesitant. Momentarily, we consider the option of walking the railroad tracks that skirt the rock outcropping. Which would be better, the unknown of the tracks or the dark mystery of the tunnel? To be caught on the tracks by a train with no place to go is not an option I want to risk. Freight trains have been passing us all day and we have no way of knowing when the next one will arrive. As I contemplate this dilemma, our friends from Bend and Vancouver suggest that we gather for a prayer circle. This definitely calms my apprehension about the task facing us. They leave us after we all share hugs. We are grateful that Linda and her "dead mouse" car will remain with us through the end of the day.

These tunnels, some straight, some curved, exist because the Cascade Mountain range spilled its volcanic flow over a 170-mile-long area thousands of years ago. The rock is two miles deep in places. Over time, the Columbia River cut a canyon through the porous lava, creating the Columbia River Gorge, now designated a National Scenic Area. In some areas, the geography left no alternatives for ground transport, so tunnels became a necessity.

With memories of the just-completed prayer circle, I entrust God to guide our steps through the five tunnels. The tunnel has a warning system consisting of a push button activator and a flashing signal light (for motorists to ignore) that proclaims, "Bicyclists in the Tunnel." The light signal button and the light itself are located on a pole on the opposite side of the highway from us. I have to run across the road to push the button, then scurry back to walk toward the black hole blasted through the rock. Ahead of us, the light is flashing, but before we can get to the tunnel, it stops. The system is not intended for the pace of walkers. Unlike bicyclists, we travel on the side of the highway

Taking steps toward the first of seven tunnels along the Columbia River.

to face traffic. There is strong probability that the flashing light wouldn't serve to alert motorists to watch for walkers. I have spent hours contemplating our passage through these oblong holes drilled through this ancient rock. I don't want to spend more time knowing we have no options now. Our support vehicle has moved on. It's time to just do it. Our eyes struggle to adjust to the intense darkness of the tunnel as we enter. We must walk on a one-foot-wide raised curb located at the edge of the driving lane. The sides of the tunnel arc up from the back of the curb, forcing us to walk single file slightly leaning to the right. As we push ourselves onward, I shine my flashlight on the bright orange vinyl traffic flag we have brought along for added safety in difficult walking locations. Our chances of startling an unsuspecting motorist are great. Fully loaded 80,000-pound log trucks are common on this stretch of road. Many have passed us today.

The first tunnel is short and straight, about 100 feet long. We view this as the beginner's tunnel. There are no vehicles approaching. The space we have to walk on seems a little wider than we thought it might be. We hug the side of the tunnel so closely that we occasionally bump into jutting rock along the roughly blasted wall. We develop more confidence in what we are doing and a false sense of security. Is it the prayers, or are we just stupid? We feel triumphant as we exit the tunnel. That wasn't so bad, we concur. The next tunnel is one-quarter mile ahead.

The second tunnel is 400 feet long and much more foreboding. It curves to the left, so we cannot see the light at the end of this tunnel. We don't think we will be fortunate enough to make it through this one without encountering oncoming traffic, but head into it we must. Our bodies are once again tense, confidence gone. We walk in silence. After the first 100 feet we begin to feel hopeful again. After the second 100 feet we can see daylight. There is no oncoming traffic. We heave a sigh of relief and relax our shoulders. Emerging from the tunnel opening we smile and share high-fives. One more to go. We know it is 250 feet long.

We proceed, knowing that the shorter distance improves our chances of not being hit, but realizing that our luck might hold only so long. I feel like a poker player waiting for a bad hand. We complete this one without facing a vehicle. As we emerge, the wind is whipping up five-foot white caps in the river. They splash against the tunnel exit, spraying us with water. It reminds us of Splash Mountain at Disneyland and brings some needed levity to the experience. The last two tunnels are over a half-mile away.

"Jer, how did you do back there?" Cindy inquires.

"I was very tense. How about you?"

"I was fine in the first one. I think, because I could see the end. Then I lost my optimistic attitude. My faith got weaker as we faced each tunnel. I definitely wasn't 'letting go and letting God.' I'm disappointed in myself."

"Don't be so hard on yourself. That's scary stuff. You are human. You've got two more chances coming up. Ready?"

We arrive at the fourth tunnel. Linda is still driving ahead of us and waiting. She is nervous, but continues to offer encouragement. No oncoming traffic in that one either. We are amazed. We're getting good at this. Our confidence is increasing.

No time to be cocky, though. The fifth and final one is short and, oh so sweet. We emerge from this last tunnel like newborn babies, but without the tears. We offer a triumphant squeal and another hearty high-five. The prayer circle of nine has accomplished all we could have hoped for. We walk over to Linda's little blue car. The mouse smell is nearly gone. So is Linda's apprehension. Down the road we now head toward the quaint little town of White Salmon, where we will spend the night.

After supper, as we sit in their home overlooking the Columbia River, our hostess and family friend Julie Ueland wants to know how our day has gone.

"So how'd you do with the tunnels?" she asks innocently.

"We're still a bit shocked. We never did face an oncoming vehicle in any of the tunnels, Julie. Is that unusual?"

"That's more than unusual. That's an out-and-out unheard of miracle, especially with traffic headed west at that time of day. There's usually a lot of traffic."

"Yes, there was, but just not when we were inside the tunnels."

"You should consider yourselves very blessed," she laments.

We do. We really do.

It's Thursday and we are walking without a support vehicle as we continue to inch our way eastward along the Washington side of the Columbia River. We like walking alone today. It is not that we don't appreciate the support people who have given so much for our cause. It's just that there is a sense of independence associated with walking completely on our own once in awhile. We feel like teenagers skipping school.

After a lunch of beef barley soup at The Country Café in Lyle, we bundle up once again and head out into the wind and drizzle. As we step out onto the shoulder, the large orange warning sign surprises us.

"SLOW. TUNNELS AHEAD."

We groan and roll our eyes in unison. We had briefly forgotten about these last two tunnels. There's nothing we can do but reach for the orange flag and the flashlight.

"Are you ready for this?" I ask Cindy with dread in my voice.

"I think so." she squeaks out.

Water drips from the curved edge of the tunnel entrance. She takes a few steps toward the entrance and then says, "Jer, I'm getting a strong message to run!"

"Let's do it," I agree with resolve.

"Hurry!" she shouts.

No vehicles are in this 400-foot-long tunnel, but it is so long and dark, we wouldn't know it until we saw their headlights anyway. We are wearing loaded daypacks and become breathless quickly. We continue sprinting toward the opening at the other end. When we reach it, we quickly step off the road into a wide spot to catch our breaths. It is then that we are nearly blown into the rock ledge by a huge, wide dump truck.

"Okay, so that message was for real, huh?" Cindy stammers.

"That was a little too close for comfort!" I shout. "There sure would not have been room for both of us in there. We wouldn't have been more than a speed bump to that big boy. Come on, let's get this over with. I've had enough excitement for one day."

The final tunnel, the seventh one we have faced in two days on 17 miles of roadway, is only 200 feet long and straight enough to see daylight. We hustle through, but don't run. We are a little giddy after the last close call. We quicken our steps in the last 20 feet because we see a double-trailer semi coming and hurriedly step out. The driver acknowledges us with a wave and a smile. We return the gesture. He has no idea why we are smiling so broadly, but we do.

We found 48 cents during this time.

Pastor Rob's Blessing

Good and gracious God.
We ask your blessing today upon your servants,
Jerry and Cindy Schultz.
Guard and guide their walking this day and
every day which now lies before them.
May the first step, and each of their many
uncounted steps, be taken knowing that they are uplifted
in prayer and protected in your arms of care.
Bless their feet that they may walk with
purpose and travel in safety.
Bless their eyes that they may see your vision
and recognize you in face and forest.
Bless their hands that they may care for your
people and embrace your creation.
Bless their ears that they may hear the cries
of heaven and earth.
Bless their hearts that they may warm the world
in compassion and mercy.
And bless them, our brother and sister, Jerry and Cindy,
that they may walk in safety, even to the ends
of the earth, and return to us in health and wholeness
as witness to our Lord and Savior, Jesus Christ.
Amen

Robert Hofstad
February 10, 1996

5

Gourmets in the Gorge

Day 19
Wednesday, February 28
Paterson, Washington

Cindy

With a friendly grin and a Saint Bernard-willingness to help, Ron Nelson, our support vehicle driver, ambles through the Torgerson's back door for the third morning this week. He brings with him news that a barge broke loose during the storm last night and is lodged against a pier on the Biggs Junction Bridge. With the bridge now closed, we must scrap plans to drive east on Interstate 84 at 75 miles an hour and travel across that bridge to get to yesterday's ending point. Instead, we will be forced to take a much longer route back to The Dalles Bridge and drive Highway 14 at 45 miles per hour. We are running late. A telephone interview has been slow and not very productive. Adding to our anxiety is the need to say goodbye to two very special people.

Lucile and Jim Torgerson have a knack for making people feel very comfortable. Founders of the local Habitat affiliate, they had offered their hospitality to us when we discovered there were no host families on the walk route on Washington's Highway 14. This meant driving across the Columbia River between Washington and Oregon each day. The more direct route choice would have been in Oregon along Interstate 84. For safety and other reasons, we have chosen not to walk on interstate highways, although some states allow it.

We have gotten too comfortable in the Torgerson's hillside home overlooking the Columbia River during the past week. Each day, they have made sure we were fed and transported. Each night we have returned "home" to them. They have let us soak in their hot tub and called Dr. Hal Sessions, friend and generous Habitat supporter, to make an 11 p.m. house call to check my infected blister. They have walked with us physically, mentally and spiritually. Today they will drive 100 miles to deliver our luggage to our next host family. Our thanks seem so inadequate but it's all we have to give.

Jerry climbs into the front seat of Ron's King Kab pickup. I slide into the jump seat behind him. We drive across the river and turn east onto Highway 14 to start the 80-mile drive over the same road we have been walking for the last four days. I expect to be thoroughly bored and have a major attitude going. I'm disgruntled about getting such a late start and dare the world to show me anything interesting.

Then we pass the red rock area where we were accosted by a tail wind last Thursday. I can't help reminiscing about the laughter we shared when that wind picked up our legs from behind and scooted us along the road like marionettes dancing on a wooden board. Giant rocks cling to the cliffs that are shaped like mushrooms and one that looks like a caricature of Richard Nixon. I see the petroglyphs, carved by the Native Americans into these golden rocks thousands of years ago.

The Columbia River Gorge is a spectacular river canyon cutting the only near sea level route through the ancient Cascade Mountain Range. The gorge is 80 miles long and up to 4,000 feet deep. The north canyon walls are located in Washington State and the south canyon walls are two to three miles across the river in Oregon State. The gorge is more than a scenic natural wonder. It is a critical transportation corridor and home to 70,000 people. We have observed barges, ships, trains and trucks carrying cargo past us each day. In these past four days we have only walked past one house on this side of the river. The gorge was designated a National Scenic Byway in 1986, 10,000 years after native fishers roamed the shores of this part of the 1,200-mile long river. Walking through this land of ancients has touched us deep in our souls. I have to admit it is good to be riding through it one last time before we head east and out of our home state.

Now, we drive by the Columbia Cliffs winery on our right. Lucile was walking with us Friday morning when we stopped there to use the restroom. We had to convince the owner that Habitat for Humanity wasn't a radical environmental group before he would let us use his bathrooms. These mile-long hills don't seem bad as I view them from the comfort of a vehicle, but they were a tough climb all day Friday. That bright green sign marking Milepost 104 gives me sweet memories of Jerry's pretend radio station that I refer to as KJRS for his initials. He had been able to get my mind off of my exhaustion when he held my hand and belted out, "Have I Told You Lately That I Love You?" and the Beatle's "When I'm Sixty-Four". The top of the hill was in sight when he closed with our family's traditional favorite, "Waltz Across Texas". Even thinking about it today gives me the same mental image I always have of our toddlers, gliding across the dining room floor in Jerry's arms as he used to sing that song. As the kids got older, they stood on the tops of his feet as they danced. I always cut in at the end, though. With me in his arms, the kids danced and giggled around us as we ended the dance with a dramatic dip and a kiss.

And now, today, we are driving through the stone fence area. When we had asked about the history of these basalt rock fences that run parallel to the highway, we had been told a folk story. It seems as though people had been told for decades that an old fellow named Shorty had built these fences in the early 1900s. The story goes that Shorty pulled a wooden cart along behind him, loaded with watermelon-sized boulders. He had stacked those dark gray stones so perfectly without mortar that most of the fences still stand. The locals told us that when a section of fence did deteriorate, others had tried to repair it, only to discover that their efforts were never as good as Shorty's. We had teased Ron about being the next Shorty because of all the rocks he had loaded into his truck during the three days he had been with us. At six-foot-five though, Ron had the wrong stature to replace Shorty.

Soon, we are driving past Jane Lee's house on the right there among the stone fences. Last week Ron had asked her if we could use her bathroom during a morning break. Jane had readily agreed and then had provided us with a history of their property. As we had walked past two Native American men working on fishing nets in her front yard, she had told us not to be concerned with their lack of comment when we had said "Hello." They don't talk much, even to Jane, she had said. They were hard workers and she was happy to let them use her yard. Jane had gone on to explain that an Oregon Trail family named Bergen had built her big white farmhouse in 1862. Their first-born child had been the first white child born in Klickitat County. When that family had sold the property, Jane's husband's family purchased the place and remodeled it in 1940.

"The Indians camped in that field to our left during the summers while they caught and preserved fish for the long winters. When Robert's family first lived here, they didn't know if the tribe was friendly or not, so they would take their five children across the road and hide them in those rock valleys," Jane had told us, motioning across the highway. "They finally discovered the Indians intended no harm, and they became friends. They are to this day."

Jane had given us a little tour of the farmyard and shown us a calf that had been abandoned by its mother. She told us the cows don't know how to count. Since they only expect one calf they often abandon the other twin, so Jane was feeding it around the clock.

I was quickly recognizing that today's unexpected detour had been a blessing of memories. How could I have ever thought the ride would be boring? With a much-needed attitude adjustment, I am ready for whatever today has in store for me.

We arrive at the milepost marker where we had finished walking yesterday and climb out of the warm truck. The menacing gray clouds now blow their mean spirited breath, chilling us and pushing us simultaneously. There are no trees to slow its speed. Ron recognizes the challenge we are about to face and offers additional warmth.

"Better add this to your layers," Ron offers as he hands me a blue polypropylene balaclava.

I gratefully put it on over my fleece earmuffs and under my plaid fleece baseball hat. I top that off with the red rain jacket hood. From the waist down, I wear a pair of polar fleece pants over long johns and under navy blue rain pants. On top, I have polypropylene underwear, a polar fleece sweatshirt and a wool sweater. I wear sock liners under wool socks and Birkenstocks. My feet are naturally very hot so that's not a problem. I am putting on my polar fleece gloves over wool glove liners as I walk across the road to join Jerry. He is dressed the same, without a balaclava and with the added insulation of one folded wool sock covering a part of his anatomy I don't have to worry about.

He clicks the microcassette recorder on and begins this day as he does all others. "It is 9:25 on Wednesday February 28th. We are back at milepost marker 146 on Highway 14. We're dressed in our Patagonia long johns and polar fleece pants covered by our rain pants. Unfortunately, we had a long trip and we are getting a late start. The sun is out. That is the sound of aluminum guard rail rattling in the wind."

I pull the cord of my hood tighter, trapping my body's warmth and mental toughness inside. I reach for Jerry's hand as a strong wind gust threatens to blow me into the lane of oncoming traffic. He hangs on tight. Although we don't show it on the outside, we have a "don't mess with us" attitude on the inside. Vehicles pass us cautiously, getting into the other lane whenever they can. Eighteen-wheel rigs rumble by, splashing muddy water on us when it's raining and blast us with cold air when it's not. It's the nature of the beast since we are on their turf. Most of them have been very friendly. One trucker just gave us a message on his loudspeaker.

"Did he say, 'You people are amazing! We know you can do it,' Jer?"

"Either that or he said, 'You people are crazy! We doubt you can do it.'"

"I prefer to think I heard it the right way, you goof. I wonder how they know what we're doing?"

"Probably pass it along on their CBs. What's this? Our seventh day on Highway 14? They probably know more about us than we do by now!"

"I just realized, those truckers will be in Olympia in time for lunch. It's taken us 19 days to get this far. I'm beginning to forget what it's like to go anywhere fast," I lament.

"That is a truly amazing realization you had. I'm definitely into thinking in 'walk time' too." Jerry confirms. "I really hadn't thought about it until now. It does seem like everyone travels at four miles-per-hour. Think about what we are experiencing though. We could not be hearing about local customs and stories from a zooming car. It's as if each slow tedious step allows us to experience more of America's greatness." Unless we stop and face each other, our words blow in the wind and so we hang on tight and walk in silence. Battling this Northeast headwind is hard work and uncomfortable. Our contact lenses are drying out while big trucks sand blast us with road grit. Even the meadowlarks are having trouble flying. The wind is relentless and taxing, making forward progress difficult. I must dig deep inside myself and pull out enough determination to gut it out. Yesterday I let a lesser wind get the best of me. I won't let it happen two days in a row.

I really need a bathroom! To distract myself, I imagine inventing some kind of a catheter device that would prevent me from having to expose any part of my body to this brutal cold. Then, as we top the hill I see Ron's white truck.

"Jer, do you suppose we could ask Ron to take us back to the Roosevelt Mini Mart to use the restroom. It's definitely break time."

"Sounds good. I could use one too."

Ron is only too happy to comply. After Ron parks at the store we walk underneath the U.S. flag flapping straight out from its pole. The warmth of the store envelops us as its old wooden door slams behind us.

"Any idea how fast the wind is blowing today?" Jerry asks the owner. We were in here yesterday. The man behind the counter wasn't much interested in what we were doing then and still isn't.

"Well, let's see," as he turns his bulky body to peer out the window, "the anemometer shows 30 miles per hour right now, but it's been gusting up to 60 miles an hour."

"Wonder what kind of wind chill factor that is?" Jerry continues, trying not to lose the continuity of the conversation.

"Ahh-well, 'cordin' to my calculations, should be 'bout minus four degrees. That's darn cold. Least it's sunny out though."

Yes, Jerry silently agrees, at least it's sunny out. We each use the restroom and load up on junk food. Fried pork rinds and a Dr. Pepper for Ron, a Diet Dew and a blueberry muffin for Jer and a pack of Hostess Chocolate Covered Donettes and a Diet Coke for me. It takes fortification and determination, not good nutrition, for us to walk back out into the wind, but walk back into it we must. Two hours later, we have one mile to go until we can stop for lunch. Ron comes by and wants to know if we want to stop now. He's got something up his sleeve and can't seem to wait. "No Ron, we better get this last mile in first. Meet us up the road in 16 minutes," Jerry suggests. Psychologically it works best for us to count off the miles up to at least 10 before lunch each day. If we stop before we have completed 10 miles we often struggle to finish in the afternoon. After lunch we count our miles downward to complete the day's 20 miles. It may not make sense to others, but it is a little mental trick that works for us. In this adventure, it seems to take 25% physical and 75% mental strength. Our mental games for coping are never-ending.

When we get to the truck, Ron has a big grin on his face. "Hop in. We're headin' back to Crow Butte State Park for lunch."

We have no idea why we are backtracking until we spy Jim and Lucile's van. The look on Ron's face tells us that we are the special guests at this little surprise party! After we left this morning, Jim devised a plan to bring us a fancy lunch. They have pushed a card table up against the concrete block bathhouse to take advantage of only wind protection available. There is a white linen tablecloth covering the card table. On it are crystal goblets with blue ribbon tied to the stems. Jim is ceremoniously pouring sparkling cider into them as Lucile seats us. Upon their finest china, Lucile has placed salmon pâté, pepperoni slices, Brie cheese, and assorted crackers, sliced fruit and cheesecake. We eat with freshly polished silver and wipe our mouths on linen napkins. We eat without removing one single item of clothing, not even our gloves, and we eat heartily. This is a special meal with special folks. It's not the atmosphere; it's the thought that counts. Although we may still be cold on the outside, their love has warmed us mightily on the inside.

It is 1:45 p.m. when we get back out to the highway to face the last 10 miles of this windy day. The sun is peeking through, and the fancy lunch has given us a better attitude about the wind. We have walked out of the geologically stunning area of the gorge. We are in a colorless, arid region now. Except for an occasional red twig dogwood peaking out of its wetland home, the orange, yellows and reds of our outerwear are the most colorful things out

Waiting to partake in the "gourmet lunch" at Crow Butte State Park.

here. Suddenly I spy my first harbinger of spring, a tiny yellow flower pushing its head through the dry, gray soil. It's enough to lift my spirits right to the 20-mile mark today.

We decide to keep our minds busy by playing tumbleweed games. Tumbleweeds come from a densely branched plant that grows about three feet high in dry areas in the western United States. When withered, it breaks off and is blown about by the wind. As tumbleweeds roll along the stark ridges to our left, I challenge Jerry, " I bet you that tumbleweed on my left will beat the one on your right side."

"Oh yeah, I don't think so!" he boasts. I cheer mine on to what appears to be an early victory, but Jerry claims the prize when mine gets tangled in a pileup at the fence and his sprints to the finish. A tumbleweed breaks loose from the mass and blows onto the road. We dart out into the empty road with arms outstretched, grasping each other's hand. With our fancy footwork, the tumbleweed rolls under our outstretched arms for what we call a goal.

Back to the business at hand now, we note that it is getting late and the sky is darkening as we pass mile marker 164. We have two miles to go today. While a runner uses her watch to track her progress, I count mile markers. I have gotten to the point where I intuitively know when we will be coming to the next marker. Each one we pass is a signal to me that we are one mile closer to a shower and a hot meal. On roads where there are no mile markers, I am constantly asking the support driver how far we've gone. I have to know. Since Jerry has calculated where we should be throughout our walk route, this drives him crazy and probably the support driver as well. The last four miles of this day seem to be taking forever. The distances seem to be off. They aren't. I am.

It is 5:10 p.m. We drag our weary bodies into Ron's truck and head to Hermiston, Oregon. We are finishing two hours later than normal. It will be too late to join Nellie, our new hostess, for dinner so we stop at Dairy Queen. Jerry looks for a table where we can seat our tired, dirty bodies without offending the other diners. The best we can find is a booth that is divided by a half wall from an adjoining booth. He goes to order while I lean my back against the half wall and stretch my legs out on my bench. Someone taps me on the shoulder.

"Excuse me, I have to know. Are you the couple walking across America?" a woman seated at the adjoining booth asks me.

"Why, yes, we are. How did you know?"

"I saw your picture and story in yesterday's paper and recognized your red raincoat. It's an amazing thing you're doing and for such a worthy cause. That Jimmy Carter, he's the best past President this country has ever had."

"Yes, he's done a lot for Habitat and a lot for the world. He agreed to be on Habitat for Humanity's International board in 1984 and since then he has sponsored the annual Jimmy Carter Work Project for Habitat for Humanity. He helps us build houses for an entire week each year. Rosalynn works right along with him. He really is a very special man," I agree.

"I wish I could afford to donate some money to your cause but I'm afraid my Social Security check doesn't go very far each month. You know, I would like to do something for you, though. Can I buy you a Peanut Buster Parfait?"

We object to her spending the money on us, but she is not about to accept our objections. Although we are concerned about her spending money that she may need for herself, in the end we accept her gift with thanks and gratitude. Her generosity reminds us of all the kind and caring people we have met thus far. At the end of a very physically demanding day, that realization warms us fast.

We found $3.37 during this time.

Jerry

J erry was born at home in Centralia, Washington in October 1943. Their house was located on the east side of the tracks facing the train station. He arrived at 11:45 a.m., just in time for lunch. The doctor couldn't make it to their house in time to assist with his birth because there was a train across the tracks, so Jerry's dad took over. Since his was the last birth in a large family, all but one born at home, Jerry's father had lots of knowledge in these matters.

They were city folk, living two short blocks from the main part of town.

Early childhood activities were generally restricted to the immediate neighborhood. Too young to venture further, all of the neighborhood children knew that if you went too far north along the tracks, the "bums," who lived in a cardboard shack community, would eat you for dinner.

When Jerry was four-and-a-half, his family moved to an old 21-room hotel above a mattress factory and a "Holy Roller" church. This was much closer to the cardboard hobo community, so his activity was now limited to riding his tricycle along the wide sidewalk in front of the hotel or playing with other kids in the alley behind their dwelling.

Family tradition often called for Sunday drives. Most of the older children had left home by now, so he was with his parents and his sister during these drives. The family seldom traveled very far. Their biggest adventures took them as far as Eatonville, Washington, 40 miles away, to visit his mother's cousin. The family car was never very dependable, but once in a while, if an older sibling came along with a better car they would all pile in for the drive to Mt. Rainier, 20 miles further. Other attempts at travel usually failed due to car problems requiring a quick return home for repairs.

Jerry's world was broadened by a bus trip to visit siblings in

California when he was 12 and later, traveling as statistician with the Centralia College basketball and baseball teams to games throughout Washington State. Those trips made him hungry to see more and go farther, but by this time his father had died, they had no car, and money wasn't available for such frivolous things.

It would be many years later, when married and a father, that Jerry would be able to start traveling to satisfy his curiosity and sense of adventure. From there, plans evolved for more trips to more places. After reading *Blue Highways* by William Least Heat Moon and *Walk Across America* by Peter Jenkins, the dream of walking across America took seed.

6

Entering the State of Confusion

Day 20
Thursday, February 29
Plymouth, Washington

Jerry

I had anticipated a problem crossing the Interstate 82 bridge from Washington into Oregon. I had written to the Washington State Patrol and the Oregon State Police seeking suggestions on how to access the bike path across the bridge. Walking onto Interstate 82 would be illegal in Washington State.

Their responses were brief and did not answer my questions. It should have been a warning to someone like me who had 30 years' experience working for the state transportation department. It didn't seem to be a significant problem because we knew the path was there and thought it couldn't be that difficult to get to. We were wrong.

We had seen the path the year before, but it had been during a 60 miles-per-hour reconnaissance trip as we towed our travel trailer across the bridge in heavy traffic. This does not give one much chance to pick out details. Still, we weren't particularly worried and decided to make our final decisions when we reached this point in the walk.

It is now decision time. We stand on the Washington side of the Columbia, peering across the interstate bridge toward Oregon. The most immediate problem is the sign telling us pedestrians are not allowed on the freeway. (Had it come later in the walk, we would have ignored it. However, we were still subject to intimidation this early into the journey.) It doesn't seem to me that risking a ticket is a good idea. I know that the path departs from the shoulder of the interstate about a half-mile away on the right. It then slants down and through an under-the-bridge tunnel parallel with the river and then back up to the bridge sidewalk. If we are successful, this route will take us up the hill to the two-lane highway on the Oregon side where we need to meet our support vehicle.

We have asked a pair of Department of Transportation maintenance employees if they could guide us to a legal access onto the path. They can't give us a clue. The best that can be said for their advice is that it is confusing and has no real value. We walk on, expecting to find the way by ourselves.

Today's support driver, Betty Whittum, meets us at the intersection to the interstate that leads across the bridge. I suggest she drive her borrowed motor home across the bridge and meet us on the other side at the top of the hill in about an hour. That seems like a good plan. I still trust that we will have no trouble finding the bike path. It is 2:10 p.m.

Finding the path should have been simple, but I am soon frustrated. This bicycle/pedestrian path connects two states, why should it be difficult to access? Why couldn't the coordinators for either state have been more helpful? Why did it seem that I knew more about alternative routes and pedestrian access in their states than they did? Why is there a National Pedestrian Safety Commission, and yet it is still difficult to find pedestrian-accessible and safe routes, even in urban areas?

All of these questions are now, of course, academic. A shred of doubt quickly enters my mind as I hesitatingly lead us down the grassy right of way to the left of the bridge. Traffic whizzes by above us on the freeway. Expecting to be nabbed by the State Patrol any moment, I am tempted to turn back. I can sense that Cindy is not convinced my route choice is the rational one. After 32 years of marriage, you know when your partner is reluctantly going along with your dumb decision.

The weather has improved and we are carrying our raincoats when we come to a barbed wire fence separating us from a railroad that crosses under the bridge. Protecting our much-beloved coats by folding them inside out, we crawl over the wire and walk down the tracks to where I thought it looked like the elusive pedestrian path began. No such luck. All we find is another fence, this time, chain link and high. We can't get there from here.

I can still see the bike path/access road in the distance. I decide we can get there by bushwhacking. A pond is between the path and us. Down and around, over and through bushes and rocks we go, looking for some sort of trail that will take us finally to the path.

It is a bonehead decision, and now I have to get us out of it. Finally we get to the gravel road running parallel with the river. It intersects with the pedestrian path. We hurry along now, finally free of obstacles and aware of the time we had promised to meet Betty. We will be only a few minutes late. Why hadn't I ignored that sign? What were the chances that a Washington State Patrol trooper would be driving the freeway across the river into Oregon? Why had I dragged Cindy over fences and through bushes instead of making a quick and sensible decision to take the shortest route? Why had I worried so over the remote possibility of having a state trooper go by at the wrong moment and couldn't I probably have talked him out of giving us a ticket anyway?

As we follow the path through the pedestrian tunnel under the freeway and begin the climb up the hill, I notice that the chain link fence post on our side is located away from the concrete wall far enough that we could have climbed over and around it. Now I am really irritated with my decisions. Unfortunately, we have only glimpsed the tip of this proverbial iceberg.

The little path on the bridge that we now walk has more loose dirt and gravel than sidewalk. Walking is difficult and dims our appreciation of the great view of the Columbia River. Exiting the path and leaving the area surrounding the bridge, we immediately come to another decision point. There are no signs telling us whether to go left or right into Umatilla. The route to the right trails out of sight, and looks as if it will dump us into heavy traffic. Left extends down the road near the McNary Dam and shows much less traffic as far as we can see. "Let's go left," I say, after digesting what little information is available. Cindy agrees. Why didn't she disagree? We walk on for what seems far too long and finally come to an intersection where workers are exiting the McNary Dam complex. We need to be heading to our right to reach the intersection where Betty is waiting. This road is taking us further to our left.

Adding to my frustration, I cannot get anybody to stop and give us directions. I finally walk up to a pickup truck and the driver slowly and reluctantly lowers his window part way. I ask him where this road would lead us, and how to get up to the highway. Still keeping his window in a protective mode, he tells me to follow the road to the end, and then take a right up the hill. I ask if that would bring us to the intersection we want, and he says, "Yes."

I feel my credibility teetering. Having already made two foolish decisions, I am building a husband's wall and putting a serious dent in my already tarnished self-esteem. We finally start up the long hill, as I still ponder the my interpretation of the directions given to me by the pickup driver.

It's a steep hill and Cindy is struggling. At this point I do something even more stupid. I turn in frustration and tell her to keep up. "I can't drag you all the way across America," are the words that spill out of my mouth before I can stop them.

Instead of apologizing and going back to help, I huff on silently. We rejoin each other at the intersection with her ego crushed and mine in a major state of remorse. It has been an intense physical and mental struggle with the cold, the wind, and the hills for both of us during these past three days. It has been hard going, and I begin to worry about the toll it is taking on us this early in the walk. I know how it has affected me and I am concerned about how it is affecting Cindy. With almost 2,700 miles to go, we can't be wearing out so soon.

In true bumbling husband fashion, however, I do not offer a clue as to what I am feeling inside. I worry about her, but fear giving in to the demands on myself. I know that she is tough when she needs to be tough, but I can't bear to see her struggling so. Now, after my three-out-of-three erroneous decisions I have capped off the day with a truly insensitive remark.

All of this could have been avoided if I had taken a two-mile ride across the river in the motor home to scout the situation. Betty has obviously given up and gone home or back across the river in search of us. She's not here.

After awhile, I mumble my way out of much of my trouble with a few lame excuses and a lot of heartfelt contrition. Now I need Betty to pick us up before I ruin a perfectly feeble apology.

"...if you are strong enough and bold enough to follow your dreams, then you will be led in the path that is best for you.

The voices of the world will drown out the voice of God and your own intuition if you let it. And most people are directed by voices outside themselves."

Oprah Winfrey
January 8, 2000
Time Magazine

7

Heading Up Cabbage Hill

Day 21
Friday, March 1
Nolin, Oregon

Cindy

The foot-deep ruts are still visible, silent reminders of pioneers who walked through this valley more than 100 years before us. We are on the old Oregon Trail between Echo and Nolin in eastern Oregon. Betty, driving support vehicle for us again today, has taken some high school boys who received community service hours for walking with us this morning, back to Hermiston. Now alone, we are enjoying this footloose and fancy-free part of the day.

We talk a lot about those who traveled this way when it was true wilderness. Their support vehicles weren't motor homes, and until very late in the westward migration, there were no hotels in which to spend the night. The early settlers relied on covered wagons pulled by oxen and their own resourcefulness to get them through. Their sacrifices were immense. They gave up the comforts of a home to strike out for unknown territory.

The people who traveled through here in the 19th Century had a dream though, and in that sense, we are alike and feel connected. They accomplished their dream. We wonder if we will accomplish ours.

The early spring sun reflects off the golden hills and onto our shirt-sleeved shoulders. We have shed our polypropylene and polar fleece cocoons. Like two butterflies exploring a new spring, we glide along the road seldom seeing a car. As we amble around the corner at the top of a steep hill, the scene before us amuses us. While her energetic black pup chases mice in and out of a prickly pile of tumbleweed, a sturdy, slightly graying woman attempts to keep it intact. When they spy us, this team stops their work to introduce themselves.

"Hi! I'm Joanne Harris, and this is Holly. Someone dumped her by my house on Christmas Day, thus the name. What brings you two to these parts?"

We are as curious about her as she is us, so we exchange stories. Joanne has recently retired and moved back to her family's homestead here. She points to a magnificent old home nestled between rolling farmland and the Umatilla River. Her sense of hospitality interrupts our conversation.

"Can I get you each a glass of water?" she asks.

"I would love one, but could I use your bathroom first?" I ask.

Jerry and his new pal, Holly, stay out by the road to watch for Betty to return from Hermiston in the motor home. Anyway, his bathroom needs are more easily met alongside the road.

"Do you have time for a quick tour?" Joanne offers as I emerge from the luxury of indoor plumbing.

This is the kind of opportunity we had hoped for when we planned the walk so with ice water in hand, she and I walk past old polished wainscoting that lines the living and dining rooms walls. Joanne pushes a heavy velvet curtain aside and we ascend a steep staircase.

"I heat the house with wood, so I normally keep the upstairs closed off to conserve heat. You are so interested in the architecture of this old house, I'd like you to see the bedrooms up here. Their decor remains exactly the same as it was when I grew up."

We come out of the dim light into a large, perfectly square foyer. The walls are painted white. Lovingly hung on one wall are 8x10 color photographs of Joanne's siblings. The four bedroom doors are closed. Each one is painted a different pastel color, creating a rainbow color scheme. Joanne opens the first door, a mint green one. It reveals a room bathed in the same color as the door. The walls, carpet, curtains and bedspreads all share the same color but in different hues. There are no patterns of any kind. Joanne is delighted by my reaction and tells about each room's past occupants.

"This room was my parents'."

She walks across the hall to the next door and swings it open. Inside this door is a room reminiscent of pink cotton candy. Once again, everything is the same solid color in different hues. It is not surprising when she says, "This is where my sister and I slept."

The door opening continues, now revealing a lavender room for her older sister and, predictably, a baby blue room for her little brother. We stand in the foyer and take in the rainbow of rooms now that all the doors are wide open.

A blast from Betty's motor home horn signals the end of the home tour. It has been a delightful repose on this warm, late winter day.

We finish our last four miles. Our high-five and kiss today put an exclamation mark on our first 320 miles. The only thing missing from this day is a pair of Disney-animated bluebirds singing on our shoulders.

Today is Saturday. Sunshine filters through the eyelet curtains in our guestroom, awakening me from a very deep sleep. I am surprised to not feel Jerry beside me until I look at the clock and discover it is 8 a.m., late for me to be just waking up. Sleep did not come easy last night. The blister under my toenail throbbed, and the heat rash on inside of my thighs had me itching like a dog with fleas.

We are staying with Nellie Neuffer in her manufactured home in Hermiston, Oregon. A widow, Nellie lives alone but stays active with the local Habitat affiliate and other community activities. Nellie has just finished preparing a hearty homemade breakfast as I enter her bright kitchen. She is talking to Jerry.

"Betty and I are going to a friend's funeral this morning. When we return we would like to take you to meet one of our Habitat families and then stop for a Wheatland Dairy ice cream cone. Word has it, you do like your ice cream," Nellie smiles.

"Sounds good," Jerry replies. "We've got work to do here while you two are gone. We'll be ready when you return."

After breakfast, Jerry gets right to work on the laptop computer while I begin sorting dirty laundry. Our clothes reek of road grime after the tough week along the Columbia River. I am already throwing away Jerry's new sport socks because they have holes in the heels. I would like to darn them because I swear I can hear my granny whispering, "Waste not, want not." But I quickly come to my senses when I realize a darned sock would be an open invitation to a blister. "Sorry, Granny, they must go."

From the living room, I hear that happy little voice coming from the laptop, "YOU'VE GOT MAIL!" America Online is singing my song. Because Jerry e-mails stories of our week's adventure each Friday night, we can expect replies on Saturdays. This has been a tough week, and we have decided to tell all, even though there is a risk of worrying them. I lean over Jerry's shoulders and we read the mail together. My sister Kay's response is first:

Hi. That was a tough one to read. I feel bad that you had to walk in such wind, but it's good to hear how you get through those conditions, and I'm sure glad people are treating you so good. I'd like to give the Torgersons a big hug for being so good to you.

Melissa and I were in Enumclaw yesterday, and it was so windy and cold, just walking a short distance. I can't imagine 20 miles of it. Please have your support person tie a rope to you both so you do not blow away. Take care of each other and once again, "I love you." Love, Kay.

And then we read Pat and Kim's reply:

Stay tough. You are in our prayers always. These are the e-mails I knew would come, but it is still hard to think of you taking crappy weather for 7-8 hours a day. As you near the Oregon Trail, it makes it clear how life must have been for the pioneers, and they didn't have e-mail to get from their families! I don't know any pioneers who had Peanut Buster Parfaits bought for them along the way. That's a nice story. Be careful. We love you. Pat, Kim, Drew and Conner

Tears are welling up in my eyes before I finish Pat's message. Their love and concern for us creates powerful emotions. I wish they were here. We hug each other and Jerry wipes my tears away. He suggests a phone call is in order. The electronic age is wonderful, but it cannot take the place of hearing their voices. I make the call. As it turns out, they were thinking the very same thing.

I return to the laundry, then pay our bills and update my journal. There are also host families to confirm for next week and packing to do. It is beginning to seem normal for us to wake up in someone else's home on Saturday mornings and then pack to spend the next two nights in a donated motel room. Staying with host families during the week gives us the opportunity to get to know a variety of new people in the evenings. By spending weekends in a motel we get a chance for some downtime. Even though we are often participating in special events on Saturdays, we try to keep Sundays free. We are pleased with the way our weekdays and weekends juxtapose.

When Betty and Nellie return, we load our luggage into Betty's car and drive across Hermiston to a well-kept neighborhood and a cute little house belonging to Habitat partner family, Elizabeth and her children.They have just moved into their new home, built with the help of many volunteers and sold to them at no profit. They will not have to pay interest on their 20-year mortgage either. This is Biblical economics and a mainstay for all Habitat mortgages. Consequently, Elizabeth is experiencing the life-changing difference that owning a Habitat home can make. For Mandy, Elizabeth's 18-year-old, physically challenged daughter, it has meant release from a depression brought on by the environment inside their formerly dark, crowded apartment. Their bathroom had been too small for her bedside chair commode, so it had to be placed in the hallway. There was no dignity in having to do private things in a public place, and so she continued to wear diapers. Now that a wide doorway and an ample sized bathroom have allowed her some privacy, Mandy wears underwear like other teenagers. Other skills are advancing rapidly too, now that she lives in a bright, new, roomy environment. She wears a smile that only a happy young woman could have.

For Elizabeth, a pretty, petite woman in her thirties, maintaining strong muscles is a necessity precipitated by a need to lift Mandy several times each day. Thanks to Habitat volunteers altering the house design, she now has a spacious area for her weight training equipment in one end of the combination living room, dining area and kitchen. Elizabeth told us that her new home is like heaven. Her choice of soft blues, mauves and white looks like heaven to us, too. Habitat homes often do. And, they are built and occupied by angels like Mandy and Elizabeth all over the world.

It's time for those ice cream cones, and Nellie and Betty prove they know our tastes well. We sit in the big red barn-turned-café, and reminisce about the interesting week we have spent with them as our hostesses. They remind us that our safety vests will be ready on Tuesday. They will bring them to us after we walk over Cabbage Hill. That will put the safety vest subject to rest. People have been suggesting we should wear them since the first week of walking, (for some reason we had never thought of them before) but with no time or resources, we've let it slide. It took a group of worker bees here in Hermiston, led by Larry Platt, to make it happen, and we are very grateful.

On Tuesday, March 5, we park at the base of the Blue Mountains and face the first mountain of the walk. Are we strong enough? It's time to find out. We hop out of Bob and Dorothy Cannon's 39-foot motor coach as we gulp down two Ibuprofen, our daily ritual, to alleviate aching legs. We tell Bob we will see them two miles up the switchbacks. Since they were with us yesterday, he knows the drill.

It is snowing a harmless kind of snow, more like baby powder drifting about the landscape. The wind isn't blowing and the temperature is mild. We start up Cabbage Hill, so named by the locals because it looks like a big old head of cabbage. For many years, this was the only way over the Blue Mountains. Now Interstate 84 cuts through, instead of over the granite that makes up this mountain. Jerry carries the video camera with him until our break. He wants to document our first mountain ascent.

He pans to the wheat fields surrounding the "Hill." The higher we climb, the more they resemble candy cane stripes of brown with white snow filling in the furrows. The pine trees that dot the landscape look like white bristles on giant bottlebrushes. Our bright colored Patagonia rain coats are in direct contrast with the white snow and now-developing fog.

We monitor our bodies with the attention of an astronaut right after blastoff and are pleased with our assessment. With each conquered mile, we become more lighthearted about the challenge. We are surprised and pleased at how effortlessly we are ascending. It is finally clear to us that we have trained enough for this walk. This realization energizes us and this mountain becomes our playground.

"Hey Mar," Jerry says in mock television reporter style as he aims the video camera at my face. "Tell the people how you are feeling as you climb Cabbage Hill today."

"Well, Mr. Schultz, it is beautiful up here with the snow quietly turning our environment into a winter wonderland. My legs are strong and the snow isn't even getting in my Birkenstocks. I'm having the time of my life."

"So, you're saying you wouldn't rather be back in your safe little home doing normal things, Mrs. Schultz?"

"No way Jose! Sounds boring to me," I quip with a grin.

With that bit of film "in the can" we continue our climb. We eventually reach Boiling

Birkenstocks in the snow on Cabbage Hill.

Point, named after the place where cars, in years past, had to stop and refill their radiators with water. Now the service station where everyone stopped is closed. Old-fashioned gas pumps and a Coca-Cola machine are there, serving as reminders of a bygone era.

At Boiling Point, we open the door of the motor home and are ushered in for what appears to be Pillsbury Bakeoff 2. Laura and Howard White are with us again today, riding with their friends Bob and Dorothy. Yesterday, the Whites had driven and the Cannons rode along. Dorothy has prepared a hot meal for our lunch like Laura did yesterday in her motor home. This is a real treat compared to the cold lunches packed in paper bags that we are accustomed to. We sit at the table and gobble down chicken rice casserole, raspberry salad and banana bread. For dessert, we are served angel food cake topped with cherry pie filling and Cool Whip. Besides their catering skills, we love these four new friends for their great story telling skills, the way they each wear their love for their spouse on their sleeves, and how they find humor in just about everything. Our similarities have made these two days feel as comfortable as a pair of old house slippers. Their warm companionship makes it hard to step outside and back into the snow.

We finish our day with confidence in our bodies and our ability to face the odds. Our accomplishment today is small, compared to the challenge of the Rocky Mountains we will face in a few months but it is nonetheless an important milestone for us. Our chances of making our dream a reality seem more attainable now than at any time during the last two years.

During this time we found $5.44.

Mapping the Route

To determine the walk route, Jerry drew a diagonal red line on a large U.S.A. map. It went from Olympia, Washington, the starting point, to Atlanta, Georgia, the final destination. He used a computer to determine straight-line mileage then added a "fudge factor" to give them a comfortable, estimated actual walking mileage. (Weekends would be spent doing fundraising walks with Habitat affiliates on Saturdays and speaking at churches on Sundays). Knowing the total miles, Jerry then calculated the total amount of time they would need for the walk. Given the date of August 30th as the date of Habitat's 20th Anniversary Celebration as a set point, he worked backwards and determined that a start time in February, midway through the winter months, would afford them a better chance of encountering favorable weather along the way.

They also needed to be in Kansas City on June 28th, to meet Millard and Linda Fuller for a planned walk day with them. In addition, Jerry and Cindy wanted to go through as many Habitat affiliate communities as they could possibly fit in along the way.

Jerry then searched for the best "walkable" highways along that red line. In Idaho, however, the line intersected at a point where there were few passable roads available, especially in the winter. That route also would have taken them over the Cascades, through the Bitter Root Mountains and into Yellowstone National Park in Wyoming. This route was too risky and isolated and did not pass through many Habitat affiliate communities.

Instead, they decided they would head south, parallel to Interstate 5 then east along the Washington side of the Columbia River. Their route would take them diagonally across northeastern Oregon, through southern Idaho then turn south toward Salt Lake City. From Salt Lake to Atlanta the route was easier. They chose not to walk on freeways and there were plenty of back roads through these areas. The Rockies gave them the most concern. A man from the National Weather Service in Reno, Nevada, cautioned them that they could be encountering snowfalls when they arrived in May. Northern Kansas was perfect and offered the opportunity to visit Habitat affiliates in Manhattan, Topeka, Lawrence and Olathe before reaching Kansas City.

Jerry and Cindy drove much of their intended route in 1995 to insure accuracy of mileages and to take notes of road conditions. Jerry created a spreadsheet to keep their road notes on and record odometer readings to calculate mileage distances that they later used while walking.

It was frustrating to find roads on maps that actually didn't exist, or weren't passable when they drove to that location. There were snow conditions, rock falls and many other pitfalls to consider. Jerry accumulated stacks of maps. Computer programs generated many of them, but occasionally they had errors in them rendering portions of them useless. In search of as much information as possible, Jerry wrote letters to government agencies, but they were rarely answered.

Jerry also knew he had to allow for weather delays and he wanted to build in some extra days just in case they encountered health problems or injuries. He figured and re-figured and spent countless hours tweaking the route. Eventually the start date became clear and Jerry would be working on his maps right up to that date– February 10, 1996.

8

Quilting The Dream

Day 23
Sunday, March 3
Pendleton, Oregon

Cindy

We are enjoying a quiet day in our motel room. Jerry is sprawled across the bed doing the New York Times crossword puzzle. I am sitting in the overstuffed chair with a Diet Coke in one hand and my journal in the other.

We have decided to take this opportunity to come up with a concise answer to our most often-asked interview question. We've danced around it long enough. It is time to figure out why a married couple, just entering their sixth decade, would decide to walk across America. It is a simple question, but we don't have a simple answer.

We realize that this dream we are pursuing has come together in much the same way as the quilt that I had finished one piece at a time before we left home. The first block of our quilt of dreams began when we met. I was just 17 and a junior at Chehalis High School. Jerry was 18-½ and in his second year at Centralia Community College studying engineering. At the end of that year he needed a job and was hired by the Washington State Department of Transportation. The department sent him to the University of Washington for nine weeks of training to be a surveyor. Jerry didn't know it at the time but that job was the beginning of a career that would change a lot and span 30 years. He would be eligible for retirement just before he turned 50. Knowing this, we realized we would be young enough to plan something really interesting to do after he retired. The foundation block was in place.

We were married one year after I graduated high school. We dreamed of having a family. Patrick, Mark and Katie fulfilled that dream during our first seven years of marriage. I loved being a mom. Our lives were full and happy. We were busy pursuing the typical American dream. I was a Den Mother, Jerry a Cub Master. He coached baseball, I was a 4-H leader. I worked part-time, he worked full-time. We began taking the kids on road trips, first to Yellowstone, then Disneyland, then Washington D.C. and finally, a six-week trip across America. We were discovering a real love for volunteer work and travel.

In 1978, Jerry read William Least Heat Moon's book, *Blue Highways*. Following his lead, we thought we could spend our retirement years exploring the back roads of America in a RV. Later, reading Peter Jenkins' book, *Walk Across America*, sparked a passion in both of us. Walking would be an even better way of getting to know some of the people across this country. Neither of us had to be convinced by the other. We had a tacit agreement. It would be the perfect retirement adventure for us to celebrate 30 years of responsible employment and parenthood. That was in 1979. Another "quilt" block was added. There were many more to come.

On a sunny October afternoon in 1979, eight-year-old Katie burst through the front door from school.

"Mo-o-o-om, where *are* you?" she had hollered. "Mom, are we going to hell?"

I was stunned by the question, but calmly replied, "Why, of course not. Why do you ask?"

"Well, I sat with Debbie on the school bus today, and she asked me if I went to Sunday school. I didn't know what it was, so I said 'No,' and then she said, 'Then you will go to hell.' So Mom, can I *ple-e-e-ase* go to Sunday School?"

It had been years since we had been to church, and we had never gone since Katie had been born. This was obviously the time to return. Jerry did not agree.

"I don't care what you do on Sunday morning, just don't involve me! I just want to go for my regular Sunday morning run and relax!" Katie and I went alone. It wasn't until she came home with a notice that she would be Mary in the Christmas program that her two older brothers and her dad would set foot inside The Lutheran Church of the Good Shepherd. Soon after that, we began worshipping as a family. On June 8, 1980, our family of five was baptized into the Christian faith. One more block was in place.

We were chaperones for many youth events over the years, but it wasn't until we agreed to accompany Katie and four other young people to the Yakima Valley in the summer of 1987 that the reason for doing the walk would get clearer and another quilt block would be stitched. We built houses with Habitat for Humanity and 80 teenagers during that week, and returned to Olympia with a serious case of "Habititus", a tongue-in-cheek affliction that keeps one greatly enthused about volunteering with this worldwide organization.

The "quilt" became bigger and brighter when we decided to participate in part of a 12-week Habitat walk in 1988. Jerry, 17-year-old Katie, and I trained 500 miles and collect $10,000 in pledges. Jerry took his three weeks' vacation and we joined the 1,200-mile walk in progress in New London, Connecticut. We completed 100 miles each week with 100 other volunteers. Now we were more determined than ever to walk across America. We figured if we could walk 300 miles, why not 3,000? Our long distance Habitat walking continued in 1990 when the three of us joined a walk from Pasadena, California to Tijuana, Mexico, concurrent with the Jimmy Carter Work Project happening in San Diego and Tijuana.

In the fall of that year, at a Habitat training event in Portland, Oregon, we proposed the idea for the walk to the long-range planning committee of Habitat for Humanity. Mutually, we decided that our walk would celebrate the twentieth anniversary of Habitat in 1996. The year was set! So was the quilt piecing. Our family and preparations were not yet ready for the walk, however.

During the next six years, son Patrick and his new bride Kim would graduate from Pacific Lutheran University. In 1992, their first child and our first grandchild, Drew Charles, was born. Our second son, Mark, graduated from California Institute of the Arts and settled into life in Southern California. Our daughter, Katie married Curtis and they both graduated from Seattle Pacific University. At that point, our children had helped us to achieve another dream. They had all graduated from college and we were thrilled with their accomplishments.

In the meantime, we had helped start the South Puget Sound Habitat affiliate. I received my associate degree in early childhood development and turned our old house into our very own Sparkleberry's Preschool while we were having a new house built

In August of 1993, Jerry retired from his job with the Washington State Department of Transportation. We celebrated in Paris at the wedding reception of Mark and his new bride. In January, Pat and Kim's second child, Conner Bond was born. Our family was growing and we were hooked on kids-in-laws and grandparenthood!

All this time, we continued to talk about and plan our walk across America. We walked wherever we could, purchased an exercise bike and jump rope. The weight bench was dusted off and put to use. I collected and began using a regimen of floor exercises and stretches. We began purchasing items we knew we would need, while we still had two incomes. Susan Howlett graciously agreed to teach us about grant writing and we used those skills to write 75 proposals to corporations, requesting donations of products for the walk and/or money for Habitat for Humanity.

Jerry had outpatient surgery on a bunion. It turned out to be more extensive than originally planned, and a titanium screw was inserted to connect the bone that had to be shortened. In place of walking during the recovery period, he worked out on the exercise bike.

In June of 1995, in final preparation for total freedom, we sold Sparkleberry's to Kim and Pat. The next week, we hitched our trailer to the suburban and headed south to build houses with the 1995 Jimmy Carter Work Project in Watts, California. While there, one of our co-workers suggested we seek donated hotel rooms to stay in during the weekends during the walk. It was an idea that many endorsed and our friend Cher Bucher began making calls to procure these rooms.

From Los Angeles, we headed east and while staying with Pam and Denney Hardesty in Arlington, Texas, Katie called to say our proposal writing was bearing fruit. Two sandal companies were interested in donating their products for the walk, Birkenstock Corporation and Chaco Sandals. While the Chacos were great for evening activities, Birkenstocks were chosen for the walk. It was while testing a pair of Chacos in Arlington that I had my first encounter with fire ants, while sitting on a curb to change socks. That encounter resulted in 38 bites to my derriere and took three weeks to heal.

We left Texas with a new respect for ants and continued east to Americus, Georgia, home of Habitat for Humanity® International. We spent five days there, organizing the walk and creating the brochures we would distribute during the walk. After driving to Atlanta from there, we began compiling road notes as we drove the walk route back toward Olympia. More corporations were responding to our proposals and in all, eight companies donated items to us. Sadly, none donated money to Habitat for Humanity.

In the fall of 1995, our third grandson, Logan Allyn Bryan, was born. He was the youngest member of a committee of family and friends who volunteered to help us with final preparation. They sent out 1,500 letters and helped us decide on the design of our T-shirts, banners and official logo. They also inventoried and organized 15 boxes of our gear, typed and laminated song sheets and produced 200 thank-you certificates for us to give to each host family and support vehicle team. Everyone worked tirelessly while we continued to train and often repeated the Holden Village prayer tacked on our planning room wall.

At that point, our quilt of dreams was almost complete. Each square had its own beauty. Some were perfect. Others were a little ragged without all the stitches in place. We chose to leave the binding off of this "quilt" though. As long as we are alive, we will follow our dreams and add more and more "blocks" along the way.

Now, all we have to do is figure out how to explain all of this to our next interviewer in three minutes or less.

Holden Village Prayer

*O Lord God
Who has called us, your servants,
To ventures of which we cannot see the ending
By paths as yet untrodden
Through perils unknown
Give us faith to go out with good courage
Not knowing where we go
But only that your hand is leading us,
Through Jesus Christ
Our Lord.
Amen*

Chapter 9

Character References

Day 32
Tuesday, March 12
Durkee, Oregon

Cindy

We are walking in a brisk wind just east of Baker City, Oregon on Highway 30 this morning. This little "blue highway" runs parallel to I-84, so we watch the traffic whizzing by us at 70 miles per hour while we plod along at 3.5 mph. Those folks could be in Brigham City, Utah by suppertime. We will be there by Easter. There are advantages to our mode of travel though. Our bodies and souls will soak up the beauty of an area that would seem boring to us if we were in a car. We wouldn't have a hand-waving relationship with the train engineers as they pull their humongous loads through these barren hills. We would not hear the spring birds singing their enthusiastic songs or have the opportunity to talk to the family driving their cattle to summer pastures. I wish the occupants of those vehicles could slow their pace and really feel the land and hear the sounds. They would most likely discover the awakening of their senses the way we are.

They would also meet a lot of interesting characters. Then again, maybe they wouldn't. I must remind myself that Jerry attracts characters the way cotton candy attracts children. To say the least, he is amused by them. Consequently, last week was very amusing.

The first character Jerry encountered as we walked into Baker City, was a guy with an unusual story. As Jerry recounts it:

"I stopped at the Cenex Station to use the bathroom. A man was standing nearby when I emerged, and he followed me out the door. (He obviously had heard me talking to the attendant behind the cash register). He began telling me how he had walked across Minnesota once, from North Dakota to the Canadian border. That in itself is an interesting geographic phenomenon, but I chose not to contradict him. He went on to explain that he did this in the winter during his Christmas break from school. At this point in our conversation, he advised me that we should befriend Greyhound bus drivers while we are walking because they had looked after him during that time. This conversation went on for a while until he changed the subject. He then started telling me about the Charbonneau family, the Charbonneaus of Lewis and Clark's time. He explained that they had cached a large gold object (he referred to it as a marker) in a box canyon that could only be reached by rappelling into it from a helicopter. That seemed strange if it were a true box canyon but I went along with his story. He said he could get within a mile of it right now but he wanted to wait and contact the *National Geographic* magazine to witness his discovery. He told me that the gold marker was valued at $250 million. He is sure that it is located between Deadwood and Lead, South Dakota.

"With the money, he plans to build a covered dome in Baker City for the locals kids to play football. He will name it the Hamilton building, according to a witch's prediction that he would build this building someday and name it after her husband.

"I actually wanted to believe him, but I kept discovering little things that contradicted much of his story. In the end, I walked away with a bemused look on my face and a better understanding of some of the characters that roam the earth."

We met our next character at the invitation of our hosts, Shirley and Don Knepp. They had picked us up at the end of our walk day last week and taken us directly to the Radium Hot Springs. Their friend Jack, owner of the springs, had met us in the parking lot. He was a young 80, lean and tall with white hair, a ready smile and a twinkle in his eye. He had invited us to follow him along a weed-choked gravel pathway and into an old building crammed full of Coca-Cola memorabilia. There, we paused to reminisce amongst the memorabilia, then went to change into our swimsuits. On our

Soaking our soles at Radium Hot Springs near North Powder, Oregon.

way to the pool, we passed several humorous signs that Jack had posted. One was a disclaimer announcing to one and all that the Hot Springs did not comply with Oregon health department regulations. It read, SWIM AT YOUR OWN RISK. Another had proclaimed that if you wanted to skinny dip, the hours were 10 p.m. to daybreak and the rate was $250 per person. There were no group rates. This character had quite a sense of humor!

Finally, we had arrived at a 40-foot long pool surrounded by green fiberglass panels. We were overwhelmed by the smell of sulphur and surprised to see ribbons of green slime floating in the water but Jack assured us that it was harmless. Hesitantly, Jerry and I lowered our road weary bodies into one of the sunken old claw foot bathtubs arranged fanned out at one end of the pool. The sulphur water turned the silver ring on my right hand bright orange but Jack assured me the discoloration would go away.

After all five of us were settled in the very warm water. Jack, still wearing his red wool stocking cap, told us about the Hot Springs. He said that the temperature of the water at its source is 140 degrees Fahrenheit but as it flows into the pool it becomes a more comfortable temperature, although still warmer than normal hot tub water. From its initial entry at our end of the pool, the water circulates through the pool and exits at the far end. Jack encouraged us to use soap and bathe since the water replenishes itself constantly. It seemed strange to soap up in a pool that smelled like sulphur, but we dutifully did as we were told. While we hesitantly took our public baths Jack told humorous stories about himself and the people who had visited the springs before the health department had shut it down.

Jack had been the kind of character we could have listened to for hours but we needed to get to a potluck at the Methodist Church. We toweled the sulphur-smelling water off, changed into clean clothes and said farewell to Jack and the Radium Hot Springs. As we drove away, we wondered what the people at the potluck would think about four people walking in, reeking of sulphur. Shirley and Don assured us no one would mind.

Our walk alongside Interstate 84 continues.

We have only walked four miles when we meet a new character. The driver of a forest green F150 pick up pulls alongside Jerry and introduces himself as John. He says he lives in Durkee. He has lots of questions about the walk. Jerry tells him the whole story. John thinks what we are doing is cool. He reaches into a shirt pocket stuffed with big bills and pulls out a $5 bill, a donation for Habitat. He apologizes for not giving more. We assure him that $5 will buy a lot of nails for Habitat houses and that pleases John.

Before we walk away, Jerry tells John that he can stop at the blue Volvo support vehicle parked up the road and get a Habitrek '96 brochure from Carl and Dotty Fehring, here from Olympia, to be our support vehicle drivers for the week. While John goes to search for Fehrings, we again head on down the road.

"What is that sitting up there on the shoulder?" I ask Jerry as I squint my eyes to get a better look.

"I don't know, but it looks interesting," the king of road litter replies.

A few more yards of walking and we discover that it is a coke can with a sticky note attached. It says,

"You're doing great! Four miles 'til lunch!"

Dotty and Carl have struck upon a unique way to encourage us. We wonder if there will be more. Sure enough, two miles later, there is another one. "Two miles to go!" it reads. We like this!

Finally, we reach the car and sit down to a lunch purchased and prepared for us by Dotty and Carl. John is the topic of conversation.

"Hey, did John stop and ask you for a brochure this morning?" Jerry inquires.

"Yeah, he did," Dotty says with a big grin. "He told us he had two messages for us. The first was that you told him to ask for a brochure. The second was that he wanted us to walk for awhile so that you could have a break!"

"That's pretty clever of ol' John. I'm sure you know that we only sent the first message but you've got to love a stranger who is so concerned for us," Jerry replies.

It's a little after 3 p.m. when John comes by, again. We both lean on his window ledge this time. He introduces us to his female passenger and tells her what we are doing. She asks lots of questions because she has never met anyone walking across America before. She loves Jimmy Carter and thinks Habitat is great. She says she will pray for us.

John's speech is slurred and his cheeks are real red. His breath reeks of alcohol.

"Hey, why doncha jushst get in the truck and I'll give ya a ride. You been walkin' too far taday."

"Sorry John, we don't take rides. Remember that we are WALKING across America, not riding," I tease. But John doesn't give up.

"Ah, come on, it's not cheatin.' I won't tell a soul. I promish."

"No, John, we only have one and one-half miles to go today and our support people are waiting for us up there. We appreciate your concern for us, though," Jerry says.

John drives away with a shrug, looking a little dejected. We worry about him getting home safely. After all, he is a caring soul.

Several hours later, we are comfortably settled at Vivian and Bill Zickman's home that perches on a hill overlooking the tiny town of Durkee. I emerge from the shower. Vivian is just hanging up the phone.

"Boy, your phone sure rings a lot," Jerry comments.

Vivian pauses, obviously trying to decide whether to explain or not.

"Well, it doesn't normally ring this much. The truth is, the neighbors are checking in. You're the big news in this tiny town and they want to know what you are like. It's not everyday that someone like you stays in Durkee. That last call was our neighbor.

She was trying to see you through her telescope but wasn't having much luck."

"We're always amused by what most people think we will look like," Jerry offers. " I don't know if they are disappointed or just surprised that we don't have that athletic, adventurer look. The fact that we are just an average looking couple seems to surprise a lot of folks. We are actually amused by it. We like that element of surprise," he concludes.

It is now Thursday, March 14 and we have crossed into Idaho. This is our entry into our third state and completes our 500th mile. We consider it an important milestone. The large paper bag banners lettered with "WAY TO GO CINDY AND JERRY!" indicate that Dotty and Carl do too. The four of us celebrate this moment over Dairy Queen ice cream treats. We have appreciated Dotty and Carl's encouragement all week. They are friends from Olympia who have come to help us under difficult circumstances. It has been a short time since their 20-year-old daughter, Dawn, was tragically murdered while studying to become a missionary. In the midst of grieving Dawn's death, they have generously given us the gift of their time and encouragement. We are deeply touched.

It is 5:45 p.m. when Dotty parks in front of the white doublewide mobile home in Parma, Idaho. We are not convinced that we have the right home, but we never think to question the date. Jerry gets out of the car and finds Bill Hall working in his beautiful yard.

"Hi, I'm Jerry Schultz. We're the couple walking across America. The Knepps from North Powder, Oregon arranged for you to be our host family tonight."

Bill gets a shocked look on his face and then replies, defensively. "That's all fine but you are here on the wrong night. We were told to expect you for supper tomorrow night."

"Well, there's lots of ways this could happen," Jerry explains. "We meet lots of different people on this trek. When we are in search of host families, they often offer to help. They just leave a message on our voice mail days later, telling us the name and address of a person who has agreed to host us. So you can see, there are plenty of margins for error. It's not a problem, though. We stayed with the Andersons in Ontario last night and they invited us to spend another night with them if we needed to. We'll just come back here tomorrow night." Jerry apologizes, backing away.

"Well now, just a minute. Let me go talk to the better half. You go ahead. I'll meet you out front," Bill says.

Jerry returns to the car and faces the three of us with the "right place, wrong date" story. The four of us are prepared to return to Wayne and Betty Anderson's when Bill returns. He is more relaxed now as he searches for a solution to a dilemma we have foisted upon him.

"We have decided we want you to stay. Only problem is, it's our bowling night," Bill says.

"Ollie is really disappointed because she had a big steak dinner planned for tomorrow night. Is there any way you could stay both nights?"

"Well sure, I think so. We were just going to stay in a motel in Nampa Friday night," Jerry says.

We begin to unload our luggage and then plan to run to town for dinner and come back after the Halls return from bowling. Bill says to follow them into Nyssa, where they bowl. There's a café nearby where we can all grab a bite to eat.

Since we are fresh off the road, we order our food and then excuse ourselves to go clean up in the restroom. When we return, Bill and Ollie are gone. When the waitress brings our salads, we ask where the Halls are.

"Oh, Bill paid for your meals and then left. He said they had already eaten but wanted to be sure their friends were taken care of and then paid for your meals."

We are amazed. "But we've only known them an hour!"

"Doesn't surprise me one bit. That's the kind of people they are," she smiles.

These are definitely not the kind of people we hear about on the daily news, I think. I wish we did.

During this time, we found $1.44.

In Training

With the goal of walking 3,000 miles, there needed to be a lot of time dedicated to training. For Cindy and Jerry, training began years before the actual walk. While at times it could be long and arduous, many of those times were great fun.

During the rainy Christmas season, Jerry and Cindy resorted to becoming mall walkers. Instead of doing a more typical five to 10 laps, they would do 20. One Salvation Army bell ringer got so intrigued that he requested a lap count every time they passed him.

When the same old routes became boring, they started walking at night. It perked up the familiarity of their regular route and gave them more time to make phone calls at home during the day. Enjoying Christmas-lighted yard displays and stores open late for shopping, they trained through the Christmas season of '95. That December, they walked through a drenching rain for 11 miles to join their family at a local tree farm for the annual tree cutting.

The mild temperatures of western Washington winters did not afford an opportunity to train for sub-freezing weather so they spent four days in the central Washington Bavarian-theme village of Leavenworth. The temperature there never rose above 20 degrees the entire time they were there.

Editor-at-large Mark Fenton of *Walking Magazine* helped them work out a computer-printed schedule that incrementally increased their walking miles up until one week before they were to leave. As the mileage increased, their time away from home increased. With all the other walk preparations, this became a full-time job for both of them. Every strengthened muscle, every push of endurance brought them closer to the day when they would begin their walk across America.

Much time was spent at the library researching historical weather patterns in the states along the route. Jerry and Cindy revisited the book *Walk Across America* and read other books written by people who had walked long distances. While training five days a week was very time consuming, Jerry and Cindy tried as much as possible to live a normal life– spending Fridays with their grandsons and attending Tuesday night bible study.

To escape the relentless rain, Jerry and Cindy used their frequent flyer miles to travel to Palm Springs, California. Once they arrived at the airport terminal, they changed into shorts and sandals, walked past the rental car counters then out of the airport with backpack-suitcases strapped on their backs and big daypacks strapped to their chests. The two luggage-laden walkers elicited curious stares from trendy attired retirees as they left the airport then turned west onto Tahquitz Canyon Way. They were headed to the Casa Cody Inn, their home away from home for five glorious days. The desert sunshine gave a much-needed reprieve from the incessant rains at home. They felt renewed and regenerated, like two bears emerging from hibernation. After a couple of days of walking around Palm Springs and the neighboring communities, they now knew that they were prepared to walk in warm weather. They returned home excited and nearly ready to roll. There was still one month to go before they would begin their cross-country trek.

10

Blessings in the Sawtooths

Since leaving Ollie and Bill's, we have spent several days in the Boise area. We talked to a large group of third graders, enjoyed verbal sparring with the crew at radio station KIDO and appreciated having Myrna and Larry Bowman, our daughter-in-law, Kim's parents, as support drivers. We then wandered through small towns forgotten by the rerouting of traffic to the interstate. The scenery was starkly beautiful and interesting too. We learned about whistle pigs and "petrified watermelon" and saw a fence made of old bedsprings. Then on a cold, snowy Saturday Lash and Peggy LaRue took us for a ride in their small plane. Hagerman Valley and Twin Falls were magnificent in their fine dusting of snow and Shoshone Falls were at record flows. Jerry's airsickness was the only thing that dampened the experience.

The following week we walked with five Habitat friends through the area that we had viewed from the plane. We were energized by their presence and deflated when they left us in a snowstorm outside "Burrrrley," as Jerry affectionately called it. That was also the day that our luggage was inadvertently left at a neighbor's house instead of our host home and our support vehicle's back window was shattered by a rock thrown by a large truck. The week ended with a bang, but our memories of that area and the people who made it so special took us right into the next week, Utah, and new challenges.

Day 52
Sunday, April 1
Burley, Idaho

Cindy

Since scouting the walk route last year, we were convinced that the landscape in southeastern Idaho would be some the most dismal of the entire route. The wind can be fierce in the valley that runs between the Wasatch and the Sawtooth mountain ranges. The ensuing dust from plowed, barren fields calls for roadside warning signs every few miles. Tomorrow we will begin walking through the valley of dread. At the moment, though, we are walking across the parking lot adjacent to our weekend hotel. We decide the fifth- wheel RV (with the Minnesota license plates) has to be them, but we're not sure. We knock on the trailer door hesitantly. The man who answers the door is the spitting image of his brother, Ken Halvorson, our friend from Olympia.

"You must be David Halvorson," we say with relief.

"And you are Jerry and Cindy?" he asks haltingly. "Come in. This is my wife, Lois. We weren't sure we were at the right place because the person working the front desk had no record of you being here. We were just going to spend the night and leave."

"That's strange, we've been here all weekend. We are sure glad you stayed. It's still hard for us to believe you are willing to do this for two strangers."

"When Ken asked us if we could help you on our way to his son, Jon's, wedding, we were immediately interested. After all, we've never had the opportunity to spend a week with someone walking across America. Probably won't in the future either. We're anxious to get started."

On Monday morning, they get their chance. We are walking with quickened steps today. It's as if we are children waiting impatiently for Santa to arrive. More about that later. For now, Lois and Dave are good company and quick to offer help as well as busily handing out walk brochures and setting up tomorrow's all-school assembly in the tiny town of Malta. They have caught on to this support vehicle thing very quickly!

We complete today's windy miles and pile into the back seat of

Halvorson's pickup for the 25-mile ride back to the Holiday Inn in Burley. Climbing the stairs to our second-floor room, we hear them before we see them. There, across the grass courtyard, are the objects of our anticipation. Our oldest son, Patrick, is pushing our four-year-old grandson, Drew on one swing while our daughter-in-law Kim pushes two-year-old Conner on the other. Our hearts leap when we spy them. Jerry does his long-recognized "dad whistle," which sets off an avalanche of human activity. The end result is a tangle of hugs and kisses mixed with laughter and joy. Words are bouncing in every direction as we all try to catch up on the happen-

Cautionary sign for the week ahead.

ings of the past seven weeks' absence of each other.

They have just driven the walk route and cannot believe what we have accomplished thus far. Are we really okay? How hard is it, honestly? Can we continue?

On the other hand, we wonder how things are going at the preschool. At Patrick's work at Infostream? Home? With grandma and grandpa?

Tonight I get to help bathe the boys and happily tuck them between clean sheets for a bedtime story followed by prayers. I've missed feeling like a grandma. It fills me to overflowing. Sleep comes very easily tonight, for them and for me.

The next day, all eight of us pack up and leave Burley. Dave and Lois depart in their truck, Pat and Kim drive us in their dark green Chevrolet Suburban. We are assaulted by rain, sleet, snow and hail much of the day, but we are together. Drew does not understand the Halvorsons' names and immediately tags them as "Davidlewis." The name sticks, and even the adults lovingly refer to them as two people with one name.

Dave and Lois feel like part of our family but still remain the official support people for the week. When walking, they take the time to pick up aluminum cans to recycle for Habitat dollars. Their RV is like a Wal-Mart on wheels, supplying us with anything we didn't know we needed until we need it. They are a blessing to us all.

Jerry is tired of the blustery wind. It has been the bane of our existence for much of these first 700 miles. There is no way to fight it. With rain, we can put on raincoats. With sun, we put on sunscreen. But wind is impossible to escape or avoid. It makes it difficult to be heard and physically challenging to walk. Finally, today, we discover a comical use for wind. While pushing the boy's double stroller, Jerry lets go of the handle. The tail wind pushes the stroller right down the road!

Before their arrival, Patrick has gone on the Internet and discovered the Mountain Manor Bed and Breakfast in the little village of Albion. This is where we will spend the night in the absence of host homes in this area. We finish walking at 4:30 p.m. and caravan out of the drab valley landscape, past four real-life cowboys driving a herd of black angus to summer grazing grounds. When we arrive in Albion, there is no snow left at the Pomerelle Ski Area but the charm of this little-known treasure is still very much alive. It casts it's magic on us from the time we partake in fresh pizza from the deli next door (owned by Renee, the B&B owner, and run by her daughter-in-law Cindy) to our homey quarters at the B&B. We have the run of the place, including the unique indoor garden room and the recreation room with toys and a television for watching our beloved Mariners play baseball. We take a moonlit stroll around town and dream out loud of developing this area into a first-class resort.

That night we snuggle into attic bedrooms complete with patchwork quilts and antique furniture. For a second night, we recognize the blessings of days surrounded by the love and encouragement of family and new friends.

The next morning Renee's graciousness continues. There is lively conversation with her husband, Ben and a feast of crispy hash browns, link sausage, fluffy scrambled eggs, brown sugar muffins, grapefruit, orange juice and coffee. Patrick and family stay behind to give a newspaper interview to the South Idaho Press

Family joins us as we enter our fourth state.

First grandson, Drew walking in the shadow of first son, Patrick.

while the Halvorson's drive us down the mountain and back on a route shrouded in sunshine for the first time this week. When the family rejoins us, we are just entering our fourth state, Utah, so everyone poses for our traditional entering-a-new-state photo.

Then it's time for lunch and a roadside picnic featuring huge deli sandwiches from the Albion Deli. It is extremely rare for us to have so many people to share lunch with and we are really enjoying it until Drew runs out into the road and must be firmly reminded about the dangers of traffic. It is a difficult lesson; given the party-like atmosphere and the one-car-an-hour traffic volume he is witnessing every day on Highway 42.

After lunch, Dave and Lois leave to go into Snowville to get the RV set up at a campground for the night. We plan to settle in a motel located nearby at the end of the day. While they are gone, we all continue walking. Even Drew walks a mile in his dad's shadow. The pace is not a stretch for him because Pat is nursing a badly sprained ankle.

When Dave and Lois return in their truck, they are anxious to know how we survived the severe thunderstorm that blew through.

"It didn't affect us. Black clouds boiled in and around the mountains on both sides of us but not one drop of rain came our way," we recount.

"That's positively amazing. It doesn't even seem possible."
They react.

When these things occur, we have learned to stop and remember which day of the week it is.

Today is Wednesday.

"I bet we can explain it," Cindy offers. "It's the first Wednesday of the month. That means Piece Corps (our church's quilting group with the funny name) is making quilts and having their birthday luncheon today. They pray for our safety each time they meet. It seems clear their prayers have diverted another storm from us."

One hour later we complete our miles and head into Snowville. We drive up to the old motel where we believe we will be comfortable for the night. But when the owner shows us a couple of crummy little rooms, which reek of Lysol, we begin to have second thoughts. The owner then tells us she will be back to help us after she "beats her kids' butts" for jumping on the beds, we decide to take our difference of philosophies and seek better accommodations. It is an easy decision but not easily accomplished.

It is over chicken strip dinners at Mollie's Café, that we decide to leave Dave and Lois set up at the RV park while we ride with Patrick and family to Brigham City, 56 miles away, to search for a motel. There is no other option in Snowville. We plan to drive back out to the route tomorrow morning, where we will meet up with the Halvorsons.

We find a nice Howard Johnson's with a "special for us" rate of $40 a night and settle in for a swim and the boy's nightly routine, while Pat and Kim go in search of a new stroller tire and tube to replace the one that blew out this afternoon. They return with an inner tube (but no tire) and a spur-of-the-moment plan.

"We found this cool-looking ice cream parlor called Peach City Drive Inn. It looks like the soda shop from the old television series, *Happy Days*. Who cares if the boys are in their pajamas? Let's go!"

Always ones to seize the moment, we enthusiastically oblige.

The interior of Peach City is not decorated to imitate the '50s; it has been here that long. The red vinyl booths are authentic. The Route 66 wallpaper is not. It is no coincidence that Coca-Cola memorabilia figure prominently into the decorating theme.

Sharing a kiss at our favorite drive-in, located in Brigham City, Utah.

We are thrown back into the time of our youth. We are tickled by the kid's reaction. Jer puts a quarter in the jukebox (inflation has raised the ante from a nickel!). Rod Stewart's hoarse voice belts out, "Have I Told You Lately That I Love You?" I melt into the arms of my soul mate then dig into a hot fudge sundae. I wonder…can it get much better than this?

Pat calls his Dad's "McGuyver" skills into service once we rejoin Halvorsons the next morning. With some good old "Jerry ingenuity" and a tube of Shoe Goo, the guys soon have the tire mended and the stroller up and rolling.

On this, the last day they will be with us, Drew is determined to memorize the walk song Paul LaRue had written and brought to us back in Vancouver, Washington.

"I'm walkin' 20 miles for a good night's sleep, 20 miles a day for a good night's sleep. I've got miles to go and promises to keep. That's why I'm on a Habitat walk."

We sing it over and over, adding new verses as he masters the last. We walk past road workers names, creatively written with tar after the road seams have been patched. Steve and Bill have left their names for us to walk upon.

"There's nothing for your legs like a good brisk walk. It's better for your body than to sit around and talk, but to do it for the exercise alone I'd balk, If I didn't get a good night's sleep."
We walk past cows' heads, disgustingly stuck on fence posts after the rest of the cow had been butchered and hauled off to market.

"A brother needs a decent roof over his head, a sister and her kids need a place to go to bed, and everybody needs a little more than bread, if they're gonna get a good night's sleep."
We stop for lunch at Morton Thiokol where space engine boosters are manufactured. David videotapes a mock interview with us on his video camera to show the folks back in Olympia. Then Jerry wanders off to look at the rocket displays. He rejoins us after awhile and has an interesting story to tell about another character. "I was reading the signs over there when a guy came over and asked if he could help. He answered my questions and then went on to tell me he had retired from Thiokol, having worked there since 1948. He said he went in for his interview with some solid rocket fuel in his pockets, which impressed the people doing the interview, and they eventually hired him. They wanted to know how he knew so much without much formal training. He told them he had read a lot of books.

At that point, Pat drifted closer and looked at me with a "what kind of nut have you taken up with now?" look. I tried to change the subject by asking him about the flares we had seen in the sky yesterday. That was a mistake. He said the flares were being tested. He told me they use them to flush out the Viet Cong. It was then that I began to wonder about the sanity of one of us. He was speaking of the Viet Cong as if we were still at war. He went on to explain how Thiokol had disposed of 400 pounds of "fletches," which are little barbed pellets that can tear a man to pieces. He had taken some of these home and I asked him why. His reply was more than a little unnerving.

"You can put them in shot gun shells and when Viet Cong come at you, you can cut them to pieces."

I told him it was nice talking to him and very slowly, not wanting to cause him alarm, I backed away. I didn't tell him about the walk, nor did I give him a brochure. I didn't want him to come looking for me. We are all anxious to move on down the road after that story.

Drew is excited to see so many Thiokol employees out walking along the road during their lunch hour. His response makes us all laugh.

"Look, Gramma and Poppa, those people are walking across America, too!"

Toddler Conner is more interested in an egg-shaped rock and a pheasant feather Poppa has found for him.

All too soon, the day's miles are completed. We drive back to the motel, go for quick swim and then get as dressed up as our limited wardrobe allows. Pat and Kim have made dinner reservations at Maddox Ranch House for all eight of us. On this, the last night they will be with us, we celebrate my birthday five days early. The staff recognizes the uniqueness of this celebration and goes all out to match their service to our jovial mood. The chicken-fried steak is the best I've ever had. There is complimentary strawberry pie to share with everyone, balloons tied to my chair and the best homemade root beer ever. As we depart, they give each adult a chocolate-dipped candy stick and the little boys 20-piece bags of candy. It has indeed been a special meal.

After a ride around the area, not wanting the fun to end, we make a ceremonial stop at Peach City Drive In. Eventually, though, we must face the inevitable. Pat, Kim and the boys are leaving tomorrow morning at eight. We all try to act like we're not thinking about it. Bringing it up would put a damper on a wonderful evening.

A night of tossing and turning, accompanied by a few premature tears, turns into a morning of what appears to be routine preparation. There is a purposeful avoidance of any conversation about their preparing to leave.

Finally, we can no longer put off the dreaded goodbyes. I had anticipated a few tears. The first hug brings sobs. And the second and the third. The little boys don't quite get it.

"Why are you crying, Gramma?" Drew asks.

" 'Cause I'm going to miss you, that's why. You have been a tremendous blessing in an area where we could have struggled every day."

Finally it's time for them to leave.

Jerry wraps his arms around me. The two of us wave until the big green Suburban is out of sight. Jerry hugs me close and wipes my eyes. Once again, we are alone and today's 20 miles suddenly seem like a trip to the dentist for a root canal.

On our ride out to the route, we talk about family ties and our struggle with choosing to be away from ours in pursuit of a dream. It's a time of questioning. Lois and Dave generously encourage our dialogue and support the decision we have made to follow our dream.

The first 10 miles of the day are emotionally difficult. It's ironic that today is Good Friday. Dave walks with us, stooping to pick up every aluminum can he comes upon. Lois supplies Cindy with Ibuprofen to numb a worsening blister. There is no doubt that the pain is exacerbated by an aching heart. The two of us acknowledge it and move through the day, anxious for it to end but not wanting to say yet another goodbye.

After a brief bout with difficult traffic, we walk into Brigham City this afternoon. Our route passes Peach City Drive Inn. We don't. We give in to the temptation and celebrate Dave's 18-mile walk accomplishment with malts. In the red vinyl seats and the comfort of air conditioning, we reminisce about the sometimes difficult, but wonderful week we've had together. We could never have planned it. It had just happened. The Halvorsons have been a big part of it and we are extremely grateful. As we think about finishing the last two miles of the day, we realize that there is no more emotional or physical energy left in our tanks. The long, lonely weekend ahead will afford plenty of time to make up the two miles. Instead, we drive to a recycler to turn in the aluminum cans, a surprising 56 pounds in all. $19.65 for Habitat!

Dave and Lois drive us 20 miles to Riverside, Utah and a new host home. The door of new friendships opens once again when Frank and Fumi Nichiguchi welcome us into their home. Then we share hugs and thank Dave and Lois, who, just six days ago, had opened another door of friendship.

"Goodbye, 'Davidlewis,' we hope we can share an adventure with you again someday."

On Saturday, the Nichiguchis drive us back to the same motel where we had stayed with Pat and Kim in Brigham City. We spend the day working on procuring host families for the weeks ahead, catching up on journals and e-mails and making plans for church attendance tomorrow morning.

When we awake on Easter Sunday, we are very much aware of just how alone we are, on this, the first family oriented holiday since we left home. There is no ham baking in the oven, no eggs being hidden in anticipation of the children who will arrive after church, and no new Easter clothes waiting to be worn.

Instead, we put on the same no-wrinkle church clothes we have been wearing since the walk began. After church, the pastor and his wife take us out to lunch and we are grateful for the hospitality. We appreciate and enjoy the time together, but when we finally admit it to ourselves, home is where our hearts are this day.

This afternoon we head out into the sunshine and make a stop at the local K-Mart to buy new earrings, shorts and a Tee-shirt for my birthday gifts from Jerry. We hope to find a nice restaurant for dinner but the only thing open is Arbys and Kentucky Fried Chicken. We choose "The Colonel's" and sit in a dining room of dismal surroundings discussing our misery. The best thing that can happen to this day is for it to be done. Walking back to the motel, hand in hand, God gifts us with an inspiring sunset. We do not miss the message. Yes, the world is beautiful, and yes, we have chosen to be right where we are today.

Today is Tuesday, April 9th, my 51st birthday. The plum trees are covered in delicate lavender blossoms. Daffodils are poking inquisitive yellow heads up out of the winter ground and stretching toward the pure blue Utah sky. Our gloomy attitudes of the weekend have gone away with the resurrection of a new week. We skip along without a support vehicle this week. Because we are in an urban area with plenty of opportunity for restrooms and meals, we enjoy pursuing the adventure without assistance.

Jerry's eyes are scanning the road for just the right treasures today–a decoration to show the world that this is my special day. He finally discovers a row of colorful vinyl flags lying in the mud and cleans them off with his handkerchief. He then ceremoniously ties them on my daypack. It's goofy but I like it. It makes my pack look like a party room decorated in crepe paper. A couple of blocks later, a young car salesman clad in a white shirt and tie, hollers across the four-lane highway at us.

"Hey, whatayadoin' with my flags?"

Jerry fires back in disgust. "We didn't get them from your lot. Relax!"

Neither party has any intention of running across four busy

Celebrating the arrival of spring on Cindy's 50th birthday.

traffic lanes to pursue the argument, so my birthday decorations stay firmly tethered to my pack.

Later, a reporter from the *Ogden Examiner* intercepts us to conduct an interview and take photos. Then we have a conversation about following dreams. He needs to understand our passion for this walk. He needs us to confirm for him that it is a good thing to follow one's dreams. We are only to happy to oblige him.

Don and Bernie Mitchell are planning to take us to lunch today. Important partners in the local Habitat affiliate, they took us under their wing last weekend and we value their friendship. The problem is, they can't find us and we don't know we're lost!

We head towards a McDonald's for a bathroom break. They have driven into the same McDonald's lot to use a pay phone in hopes of reaching Al McGuire, our host from last night. Don gets out of his car and reaches into his pocket for a quarter just as we walk by. He looks shocked but pleased.

"There you are! We have been trying to find you in case you needed any assistance. What are the chances that we would just happen to pull into this McDonald's, out of all the fast food restaurants along this stretch? Amazing!"

We are amused but not surprised. "You know, Don, nothing really surprises us anymore. It's as if God has His own little beacon attached to us."

During this time, we found $2.20.

Arnold's Advice

In May 1994, Jerry and Cindy wrote a letter to Arnold Schwarzenegger's fitness column, "Ask Arnold".
It was printed, with his response, in USA Today's Weekend.
His advice was followed to the letter!

Q. My husband is 50 and I am 49. We plan to walk across America in 1996. We will cover 20 miles a day, five days a week. We now walk and run. Could you help us with an overall fitness plan?

A. I envy you: walking, especially with my wife, is one of my favorite activities, and it is a terrific way to see this beautiful country.

The walking and running that you do now are working your cardiovascular system. Add a general strengthening routine twice a week, working the major muscle groups of the upper and lower body.

It's also essential that you stretch daily, especially those muscles that can tighten with walking; the calves, hamstrings and upper back. Plan a 10-minute stretching routine that you can do every day of your walk, before and after you cover your daily distance.

There's an excellent article on distance walking by Mark Fenton in this month's issue of *Walking Magazine*. For walkers like yourselves who will cover hilly terrain, he suggests adding at least an hour of hiking once a month to your routine. He also recommends regular time trials to see how you're doing and details three workouts to do each week at short, medium and long distances.

Enjoy your training and your trip. Send me a postcard!

Arnold Schwarzenegger

11

When the Saints Come Driving In

Day 61
Wednesday, April 10
Salt Lake City, Utah

Jerry

It is week 10. We are in Salt Lake City heading south on Victory Road, also known as Highway 184, toward the State Capitol. Head down, I am trudging and begrudging, as I lead our walk up the long hill. Victory Road seems ill named for us today. The only victory we can be assured of is the completion of today's 20-mile walk and the assurance that our other two families will be joining us this weekend. Our hope for a welcome from the Salt Lake City Habitat affiliate is not to be. We are reasonably sure that someone will eventually come to get us, but who and when is a puzzle now.

There once had been a set plan for our pickup and transportation to Park City at day's end, but that has evaporated along with any benign thoughts we had about the people who seem to have let us down. We don't know what we will do when we reach the top of the hill. Our carefree walk from this morning now seems destined to end in frustration and befuddlement. Cindy, trailing about 20 feet behind me, is unhappy, and I am unhappy that she is unhappy. We have just walked through a loud and dirty battlefield, and it has taken its toll.

The morning had begun very well after a good meal and a good night's sleep. Our host for last night, drove us from his home in Layton to Farmington to begin our 20-mile trek into Salt Lake City. The early morning overcast sky soon burned away under the persistent sun and we basked in its warmth as its rays recharged our inner batteries and lightened our steps. We were far from the cold winds of southeastern Idaho and northern Utah, clad in walking shorts and Tee-shirts, and enjoying the freedom from our heavy, bulky winter clothing. Our few necessities for the day, which now include Neutrogena SPF 30 sun block and lip balm, are stashed in our daypacks.

At this point in the day, we were on our own, once again feeling like teenagers, cut loose from parents. We held hands as we explored new territory. The sun continued to brighten our day, and lighten our spirits as we wound our way in and out of the communities along Highway 106. The mix of rural and urban areas provides us with a variety of pleasant distractions and many opportunities for snacks and bathroom breaks. We enjoyed the early morning bustle of each community and stopped at a bagel shop for our morning break.

The miles and the morning had nearly past when we reached North Salt Lake. The temperature had reached 80 degrees for the third day this week. The warmth of the day erased any remaining memories of the cold, windy days we struggled through in the past two months. We were not sure what we should do about getting lunch since we couldn't tell if there were any food opportunities beyond the long curving road ahead of us. The young lady at a convenience store located just short of our entrance into oblivion had told us that there would be nothing ahead. Our best chance for food was at the deli in the grocery store a short distance back up the road.

So we retreated back to the store and sought out culinary delights from the deli. Our orange vests and brief attire attracted attention and a few furtive glances our way. Since we were road-grimed and sweaty, we paid and went outside to enjoy our noon repast at the curb near the entrance. We had positioned ourselves on the curb, so as not to interfere with any customers, and dined in the noonday sun. Chicken fingers, corn dogs, baby taters and fruit-flavored yogurt washed down with Diet Coke and Diet Mountain Dew satisfied our immediate hunger as we watched the shoppers come and go. As further insurance against famine in the next few miles, we also downed the last of the bagels we purchased this morning.

Excessive calories and fat grams devoured, we tidied up the area and ourselves and then set out toward our destination somewhere in Salt Lake City. We did not know it yet, but we were saying goodbye to our carefree and balmy day. There should have been a warning sign where the sidewalk ended similar to the ones in northern Utah that had cautioned us about the possibility of severe winds for the next 25 miles. This one could have read, "You are about to enter an area of industrial blight. All your senses will be assailed. Permanent negative impressions of this area may occur. Welcome to Salt Lake City!"

Now, rounding the sweeping curve onto Highway 89, we are introduced to the black hole that will extinguish our morning zeal. Too soon, we are intimidated by huge trucks and assailed by blowing dust and sand as we pass the cement plant and earth-devouring operations on our left. Above us, the large trucks appear to travel so close to the edge of the lofty, steep cliff that they might tumble over the side and land upon us any second. The dirty-looking refinery across the freeway and to our right is belching fumes, and the dark vapors cast additional pall to the area. The noise and intensity of the traffic on Interstate 15 immediately to our right further assails our visual and auditory senses. We watch high-speed vehicles on a rampage attempting to pass each other or maneuver to enter or exit the freeway. Senses once dulled by low-volume traffic and the beautiful, relative quietness of small towns are now screaming in protest and concern of what lies ahead.

We have no choice but to walk on as we continue seeking the best places to be. Eventually, we must share the road with the truck traffic as it buzzes along in and out on the road below its hilltop hive. The swirling dust bowl they generate coats our contact lenses and nostrils. When we are nearly through this minefield, Cindy's noontime Diet Coke and my Diet Mountain Dew strike us with urgent need at the same time. Bladders, perhaps reacting to the nervous tension we feel, are telling us that they can't wait to see what opportunities for relief lie ahead.

Having walked over 800 miles now, we long ago learned to put modesty aside for these types of urgencies. We usually have managed to conceal ourselves from motorists and the rest of the public. The freeway to our right and a cliff with trucks traveling close to the edge affording a near vertical view on our left allow us no room here to completely conceal our actions. There are some sparse bare bushes at the base of the precipice, so we devise a plan. Using one of the larger bushes to slightly break the clear line of sight from either direction, we take turns standing as a screen while we each take care of our pressing urgency. No trucks fall over the side of the cliff, or drive past, and hopefully traffic is moving at such a speed on the interstate that drivers and passengers never realize what they are seeing.

Now relieved, we rebuckle our daypacks and walk on to the far reaches of this dismal setting. The din and frantic activity are finally behind us when we reach Beck Street.

I calculate that we are within an hour of finishing the walk and at our first opportunity to use a phone, I make the appointed call to Marc Miller in Park City. There's a problem though.

"I'm in a meeting. I thought Walt Nelson was going to meet you. Was he able to reach you?"

"No one has gotten a hold of us. We thought the plan was for you to come get us."

"Well, I can't come right now, this meeting is going to last awhile. If there is no one to meet you when you get to Salt Lake City, give me a call and I'll see what we can work out."

Too numb to argue, I give up and hang up.

Cindy is waiting at the sidewalk, looking disheveled and drained by what we have just walked through.

"Is he going to meet us? What did he say?"

I tell her what little I have understood of the conversation, including the part about Walt Nelson, not realizing it could be the same person as the Willard Nelson that the Salt Lake City Habitat folks had referred to on the phone a few days ago. We are parched by the dust and without mental energy to think clearly right now, so the names mean nothing to us.

"What are we going to do?" she asks. "What did you two decide?"

Her question intones that I can fix this situation. I wish I could. I am afraid I cannot, but I don't want to admit it.

I have no answer. "I guess we'll just walk into Salt Lake City and see what happens. When we get wherever we are going we'll call him again. Hopefully he will come and get us like the original plan."

"You mean he just told you to call him when we get there?" she asks, her voice increasing in volume and tension.

"Yes," is all that I can say.

She needs more details. I don't have them. I can't tell if she is angry with me, him, or is just tired of this day. My best thoughts are to extricate myself from further conversation by heading on.

We face an option at the base of the hill, but I elect to take Highway 184 (actually a city street) up the hill in hopes the Capitol grounds will provide a brighter ending to this day.

As we near the top of the long hill in silence, a blue van turns left into a driveway behind Cindy. The passenger opens the window and shouts something to Cindy. It is out of my hearing range.

"Jer!" she hollers with a big grin, once again willing to talk to me. "It's Janet and Walter Nelson!"

At first, my dulled senses don't comprehend what she is saying. There is no reason for us to expect them yet. They are to join us, as support drivers, on Sunday. Puzzled, I turn toward Cindy, then look beyond and see the two saints who have come in our time of need. Walter Nelson is the "Willard" and "Walt" that we have briefly heard mentioned in conversations recently. They have come early to see if we needed their help. We certainly do! They will gladly drive us over the mountains to Park City.

Hurrying now, we jump into the back of the van without losing any continuity in the excited conversations. The Capitol grounds, only a couple of blocks away, no longer have any significance as an ending point. All we want to do is get our luggage and get out of town. But first, we must soothe our dust-parched mouths and throats and slake our thirsts at the nearest convenience store.

We first met Janet and Walter in Eagle Butte, South Dakota. They are full-time RVers, wandering the country while keeping a taproot in South Dakota. We had come to Eagle Butte to build houses with Habitat for Humanity as part of the Jimmy Carter Work Project in 1994 on the Cheyenne River Sioux Indian Reservation. During that time, we stayed at the same campground and became friends in the short time we had together.

We discover they would have been very willing to accompany

us this day, but were unable to find us, or find out where we were walking, although they tried several times. Frustration now turns to jubilation. We stop long enough to retrieve our luggage from the Habitat office, then drive to Park City to meet with Pastor Marc Miller.

Tonight, we are once again excited to have more of our family arrive. Our son, Mark is flying in from his home in Los Angeles. Our daughter, Katie and her husband Curtis and now seven-month-old son, Logan are arriving from Olympia. Because we will have a scheduled three-day weekend, (our reward for no illness or injuries so far) they will not get to walk with us. Instead, they are looking forward to skiing in some of the best snow in the country.

We have not seen Katie and her family since that tearful Valentine's Day farewell in Kalama, Washington. It has been a full year since we have seen Mark, and more exciting, this will be his first meeting with his newest nephew. So it is with much excitement that we all ignore the lateness of the hour and sit on our bed to gab happily with each other. I revel in my appointed duty to give Logan much-needed crawling lessons while Cindy opens her belated birthday presents. Once again, we are privileged to hear the latest news from home and about Mark's latest art and music projects. Like Pat and Kim before them, we are prodded about how we are *really* doing and receive more comments on our too-tanned bodies. It is 1 a.m. when we all fall into our beds, tired but extremely connected and fulfilled.

Today is Thursday, April 11, and our 32nd wedding anniversary. The Nelsons have set up their motor home in Pastor Miller's church parking lot. That will be their home base until Monday morning when we once again set out. Pastor Miller has driven us back to Salt Lake City to complete this week's miles by walking through Emigration Canyon. Although very hilly, it is a scenic walk and we are amused at spending an anniversary in such an unusual way. Katie and Logan join us near the end.

Arriving back in Park City, we walk into the local newspaper office for a prearranged interview. While there, I get the opportunity to buy Cindy an anniversary bouquet of long-stemmed red roses from a door-to-door salesman making his weekly rounds.

After three days of fun and relaxation with our family, it is time, once again, to gather up the courage to say good-bye to the ones we love. They plan to join us in Atlanta for the celebratory end. After the tears that flowed when Pat's family left us in Brigham City, Cindy has been practicing controlling her emotions a little better this time. I assure her that there is no need for heroics here, but she is determined. She does pretty well when they are within range, but as soon as the rental van is out of sight, the tears flow. This is not something she trained for. Moms shouldn't have to.

It is a cold, crisp 20 degrees on Monday morning, but the sun is shining. Janet and Walter have driven us to Heber City where our route resumes. Our destination today is the summit of Daniel's pass on highway 40. We make the climb to elevation 8,000 feet

Katie and youngest grandson, Logan, enjoy a day with us near Park City, Utah.

without much difficulty and go into the café and mini-mart there for soft drinks. The young woman behind the counter says to me, "Those are some buff legs you have there!"

I crack a joke about her comment and return to where Cindy and Janet have sat down. Remembering that at almost 70 years of age, Janet may not know what the clerk's comment means, I repeat the story. Janet replies, "Well, they are pretty tan."

It's always good to end a long day with a good laugh. We share many with the Nelsons.

We return to Heber to spend the night with the Hathaway family, sleeping on an air mattress in their living room. We resume walking at the summit on Tuesday. Walter checked our miles from yesterday and finds that, unfortunately, we had only made 17.8 miles. Miscalculations yesterday mean longer than normal miles today.

The walk along Strawberry Lake is scenic and pleasant. Bluebird houses are erected everywhere. We hope to catch a glimpse of one, but never do. By now our minds and bodies know when we have walked 20 miles, which is part of the reason we checked miles yesterday. We know we are going to have to push ourselves to add the extra two-plus miles as we near the end of today's 20 miles. We must fight psychological and physical fatigue at this high altitude as we try to convince our bodies to continue on.

Just when we need an added incentive, Tom Guyer and Susan Baker arrive from the Salt Lake City Habitat affiliate and announce that they are going to walk with us. It is the boost we need and a blessing, especially from a Habitat affiliate that we hadn't had a lot of contact with while in the area. They walk almost five miles with us, far more than they intended, before Janet returns them to their pickup for the long ride back to Salt Lake City.

We must spend this night in the motor home at the Fruitland RV Park because there are no host families in this area. Wednesday morning, Walter takes the van to Duchesne to purchase replacement lug bolts for the ones that broke on the right front wheel of the motor home. We walk away from the campground in light hail and wet snow. Thankfully, it doesn't last long and we are soon walking in sunshine. My body is sore today, and my energy level is low. Cindy wants me to keep up, but my legs are aching seriously. We begin to argue about petty little stuff that has built up over the last week. We've had no time alone. We come upon Janet in the van, parked along the road waiting for us. We wave at her and keep walking and arguing. She looks puzzled and drives slowly past. We hold up two fingers, signaling her to drive two more miles. She does. We keep up the heated dialogue. By the time we come upon Janet again, we are communicating well and making progress toward a truce. Had she really gone two miles further or had she stopped short, out of curiosity for our strange behavior? We signal that we are continuing. Two fingers in the air again. Another even more puzzled look from Janet. She's never seen us like this.

We finally resolve our differences and now are devising a plan to not let us get into another situation like the one that precipitated the dispute. We come to Janet parked in a wide spot along the road. We kiss and make up and then walk over to the van.

We have walked six miles without a break. I go to the back of the van to relieve myself while Cindy flings open the van door and uses it as a shield behind which to hide and uses her Feminine Urinary Director. Since Janet is in the driver's seat across from the door, she asks Cindy what's been going on. She gets a condensed version, Cindy assures her that all is well with us now and asks her if she can reach the ibuprofen bottle.

Ibuprofen finally numbs my discomfort after noon when the second dose takes hold. Walter returns in the motor home in time for us to have lunch. This afternoon is partly cloudy, but we walk under blue skies and sun most of the time. We are near the end of the day when the wind and cold strike us from behind, suddenly making it difficult to finish. It is blowing so hard that we must hold onto the motor home door to keep it from being wrenched from our grips. Once again, we must spend the night in the motor home.

Today we are back at milepost 80 to resume walking under somewhat pleasant skies. Before we walk a half-mile, a thick, wet snow comes down the mountain and once again catches us from behind. Before Janet can take a photo of us walking in the snow, it stops as quickly as it has begun. Later in the day, we are finally warm enough to take off our sweatshirts and walk in our wind shells. Janet waits for us to shed our extra clothes, then takes off toward our next rendezvous point. She is barely out of sight when a cold, blowing rain suddenly assails us from behind. I have on rain pants, but Cindy is wearing only leggings and her raincoat. I am soon worried about hypothermia, especially for her. I am losing body heat rapidly, and I worry that she must be doing worse. Janet notices the weather change and hurries back. At first we think about adding clothes and continuing the last three miles of the day, but our core temperatures are down and I am not convinced we can warm up under these conditions. Reluctantly, we give in to the weather and drive into Myton to park by the Presbyterian Church where we will spend our third night in the motor home. Once again, we are faced with make-up miles tomorrow.

The past few days have drained our reserve energy. We choose to not make up the miles on Friday. Cindy experiences a very sore shin by the end of the day, and we elect not to go on. Instead, we will walk three miles on Saturday to put us at 1,000 miles for the walk.

We have the pleasure of meeting Father Tom Culleton, the parish priest in Roosevelt. He is interested and excited about our walk and arranges for a night's stay in the motel owned by one of his parishioners. We dine at the Frontier Restaurant, feasting on more food than we can imagine for $7.95. Chicken fried steak, baby carrots, fries, scone (Indian fry bread), salad bar, soup and rice pudding. We eat it all, soon regretting our gluttony, as we sluggishly walk back to the motel room. We spend a pleasant evening alone for the first time in over a week.

On Monday, Walter brings Father Tom out to join us about two miles into our walk day. He is excited to join us, but not long after we begin, I stop abruptly to pick up a coin, and in his haste to stop, he slips on the loose gravel and hurts his knee. Cindy is a racehorse today, and there is no slowing her down. I keep suggesting she ease up on the pace so Father Tom can keep up, but she is programmed to go this pace and soon resumes our normal cadence. Father Tom does well for a man his age that has not had the opportunity to walk much, but he is extremely relieved when we call it a day a few miles west of Vernal.

Walter and Father Tom sit with us at a booth inside Burgers Unlimited in Vernal. We have come here to celebrate Father Tom's completion of 18 miles with us today. This former monk, now a priest at St. Helens Catholic Church, is a youthful 69 years old. We had asked him if he would like to spend a day walking with us when we met last Friday. He still loves the concept of walking a great distance but his muscles do not. They actually started objecting at mile 12, but Father Tom understood the drill about mind over matter. He wouldn't quit. Now, as we slurp on shakes and laugh about the things we experienced today, he has renewed energy to dream about the future.

"So, what's next for you two? Are you walking home, too?" he quips.

"You would be surprised at how often we get that question, Tom," I smile and say.

"Actually, we don't have a clue what we will do after the walk. Always ones for a five-year plan, we were so busy planning this that we forgot to look to the future."

"Well, I have a plan for you," says Father Tom. "Let's walk across Ireland, we three. It's my homeland, so I know it well. Would you enjoy that?"

Ireland is a country we have much interest in exploring and so we nod in agreement.

"Well, you can't do it without us," Janet chimes in. "We

A celebratory meal with Janet, Walter and Father Tom in Vernal, Utah.

are a team, after all, and no one could provide a support vehicle for you like us!"

The plan is cemented with a clinkless meeting of our Styrofoam cups and a promise to make it happen in the future.

We found $1.38 this week.

The Support of Many

When Jerry and Cindy were planning the walk, they considered trekking east without the use of support vehicles. Their children thought otherwise. Jerry and Cindy reconsidered.

Finding folks to assist them seemed like a formidable challenge until they remembered Habitat for Humanity's group of volunteers known as the Care-a-Vanners. These folks normally travel around the U.S. in their RVs, gathering in communities to work with the local Habitat affiliate building houses. Care-A-Vanners coordinators, Jack and Lois Wolters, asked their volunteers if anyone would be willing to drive along with Jerry and Cindy as an alternative to building.

From family members, friends, and Care-a Vanners, 30 teams had signed up as drivers before the walk began. Some agreed to help for a day, some longer. Janet and Walter Nelson signed on for five weeks! One person cancelled his two-separate-week commitments weeks after the walk had begun and had to be replaced. Filling these voids proved to be very challenging and a bit daunting. Eventually, they found individuals who were willing to participate for a day or more to help them. There were other schedule holes to fill too. In the end, a total of 41 support vehicle drivers, and often their spouses, helped to make the walk successful.

They were each a godsend.This was not an easy job and the folks who carried it out were a patient lot indeed! Most were accustomed to driving several hundred miles a day. During their time with Habitrek '96, they drove 20 miles a day at the painstakingly slow speed, traveling less than four miles in an hour. Fortunately they were creative! Some were master chefs and Jerry and Cindy were their eager tasters. Some created beautiful quilts, wrote letters, read volumes or picked up aluminum cans to support Habitat's mission. Some walked part of the time, some much of the time.

These generous souls were many things to Jerry and Cindy. They served in a variety of ways, including acting as surrogate grandparents, nurses, press agents, marketing experts, cheerleaders or psychologists. All became friends. When the occasion called for it, they would knock on strangers' doors in hopes of the person agreeing to let Jerry and Cindy use their bathroom when they arrived. The stranger usually said, "yes" to their request, and these chance meetings added greatly to the overall walk experience.

Support drivers were protective, caring, kind and generous. As with Jerry and Cindy, these folks spent their own funds without expecting anything in return. They were also confident that their assistance would get Jerry and Cindy safely through another day of walking. They were right.

Jerry and Cindy needed these support folks to help them achieve their dream. The way in which these folks responded to that need allowed them to vicariously participate in the walk. Most of them would never consider walking across America, but they could spend their days with someone who would. In that way, each gave to the other.

Jerry and Cindy cannot think of Habitrek '96 without remembering these wonderful people. They are forever indebted, and immeasurably grateful to them all.

12

Sleepwalking in the Canyons

Day 75
Wednesday, April 24
Dinosaur, Colorado

Jerry

We have departed Utah and celebrated the entering of Colorado, state number five. Janet has taken our traditional photograph beneath the "Welcome to..." sign. It is important for us to be reminded that we are making progress. It seems strange to many folks that we are traveling at such a slow pace. We are often asked about this during interviews. It has become a way of life for us over these last months and we have trouble understanding their fascination. We forget that this is unusual. Explaining it sometimes becomes tedious.

The road construction through here coats us in dust, aided by a 20 mph wind out of the south. We are at an elevation of 5,900 feet and our lungs remind us of this as we climb this last hill before lunch. While we take a 45-minute lunch break in the motor home, Walt shows us the Vernal, Utah newspaper. It contains an interview we had yesterday. The article reminds of the "rest of the story" as recounted by Walter after the reporter left with her story yesterday. It had happened early yesterday morning.

"After you guys left in the van with Janet, I ambled into the

Vernal Express office to see if anyone would be interested in doing a story on Habitrek. I noticed two reporters leaning back in their chairs discussing something as I was explaining my presence to the receptionist. She pointed me in their direction, so I walked over to introduce myself. I was surprised at their enthusiasm for covering the story until they told me of a slight predicament they were in. They had planned for a story that would fill a front-page space in today's edition. A few minutes before I walked in they were told that the story had been cancelled. They didn't have a clue how to fill the space and were beginning to panic. They would be thrilled to cover the story if I would let the young female reporter follow me out to your route. Isn't that a great story?" the always-enthusiastic retired minister asked us. Yep, it is Walter.

We are two miles west of Dinosaur, Colorado. Janet just stopped to check on us then said, "I'm going into town to meet up with Walt. We understand there's an RV park where we can spend the night. I'll meet you at the Shell mini mart in about half an hour, okay?"

We arrive at the Shell station and see Janet waiting.

"The people here are amazing," Janet says as she bounds out of the van. "Remember Mick Benz from the Presbyterian Church in Myton? Well, his sister, Dixie Simms lives here. Mick had told her about the walk and when we would be coming through. She saw the van with the Habitrek banner on it and stopped me. She gave me this huge German chocolate cake, seven turkey sandwiches and a big bag of chips for dinner. She also got us a free night at that RV park over there. Can you believe it?" Then Janet continues the story. "Dixie had no more than left when Walt drives up. He had just stopped to use the pay phone at the only motel in town and began talking to the owner about your walk. Upon hearing that you had no place to stay tonight except the motor home, the owner offered to let you stay there for free!" Janet concludes enthusiastically.

This little town of 324 people has mighty big hearts. Ours are touched once again.

We never did meet our benefactor, Dixie Simms.

And now, this morning we walk past street signs in the shape of a stegosaurus and onto Highway 64. It is 30 degrees F and overcast. We are immediately delighted by the antics of the beige-and-white-striped pronghorns. We are walking through their territory and they stop to stare at us. When we dare to attempt a conversation with them, they make a coughing sound and dash off along the bluffs of the rocky outcroppings like ballerinas exiting a stage.

There are prairie dogs in this same "neighborhood." They sit on their haunches, ears tensed and eyes unblinking. They too amuse us as we approach. They make a high-pitched, rapidly spoken "chip, chip, chip" sound to notify their neighbors of our presence, then they all scamper into their tunnels to hide.

On our right, an electric-powered train passes almost silently through the rocks, carrying its load of coal to the power plant west of us. After having seen many shepherds' wagons over the past months, we finally see our first shepherd today. It is interesting to watch him, hunched against the wind and cloaked in dark clothing, keeping watch over his sheep as they graze around him. We can identify with his dusty appearance for we are pretty well coated ourselves. However, we know that he will spend the night out here under the stars while we are enjoying a warm shower, hot meal and soft bed at our host family's home.

We leave the shepherd and as we crest the hill, we come upon a scene that is in sharp contrast to what we have been experiencing during the past couple of hours. There are drilling towers the size of skyscrapers rising throughout the stark, sandy landscape. Workers scamper around and about the towers with precision and a sense of urgency. We are told that Chevron Oil Company owns this operation and that it is their sixth largest in the world. We move swiftly through this area, our steps in sync with the rhythmic motion of the huge black arms pumping crude oil out of the earth.

Unfortunately, as we make our way through this area of heavily populated wildlife, we also must deal with lots of road kill, usually lying in roadside ditches. We usually smell the carcasses before we see them. Rotting meat that has lain in the sun far too long lets off a putrid odor. We must breathe through our mouths until we get well out of range. The encounter with the odors varies with the direction of the wind. Sometimes we meet it face on and other times, we endure it while walking beyond the dead animals.

We wish that there were more live wildlife to enjoy and less to smell.

We complete our miles a short distance south of Rangely today. With 2,278 population, it seems like a metropolis compared to the towns we have been in recently. We are anxious to get to our host family home. We are anxious to meet new people and share a hot, home-cooked meal, our first in two days.

We are having a good conversation with his dad, when 12-year-old Daniel steps into the doorway that divides the kitchen from the living room. "Are we just gonna eat in front of them?" he yells to his mom, as he tries to be heard over the sound of the electric mixer. Our adult conversation comes to an abrupt halt. Part of the problem with this scene is this young man. He has made it clear from the moment of our meeting that he's not happy about us being here. We have been given his room for the night because it is the only room with a double bed. He's never heard of us and thinks that what we are doing is dull and not particularly difficult. "Anyone could walk 20 miles a day," he proclaims.

"Well, that may be true. Why don't you join us tomorrow and we'll see if you can put your feet where your mouth is?" I challenge.

"Okay," Daniel replies.

Daniel's mom intervenes, suggesting that a day of school is more important than walking and that he will not be joining us. We are both relieved, although there is a part of us that will miss the opportunity to show this young lad a new view on the world.

Meanwhile, we are stuck in this awkward position. Daniel's dad offers a temporary solution.

"Would you like to go down to the basement family room and watch the news?"

Cindy takes his cue, stopping by our bedroom to stuff some snacks in her shirt. I miss the hint.

Cindy is sitting in the basement wondering how we manage to get ourselves into these predicaments when the doorbell rings. It is Janet, back from doing laundry. They have decided to go eat dinner at a local restaurant and want to know if we want to join them. I leap down the stairs to rescue Cindy and we graciously take leave. I had alerted Janet earlier that there might be a problem, when she said that they were going to go do laundry.

"What's going on in there?" Janet quizzes.

"We're not sure what happened. Thanks for coming back to rescue us. Cindy's shins are too sore to walk back to town so we weren't sure what we would do. They are a very nice family, well, except for the 12-year-old boy with an attitude. Obviously they did not realize that part of the agreement to host us includes an evening meal. They have a lot on their plates right now besides food. The husband, Jerry, was told today that his job as an associate pastor is ending soon. Their daughter just got out of the hospital with complications from her diabetes and they got a call that Grandma is critically ill in Wyoming so they need to make plans to get to her bedside as soon as possible. It's a family in crisis. They need our prayers more than our presence." I explain to Janet.

The next day, Friday, we join Janet and Walter in their RV for buttermilk pancakes, say goodbye to the family and then begin walking south towards Meeker. We have watched contrails, created by commercial jets, criss-crossing the sky all day as they approach and depart Denver International Airport. They are only minutes away from Denver as they fly overhead. We are still three weeks away!

Cindy

I bark at Jerry as we descend the steps of the motor home in downtown Meeker. He gives me the distance I don't seek, but my words seem to demand. In a 26.2-mile marathon, runners often hit the wall at their 21st miles. In this 3000-mile "marathon," I have hit the wall at the 1,100th mile. I am suddenly emotionally and mentally exhausted. It isn't that I don't want to walk the remaining 1,900 miles. That seems like the easy part. What I don't want to do is pack and unpack any more. I don't want to sleep in any more unfamiliar beds. I don't want to be public property either. I want to wake up when I want to, walk as far as I want and not explain anything to anyone. My adaptability, flexibility and patience are nowhere to be found. I am just plain cranky!

This is out of character for me. I usually go along and get along. People are giving a lot to us so that we can make this crazy dream of ours a reality. I believe they would consider me an ingrate to whine and complain. They could even view my situation as cushy. After all, no responsibilities or work to do, just be quoted in newspapers and speak to groups of people who hang on every word. I would argue that I am tired of being totally dependent on others for my every need, even water. "Pretty lucky to have water," they would say. I'm sure they would say that. And so I remain painfully silent, for I am convinced that no one would understand what I don't even fully understand. It is like the walk has suddenly changed me and not in a good way.

Jerry lets me have my space tonight. He is happily engaged in a theological discussion with our pastor-host. I say good night and shuffle off to the bedroom. I need some time to myself. I have one ray of sunshine to focus on as I drift off to sleep. We have a motel room reserved in downtown Meeker. We will have two whole days to just hang out. We will eat when we're hungry, sleep when we're tired and maybe even…We'll return phone calls, watch TV and receive e-mails from family and friends. It's a dream I can't wait for and I haven't even gone to sleep yet.

It is Saturday morning and sunlight wakes me at 6:45 a.m. It's a new day and my thoughts for a perfect weekend are only hours away. I'm happy to be up early, even happy to be sociable after such a good nights sleep. Jay and Walt Silveria have been wonderful hosts. Jay and I make easy conversation as she prepares pecan waffles for our leisurely breakfast. By 10 o'clock, we are packed. The motor home and Janet stay in the driveway while the two Walts take us to the motel in the van. I like it and its proximity to downtown. We will not need a vehicle to live the independent life.

The guys immediately point out a problem that I haven't considered. There's no room for the motor home. That doesn't seem like a problem to me. In my mind, they can go to a RV park and pick us up Monday morning. Without even asking what I think, the guys decide to go look at a motel with an adjoining campground two miles out of town. I'm silently devastated.

The owner of The Stagecoach Motel and RV Park is intrigued with the guys' description of our walk and wants us to stay here. As a Christian who really believes in what we are doing, she offers to rent us a cabin and RV space for only $15 a night. She mentions that there are no telephones or televisions, but the guys seem so taken by this rustic setting on the White River that they don't seem to hear her. Walter generously pays for three nights as he turns to ask me if this will be all right. What can I say? I feel like I can't ruin their enthusiasm. Jerry thinks we can make the best of it and encourages me to think the same. I don't.

We unload our seven pieces of luggage onto the little covered front porch and then the Walts return to town to get Janet and the motor home. I roll my eyes at Jerry as he silently unlocks the door. We walk into a little living room and look ahead into a darling little kitchen. The separate bedroom is one step down and has an adjoining bath. The entire place is paneled in knotty pine, varnished to a deep yellow luster. It is furnished in bright colors with cute curtains. The bedspread is a rose-colored print and there is a fabric wrapped prayer rock on the pillow with a poem attached. It is quaint and inviting and reminds me of the place Alan Alda returned to each spring in the movie, *Same Time Next Year*. It's beginning to grow on me.

I can live happily without a television. I am concerned about the lack of a telephone. I take a walk to scout out the grounds while Jerry unpacks. We appear to be the only ones here. The sound of the river is so peaceful and the tall aspens and firs absolutely beautiful. My attitude is changing rapidly.

I finally find a pay phone attached to a public restroom, 50 yards from our cabin. I believe this to be totally unacceptable. God clearly has other ideas. I have been whining about needing some space all week. Space to get in touch with my spirit, spread out and relax. Now here it is. We have a quiet place in which to talk and, more importantly, to hear each other.

While I am suddenly seeing things in a positive light, I realize that the kitchen affords the "Queen of Nesting" to do her thing and cooking is my thing. I'll need a few supplies though.

"Jer, do you suppose we could borrow the van and go to town?" I suggest after we are settled.

I have not cooked a meal or washed a dish in three months. To many, that may seem heavenly, for me, it is a part of a daily routine I do not realize I have missed. Perhaps my soul is a little out of kilter.

And so we go to town in the Nelson's Dodge van tow-vehicle.

We stop at the post office, wash clothes at the laundromat and call our son Mark from a pay phone while we wait for the clothes to dry. Then we find a grocery store. We buy everyday things; baked beans, cottage cheese; Kraft macaroni and cheese, canned green beans, Grape Nuts, bagels, peanut butter, whole wheat bread, hot dogs and cheese. My spirit is awakening with these simple acts.

This place God had dragged me to, kicking and screaming inwardly, is exactly the place He knew I needed to be. This is a pivotal point in the walk for me.

With snow on the ground and us snuggled deep into the comfy

bed with the puffy blankets, it is difficult to roll out of bed today, but roll out we must. It's a new week and I have a new attitude! We layer our clothing against the 21-degree-morning air and step back out onto Highway 64. It is later than usual because we have ridden 35 miles back to Friday's stopping point. We still have almost two walking days before we officially walk into Meeker.

Before long, we walk past some horseshoe art decorating the yard. Sort of an outdoor art gallery of an unusual kind. In the midst of the sculptures is a well-maintained little house painted bright apple green. Someone has put a lot of effort into creating a full sized cactus, a wishing well and many other objects, all from horseshoes! This unexpected display begs for a photo. We oblige.

We are stopped by a mailman a couple of miles further down the road.

"I've seen you walking on the highway for three days now. Whatcha up to?" he inquires.

Jerry props his elbow on the open window ledge and gives the guy our condensed version of the walk, the basic who, what, when, where and how.

That satisfies the mailman's curiosity, but he has more to say.

"Are you Christians?" he asks.

"Well yes, we are. Why do you ask?" Jerry replies.

Jerry at the horseshoe sculptures outside Meeker, Colorado.

"I am, too. I messed myself up pretty bad on drugs, brain damage and the whole bit. Now I'm right with God. I go to the Assembly of God Church and God has called me to be an intercessor. I'm the fourth generation in my family to live in this valley. I believe God wants me to stay right here and do His work. There was a guy speaking at our church last night. He believes that all the churches will eventually come together. Pentecostals and Baptists; Methodists and Mormons; everyone getting along." The mailman thinks that would be great.

So do we.

After lunch, we come upon a cattle drive gone awry. Four calves have gotten spooked and have run away from the herd. They start bawling for their moms and the moms are mooing in response. In the confusion of the moment, they can't find each other. The ensuing noise is deafening. Somehow we find the scene entertaining. Jerry stops to inquire about the whole situation and the head honcho explains that it will take a lot of work to get the cow families reunited. Once this is done, they will hold them in the pasture to our right overnight and attempt to move them again tomorrow. We have walked by and talked to a lot of cattle over the past months. Jerry always warns them to stay away from trucks with ramps as we secretly root for their survival even though we know that survival is not to be. Today we root for the little calves to be reunited with their moms and dads. We actually thank them for throwing a calf-sized temper tantrum. It has saved us from having to dodge highway cow pies all afternoon.

It is May first and the day we must leave our little haven on the White River. We are moving down the highway to Rifle. We have settled in to our temporary abode a little too much, so packing is a challenge. So are the stupid blisters, which Jerry is bandaging and padding carefully before we can leave this morning. Consequently we get a late start. We are heading to an elevation of 7,000 feet above sea level today.

Jerry's legs are aching severely and he is sleepy. The altitude is the likely culprit. The two of us will have to gimp along, each with our own challenges. We divert our attention by talking to a herd of llamas. They appear to display keen interest in what we have to say, which encourages us to say more. Two farms up the road we come to a herd of black-faced sheep that draw our attention away from our aches and pains. We see one that reminds us of

Janet saves us steps by picking us up at our last mile marker today.

"our" peaceful sheep south of Chehalis but without the red collar. This guy has no such message for us, though.

After a brief construction detour, we both begin walking in autopilot. Jerry is quietly trudging along while I turn my attention to the colorful boulders that dot the mountainside. I think there must be mountain lion in those rocks. I strain my eyes in search of one. All of a sudden I realize that Jerry has not said a word in over a half an hour.

"Jer, you're awfully quiet. Is everything alright?"

"Uh, what did you say?"

"I said, is everything alright, you are awfully quiet."

"Mar, I think you woke me up. Is it possible that I was sleep-walking right through these canyons?" He asks in amazement.

"It's hard to believe. Are you sure you weren't day dreaming?'

"No, I think I was asleep. Wow, it actually wasn't that hard. I kinda liked it," he teases.

It's a struggle to finish today's miles. Janet knows we will not cut the day's miles by even a few feet. She also knows we are both in discomfort. Instead of parking across the road and waiting for us to hobble the few extra feet to the van, she whips across to our side of the road and backs the van up to milepost marker #9 where she knows we will stop for the day. Then she rolls down the window and sticks her now familiar fleece baseball capped head out the window and smiles.

"Is that close enough for you two?" she chides.

Her keen sense of humor has once again tickled us and we do not have to take one extra step on a day when we didn't think we had any left in us.

We found $2.44 during this time.

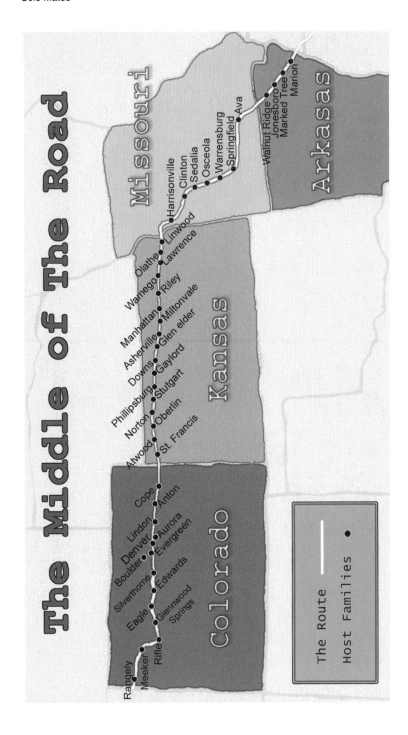

The Middle of The Road

Missouri

Arkasas

Kansas

Colorado

Harrisonville
Clinton
Sedalia
Osceola
Warrensburg
Springfield
Ava
Walnut Ridge
Jonesboro
Marked Tree
Marion

Linwood
Olathe
Lawrence
Wamego
Riley
Manhattan
Miltonvale
Asherville
Glen elder
Downs
Gaylord
Phillipsburg
Stutgart
Norton
Oberlin
Atwood
St. Francis

Cope
Anton
Lindon
Aurora
Denver
Evergreen
Boulder
Silverthorne
Edwards
Eagle
Glenwood
Springs
Rifle
Meeker
Rangely

The Route
Host Families

"The difference between the impossible and the possible lies in a person's determination."

Tommy Lasorda

13

Resurrection in the Rockies

Day 84
Friday, May 3
Glenwood Springs, Colorado

Jerry

We have entered the Glenwood Canyon bicycle/pedestrian path at the east end of Glenwood Springs, Colorado and are immediately facing an onrush of freeway traffic that is separated from us by a concrete barrier and chain link fence. It is intimidating, and we are relieved to leave the view of the onslaught of frantic cars and trucks as we cross Interstate 70 on an overpass. A sweeping curve in the trail takes us away from the freeway. The majestic mountains surround and soon dwarf us. Their beauty and ruggedness overwhelm us. Towering peaks sport traces of snow from the storm that closed Interstate 70 a week and a half ago.

We were unable to train for walking through the mountains before we left home. Now that we are here, we are pleased to find that our bodies and stamina seem equal to the task. Our senses continue to be overwhelmed by all that we see. The spring foliage is slowly emerging, even though it is early May. Groves of aspens send nutrients to their nearly bare branches producing leaves that will soon quake and rustle in the mountain winds. There is so much to see and absorb.

We stop occasionally to watch the fast-flowing, clear Colorado River on its journey west and to soak up the moments. The stops give Cindy a chance to get off of her badly blistered feet too. The mountain roadside rest areas blend into their settings. At Grizzly Creek Rest Area, we stop to watch a father and son fishing in the creek adjacent to our path. I tarry as I watch and yearn to fulfill my desire to be doing the same. Grizzly Creek is small and runs fast with one small pool directly beneath us. I am surprised to see the man catch a fish there. Cindy joins me to watch in bemusement as the father tries to choreograph his son's use of the net while he struggles to control the strong, feisty, fighting fish on the end of his line.

They are so close below us that we dare not laugh at the sight before us. It brings back my memories of similar fatherly incidents with our children. I am inwardly rooting for the son's success, but it does not look probable. He is a bit inept and can't seem to coordinate his movements with those of fish. The father, no longer able to restrain his impatience, takes the net from his son and captures the fish in one smooth swoop while the son, slump-shouldered, watches. The fish is large. Compared to what I usually catch, it could pass for a small salmon. I am starting to salivate as I watch, astonished and engrossed with what I see. We must walk on before I seek out Janet's van, grab the fishing gear I found on the road in Utah and jump in and join them.

This afternoon, Janet and I try to convince Cindy to ride in the van for the last three miles. Her blisters are full of fluid, and walking on them is excruciating for her, but she will not give into the pain. She says the natural beauty of this area will be lost on her if she encloses herself in a vehicle. I concede. All I can do is walk with my right arm wrapped tightly around her waist. Each time she steps on the right foot I rythmatically lift her weight on that side to alleviate some of the pressure. She says more than the weight, she feels my energy and support helping her along these beautiful pedestrian paths. I'm glad I can help her. I am always concerned about her struggle with her blisters. I feel helpless, since I am able to do very little to alleviate her discomfort. Knowing that the alternative is to quit the walk, I try to give her positive support.

On Wednesday, May 8, local Habitat board member, Sandy Apps, has planned a five-mile walking tour around Vail for us. It is a short walk, but Cindy has to muster the spirit to do it since she is once again struggling with her painful blisters. She is anxious for these miles to go away so that she can get off her feet. It was intended to be a group walk, however, the folks that were expected to join us did not show, so it is the three of us walking.

Once we are done, Sandy offers to drive us up to tomorrow's starting point. Disappointment comes there at Vail Pass. This was to be our crossing point for the Rockies. Now we see that the path is covered with five feet of dirty remnant snow. Sandy and Cindy toy with the idea of using snowshoes so that we can still walk the path. I am not in favor of this option. The pathway ahead of us is clear for the first few hundred feet, then disappears out of sight, to emerge again in the dirt and gravel along the shoulder of the freeway. It then diverges down and away to locations we cannot scout from the car. We have never used snowshoes before, and once we would leave the freeway area, we would no longer be able to communicate with Janet for nearly seven miles. It's a risk I do not want to take. Reluctantly, I lobby to skip this 10-mile segment of the route and make up the miles elsewhere. I do not want to disappoint my spouse, and I know she is disappointed after looking forward to this crossing since we drove through here last summer. Although she does not disagree and seems to accept my reasoning, I once again am burdened by the feeling that I can't make things better for her.

Cindy

Sandy drives us to our host family's home at 8 p.m. Michael and Molly Wasmer have waited supper for us, so we wait to take showers and sit in their terra cotta tiled dining room and dig in to the penne pasta dinner Molly has carefully prepared for us.

This lonesome Gramma is immediately delighted when 21-month-old Madison scoots a little straw seated chair across the tile and pushes it up right next to my chair. She toddles up onto the chair and stands up, her chin barely reaching over the tabletop. With a smile and a look of trusting friendship, she reaches over and pinches a piece of my pasta into her pudgy fingers. Molly is mortified.

"Madison, come get in your highchair and eat your own food. Cindy would probably like to enjoy her own food."

Madison and I object! The two of us were enjoying my food. She gets to stay. Not only did I like being reminded of our little guys back home, Madison was keeping my mind off of a few things that were troubling me tonight. Solutions would come, as they always do, but not before the situation got a little more troubling.

As Molly excuses herself to put Madison to bed and Michael and Jerry sit down in the den to talk Habitat. I excuse myself to go shower, write in my journal and check our voice mail. A message received from Walter Graham saying he will not be able to support vehicle us through Missouri in July, troubles me further.

I pull out my journal and write about the day's events as I do each evening. I look forward to this time to rest, relax and reflect. Before closing the black cover journal, adorned with Mary Englebreit flowers, I write,

"My blisters are so bad tonight, I don't even know where to begin. I'm getting weary of them. I soaked the two big ones on the ball of each foot along with the horseshoe shaped one along the ridge of my left heel. I'm feeling discouraged."

I remember getting blood poisoning in a heel blister during the 1988 walk and I do not want that to happen again. At the risk of desperation causing stupidity, I take a pill meant for bladder infections and two Tylenol. After all, I convince myself, how could my body tell the difference between bladders and blisters? I drain all the blisters with sterile needles, bandage them and then wrap the extremely hot feet in two cold water-soaked hand towels. I pull the covers up so my feet are exposed to the cool air and finally fall asleep next to a soundly sleeping Jerry by 11:30 p.m.

The 6 a.m. alarm awakens me too soon. The towels are wadded on the floor and there has been no magical cure while I slept. At least I do not have a red sepsis stripe running up my leg. I take another bladder pill, pack my things and duck walk out to the van on the only unblistered part of my feet. I carry my Birks, socks and foot pharmacy bag and slide in the middle seat.

During the 13-mile ride to McDonald's in Vail, my usual upbeat mood plummets with the draining of each yellow fluid-filled blister. In contemplation of a solution to this predicament, I am barely aware of Janet and Jerry's absence until the door slides open and Jerry stares at the bottom of my feet and sympathetically asks, "What are you going to do?"

He hands me a Diet Coke and an Egg McMuffin.

"I don't have a clue." I hopelessly reply. I have 14 more miles to figure it out before we come to the place where Jerry has confirmed we can enter the bicycle path free of snow.

Jerry's concerned voice startles me again.

"Have you tried praying for a solution?"

"Yes, I have."

"And what was the answer?"

As I put the answer into words, an unexpected flood of tears accompanies my reply.

"I heard the words clearly. They were, 'Don't walk today.'" I blurt out with a tearful onslaught.

I want to fight the words I have uttered. My sleep deprived body shakes with pent-up emotion. I reach down and shake the contents of the foot pharmacy bag. The contents tumble onto the van floor. There are blue and gold packages of Dr. Scholls foot products; foot soak and bunion guards; cracked heel cream and callus scrapers and powders and lambs wool insoles. I throw the bag on the floor and survey my options. The brown block letters on the discarded bag read "BIRKENSTOCK". It seems to be telling me that my sandals, not my feet, may need modifying. The message is lost on me for the moment.

These sandals have caused enough comment already. I think of that lady in Hermiston, Oregon chipping at me one day as I emerged from the motor home.

"You know, you probably wouldn't be hobbling like that if you'd get yourself a good pair of Nikes." She was the first of many who had questioned our choice of footwear. I couldn't expect them to understand why we had chosen Birkenstocks.

It had begun back in June of 1988. In less than a month we would be leaving home to do the Habitat for Humanity House Raising Walk. We had been two miles from home, during a training walk, when I took off my new walking shoes and walked home in my socks, declaring,

"Anything is better than those darn shoes!"

That night we counted 13 blisters on my two feet.

I was desperate for a pair of shoes that would give better air circulation for my overheated feet. I wondered who on earth made walking shoes with holes in them. I prayed for an answer. We began making the rounds of shoe stores and found a funny looking sandal called Birkenstocks. They were made of leather and had a cork foot bed that molded to your foot shape as you wore them. The salesman assured me that three of their models could be worn to do long-distance walking. The problem was the price tag, $75. All of our extra money had been spent on the new walking shoes and airfare to the east coast.

After church on Sunday, Dotty and Carl Fehring came up to us and asked if there was anything we needed in preparation for our trip. I admitted my need for different shoes and that the ones we had found were out of our price range. Dotty pulled out her checkbook and wrote me a check for $75 on the spot! That day, I became the proud owner of my first Birkenstocks. I never walked long distances in anything else after that. My blister problems improved by a good 75%. I convinced Jerry to try them two years later and he was hooked.

Once again, that BIRKENSTOCK logo jars me back to the problem at hand. I can't stand the thought of Jerry walking through this beautiful area without me. If I were Madison's age, I would throw a good temper tantrum. Maybe God would give into me. As an adult, I resort to good old begging.

"Lord, this is the area I have most wanted to walk. Jerry has worked hard to come up with these alternate miles for me. The sky is so blue, the sun so bright. Please, Lord, please help me figure out a way to walk today."

Over Vail Pass and through the tears, I beg for an answer I can accept. Things are very quiet in the front seat.

Then, Jerry's calming voice floats to the back seat.

"Mar, maybe those lambs wool insoles would cushion your blisters so you could walk without pain. Is there any of that double-sided tape in the bag?"

"It's worth a try." I blubber. "I've only considered them as insulators on cold days, but I think you may have a good idea."

The tears that had washed over me like an incoming tide finally lapped gently at my shore. They had cleansed my soul of debris deposited over the past three months, sterile needles and band-aid wrappers, used gauze and wads of Johnson and Johnsons' Elasticon tape, gel-filled shoe liners that hadn't worked and Compeed pads that had. As the emotional tide gently washed back out to sea, I was left renewed, uplifted and hopeful.

Jerry's solution had given me a sense of purpose and with it, energy. I quickly cut the lambs' wool insoles to fit in my sandals and Jerry attaches them with the tape. In the meantime, I cut mole foam "donuts" to fit around the blisters. I stack another one on top of the first so the actual blister floats in the hole, allowing no pressure

After the blister "resurrection" near Vail, Colorado.

directly on the blister. I fill each hole with antibiotic ointment and cover that with lambs' wool tufts. Then I wrap my feet completely with the stretch tape. I pull the Ziploc bag full of powder from my pack and dunk my feet into the bag. Holding the bag opening tight around my ankles, I shake my foot to completely coat my foot in powder. I have found this to be an effective way to keep my feet dry. My feet emerge looking like powdered sugar doughnuts. I put on a thin pair of cotton socks and a thicker pair of sport socks. Then I strap on my newly "upholstered" Birks as Janet pulls into the parking lot of the BP mini-mart at the trailhead near Copper Mountain ski area. With Diet Coke, I wash two down Ibuprofen as Jerry slides the open door.

"Well, what do you think?" He inquires with an edge of concern.

"I think I'm as ready as I can be. I'll walk into their restroom and test the results of our prayers and ingenuity. You stay here. I'll be right back."

I step down from the van and touch the asphalt as if it were eggshells. I am pleasantly surprised. Entering the store, I hear two men discussing today's ski conditions. I purposely avoid eye contact and zigzag my way through the Frito chips and Hershey candy displays to avoid conversation. I am too focused on my feet to answer questions about my presence. Those guys do not matter to me. Who matters is waiting for me outside.

Jerry's inquiring face stares in anticipation as I emerge.

"Well?"

My response is more physical than verbal. Somewhere among the laughs and hugs I manage to convey that the blisters do not hurt. I have made an honest appraisal. Jerry is not convinced.

"Are you being honest?" he pushes.

"Yes, I have no intention of being heroic here. They really do feel good. To be sure, let's do a test mile and have Janet park at that first rest spot and wait. If I'm having trouble, I will admit defeat and ride today. Honest."

He grabs my hand and we head across the little log footbridge spanning spring runoff. Janet leaves to find the next exit and await my verdict. We head off onto the snow-lined pedestrian pathway that I have looked forward to walking on for almost a year.

The white barked aspens stand tall against the Colorado Rocky Mountains. They look like soldiers saluting us as we enter their magical kingdom filled with beauty. There is a woodchuck lounging on a boulder right next to us. He stares at us and does not move. His buck-toothed smile seems to be saying,

"Have a nice day."

Do angels come in the form of woodchucks, I wonder?

I have emerged from the darkness of desperation and emerged into the heavenly sunshine. I feel like I have been resurrected. This is another important victory during seven months of challenges. Today, Jerry will not walk alone.

Jerry

Today is Friday, May 10. There is good news! We have an unexpected opportunity to walk across the Rockies by way of a mountain pass. Paul Haige, last night's host, has told us that instead of having to be driven through the I-70 tunnels, we can walk over Loveland Pass. I had eliminated this route from our itinerary before we left home because of the additional miles it would add to our journey. Now the miles will replace the ones we did not walk on Vail Pass. Paul drove the route this morning on his way to work near Denver and reported via cellular phone that it is relatively clear of snow, and quite passable. Cindy stands within hearing distance of the phone conversation and waits with anticipation for the conversation to end.

I am excited that we can do this, since I have carried the burden of Vail Pass with me for over a week now. With renewed incentive, we are driven out to our drop-off point on the road to Keystone. It is 8:30 a.m. Janet and Walter will return to Vail to retrieve their mail from a post office box and rejoin us in time for lunch. We are alone for the morning. We stop briefly at a convenience store for snacks and drinks before beginning our ascent. As we begin climbing, we both begin to experience headaches. I recall having a conversation regarding our route with a woman in Hermiston, Oregon who had worked at a resort in the Rockies. She told me that they always advised "flat-landers" to take *Tums* and drink lots of liquids. I have some *Tums* in my pack, so we ingest them and drink our liquids per her advice. The headaches soon disappear.

Cindy's blisters continue to improve and her new padding device from yesterday is once again providing a soft foot bed for her feet to rest upon.

The mountains and the road ahead look formidable as we trudge on at a moderate pace with relative ease. We are amazed to find that we only add one minute to our normal pace per mile as we start to climb higher. The joy of walking together up this pass seems to catapult us toward the top. We are happy to have the opportunity to attempt this climb.

When Janet and Walter return at 11:45 a.m., they don't find two struggling, tired middle-age adults on an arduous trek. They find giddy teenagers on a whimsical walk. We eat an early lunch, have photos taken for a local newspaper and borrow a walking stick to make the upcoming switchbacks easier to maneuver. We also drink extra water and replace our empty water bottles with full ones.

We pause frequently to absorb the panoramic scenes before us. Heaped snow looms above us at the edge of the pavement. The road is generally clear and mostly dry. Skiers on Arapaho Basin now are below us on the adjacent slopes and oblivious to our upward trek. We are amused with the realization that they had taken a chair lift to their playground. We have surpassed them in elevation by now and have done it by walking. We are pleased with that thought. We do caution each other that we have a ways to go before we summit. We do not know what lies ahead.

Huge trucks provide the only discordant sounds of our climb

as they decelerate down the mountain road on their journeys to rejoin the freeway at Dillon. Like us, they are barred from passing through the Eisenhower tunnel on I-70. Infrequently, cars pass by. Driver and passengers cast brief, puzzled looks in our direction. Within sight of the top, we take deeper breaths and remind ourselves to keep a slow, steady pace. We struggle more as we come to the final and steeper grades, as we now cope with colder temperatures and buffeting winds. The skies have become cloudy, but no snow falls. The motor home moves ahead once more, only one mile this time. If we are going to have problems, this is the area where it is most likely to occur. Our legs are fatigued, but not aching. We know that the past three months have slowly been preparing us for this day. Any doubts we may have had about our abilities are quickly dissipating. We are undeterred now, plodding on in the pure silence of this mountain, alone with our thoughts.

We step gingerly across a swiftly flowing runoff of melting snow and round a curve in the road.We have no idea how much farther we have to go.The motor home is not in sight. Within a short distance we see it in a sitting in large parking lot. We have reached the summit! We have done it. We are elated! Four hours after we began our assent, we are standing at the top of Loveland Pass in the middle of the Rocky Mountains. It is 2:11 p.m. Mountain Daylight Time.

After conquering the divide on Loveland Pass.

We are exuberant! The long awaited day has come and we have conquered our mountain. Day 89 of the walk is a day of triumph! The rarified air, at elevation 11,990 feet above sea level, has no effect on our enthusiasm and delight as we linger at the summit wanting to further appreciate our accomplishment. We have made it by foot to the top of the Continental Divide. I found a ski pole along the roadway and I plant it in the snow approximately 10 feet above the roadway so that we can say we reached 12,000 feet.

No terrain lying ahead of us should stop us now. We want to savor this moment over and over, and to tell everyone in the parking area what we have done. These once curious motorists, however, display no interest in two broadly grinning walkers posing for photos then high-fiving and kissing alongside the summit sign. Janet and Walter, however, recognize the importance of our accomplishment and are more than happy to make up for other people's lack of interest.

Far below and beyond, a plethora of vehicles and the low drone accompanying them signals to us that the remoteness of our mountain walk is approaching its end. The vehicles look like toys moving along the road far away and below us. We struggle to concentrate on the need to start down the switchbacks to complete today's walk and rejoin I-70 once again. The bounce in our steps fades with every step we take as we trudge down the circuitous route toward the freeway. The challenge is over. We have used up our energy climbing the mountain and we are now coming down from a mighty big high.

We found $3.48 during this time.

From Strangers to Friends

Jerry and Cindy knew that the only way to really feel the pulse of America during the walk was to stay with host families. When they started the trek, they had secured 25 host homes. Many more were needed. Finding people willing to do a good deed for a couple of strangers was often a challenge but always interesting.

Once, after Jerry and Cindy had completed a Sunday afternoon tour of the Oregon Trail Interpretive Center, they met Mary, a volunteer at the center. While chatting with her, Jerry explained why they were in the area and what they were doing. She was very intrigued and asked him where they stay each night.

"Funny you should ask." Jerry had replied. "We know where we are staying tonight and tomorrow night but we have no idea where we will stay Tuesday night. We'll be ending that walk day in Durkee and we understand it is a tiny town with few families living there."

To Jerry's surprise, Mary said, "You're in luck. I used to live there. Let me see what I can do."

Mary retrieved a phone book, took out a large magnifying glass to improve her diminished eyesight and attacked her mission with intensity. She would look up a familiar name and phone number and then dial it. When there was no answer, she would find another and repeat the process. For a while, it seemed like she would call everyone in town! It was on her sixth phone call that she hit the jackpot! Her mission accomplished, she proudly handed the phone to Cindy and Tuesday night's plans were finalized.

Meeting people like Mary was not unusual and not by chance. Jerry or Cindy gave the password and God's angels did their mission.

So it was, when Jerry and Cindy arrived at Miss Willie B. Dancy's home for an overnight stay. They knew they did not have a host home for the following night and commented to Willie B. that would probably have to find a motel for the night. That

A cool guest room amongst basement "treasures."

night, Jerry and Cindy went to bed listening to Willie B. making phone calls. There was nothing to do but pray for her success. In the morning, there was no sound from Willie B.'s room so Jerry and Cindy crept quietly toward the front door, wondering where they would stay that night. It was then that Willie B. came hustling out of her room declaring, "I finally found you a host family late last night. Here's their name and number. Give them a call when you get into town." Another angel had come to the rescue!

No matter what the circumstances of a particular family, be it busy or boring, it was always interesting. Sometimes the dining room table was overflowing with the culinary offerings of fine cooks. Other times, cooks struggled to use a can opener and meals were a bit meager. No matter, the meals were always appreciated and heartily eaten by two people who had just burned 2,000 calories that day.

Sleeping accommodations varied wildly, also. Some mattresses were fit for a king and the rooms could have been featured in *Better Homes and Gardens* Others were just fit and smelled more like *the* garden. During the warm summer days, if the room was cool, there was nothing to complain about. If it wasn't, Jerry and Cindy made do. Every home came with a guarantee of a safe, secure place for two tired bodies in need of a warm shower and a good night's sleep.

Families gave support, encouragement and friendship, without expecting anything in return. So it was that Jerry and Cindy left 82 thank-you certificates for their hosts on a variety of beds across America. At the end of most walk days, it was strangers who greeted Jerry and Cindy at the front door. With a hug and a hearty thank you, they parted the next morning as friends.

14

Grace in the Heartland

Day 101
Monday, May 20
Byers, Colorado

Cindy

Our three-day, carefree weekend in Denver is brought to an end by the obnoxious alarm clock at 6 a.m. We have spent the past 10 days on a "Rocky Mountain High." From a sun-filled and unforgettable Mother's Day weekend in Boulder, to a week of walking through the majestic eastern slopes of the Continental Divide. We have made new friends, visited with old ones and laughed heartily. My blisters are healing and we are rested and ready for a new segment of the walk. We are at the foot of the Rocky Mountains feeling like we are on top of the world.

By 7:30 a.m. we have hooked up with our new support vehicle drivers. After being with us for five weeks, Janet and Walter have returned to their summer quarters in South Dakota. We will miss them greatly. They have given us the stability and support we very much needed through the mountains of Utah and Colorado.

This is the first time we have met Ruth and Fred Hyde. They are committed Habitat volunteers. The Hydes have driven from Carlsbad, New Mexico to help us. Ruth lives with the daily frustrations of severe arthritis, but never complains. Fred is a feisty fellow who says if he keeps traveling, God will have a harder time finding him to call him home.

Fred likes to drive their little motor home at 52 miles an hour on the freeway, so we take it slow and easy out to Byers. We begin where we had stopped on Thursday with our "plains loving" Janet. Janet had finally admitted that she would miss the mountains after showing little appreciation for them during her time with us. She also left with a new name from us, "Mountain Mama."

The landscape of Eastern Colorado is stark and flat, hypnotizingly flat. Trees are rarely seen on the gently rolling hills. Our days of walking through the mountains and evergreen trees fade in the distant horizon behind us. It seems to us that the Kansas state border should begin here. Around us, we see acres of ripening wheat swaying gently in the soft breeze. It is sunny and 73 degrees.

"Mar, watch out for that snake!" Jerry shouts. Startled by what I hear and see, I do a clumsy, leaping dance over a bull snake that is sprawled across the entire width of the roadway shoulder. I had thought it was looking at a big stick. I have coped with a fear of snakes most of my life. Knowing that, I have continued to pray for courage assuming I would encounter snakes on this walk. Has God caused my eyes to see snakes as sticks? Although I was startled, and reacted accordingly, I am relieved that my first instinct was not to scream and I did not break out in cold sweat. This, I believe, indicates that I am doing better with the snake issue.

During my snake dance, a white travel van, bearing Washington State license plates, pulls onto the opposite shoulder and stops. We look over, expecting the driver to offer us a ride as so many have before. We are stunned to see friends Jeanette and Roy Friis from Olympia! They are on their way to Ohio and have gotten our itinerary from Julia, our church secretary. Since leaving Denver, they have been looking for us. They have found us on the first day of their search and are surprised to find us so easily. The hugs and conversation about what's new at home are wonderful. After 15 minutes of gabbing, they must be on their way. We ask them to stop two miles down the road and tell Ruth and Fred why we have been delayed.

The bull snake's relatives occasionally occupy the shoulder as we move on. I'm actually getting used to seeing them. We even observe two snakes mating right on the shoulder. I am amazed to find that I can watch without a pressing urge to hurry from the scene. It's an odd place to put this phobia, if that is what it is, behind me. God always seems to have impeccable timing.

This evening we are riding around and across farm fields in a pickup truck with our new host, Gerry Ohr. We have been learning what it is like to farm 5,000 acres of wheat and millet. His ranch is located in the tiny town of Lindon. He and his wife Julie and sons, Brandon, six, and Derrick, nine, will be our hosts for the next two nights.

We slide effortlessly into their life and appreciate the time they spend helping us to understand it. They are good teachers and we are willing students. We are enthralled with the old sod house Gerry shows us located on land he has inherited from his family. His grandparents lived in this tiny home made of dirt and grass when they first settled this area.

We walk during the day and immerse ourselves in their family's life each evening. We feast on huge farm meals prepared by Julie. Jerry plays baseball with the boys. We are entertained as Gerry feeds his tamed squirrels. We are impressed when the boys show us Gerry's collection of 119 rattles from snakes he has killed since he was a boy. We learn of cheat grass, crop rotation programs and subsidies and pheasants forever. We hear the story of Gerry and Julie's mentor, Ray McBeth, and his untimely death in 1984. During our walk through Lindon, we visit the memorial to his life. Two criminals murdered him inside his Lindon Mercantile. They stabbed him 31 times when he wouldn't accept their stolen check to pay for their gas.

Too soon, it is time to say goodbye to our new friends and move on down the road. We never quite get used to this pattern of developing friendships, then having to leave. These folks live on in our hearts, but there are rarely opportunities to rekindle the friendships.

While stopping to use a restroom at a Dairy King, an enthusiastic boy of 13 stops us to ask if he can photograph us. He is on a field trip with other students from a Denver inner city school. Each child's assignment is to take a photo of someone or something and then to write about it. He is amazed to learn of our walk and thinks he has scored quite a coup. We give him an autographed brochure to provide him with additional information and wish him well. He can't wait to get back on the bus and brag to his friends.

This afternoon, we meet Gerry for lunch at his Aunt Elva's Café in Anton. We have planned this in celebration of our 1,500th mile today. We are halfway to Atlanta and this is a big deal to us. We are pleased that Gerry recognizes our need to celebrate and

Looking forward to the second half of Habitrek '96.

disappointed that Fred and Ruth choose to stay in their RV for lunch. On this 90-degree day, we are confused at Gerry's drink order of "half-n-half". Folks from the Northwest know this to be half-milk, half-cream. Seeing our questioning faces, Gerry explains.

"Oh, in these parts that is an equal mixture of lemonade and iced tea. Would you care to try some?"

We do and I quickly become a convert to this thirst-quenching concoction.

Tonight we stay with Gerry and Julies' friends, the Rodwells in Anton. They are ranchers also. We are glad get to continue learning about ranching, although this time on a smaller scale. We also learn what it's like to be a paraplegic for their 28-year-old son, Shawn, who was paralyzed in an auto accident a few years ago. Their 18-year-old son, Carl saddles up his horse and teaches us the basics of being a junior champion rodeo rider. We love this stuff.

By Thursday we have made it to Cope, east of Joes. We meet the town's postmistress, and tonight's hostess, Georgia Mason. She hands us a letter from Millard Fuller and we buy a book of Civil War stamps for Jerry for a Father's Day gift from me. With directions to her home, we leave the post office carrying a large box mailed to us by Katie.

"I'm excited to open our new supply box from Katie, Jer," I reflect as we head on down the road. "She was telling me that she's on a first name basis with the UPS lady, because of all the shipping she does to us these days. She said the lady is used to her writing checks from our checkbook, now that she knows the unusual story and even asks how we are doing. That's pretty cool, huh?"

"Yeah it is. I don't know what we would do without Katie doing all this from home. Besides shipping supplies from our inventory, she said she fields lots of questions on the phone from curious friends who want to know how we are progressing."

We complete our last four miles of the day, let ourselves in to the Georgia's home and anxiously open the box. Katie has sent us our expected refill of supplies and a surprise as well. She has managed to elicit a donation from Sun Precautions Corporation, something we briefly attempted and failed before we left. We unwrap two shirts, two pairs of pants and a hat for each of us. They are a Northwest company who makes clothing from a special 30 SPF (sun protection factor) fabric that protects the skin like sunscreen. The lightweight fabric promises to breathe better and dry faster than the heavy Tee-shirts and shorts we have been wearing. We get on the phone immediately to thank Katie. She is pleased with her acquisition and proud that we are so psyched.

Our excitement over new gear is soon overshadowed by the news on television warning of a tornado. We do not know about storm cellars and bringing pillows and blankets down with us to protect us from flying debris. After a typical evening with our new friends, we lay our heads down tonight with an ear alert to the wind and our eyes on the flashlight.

The next morning, we eat a celebratory meal of biscuits and gravy. The tornado has moved north without doing any damage, leaving nothing but rain in its wake. Donning our rain gear for the first time in weeks, we once again head out into the bleak, flat landscape that is eastern Colorado. Today's rain and gray cast reminds us of the opinion we formed of this area from the year before. It's depressing.

"Hey Jer," I ask. "Do you think you've lost any weight so far?"

"It's hard to say, the last time I stepped on a scale, I hadn't. How about you?"

"I weighed myself last week and I had actually gained five pounds. It's hard to believe that after three months of intense exercise we wouldn't lose a few pounds. My clothes fit fine, if not looser. I wonder what's going on? Of course, it could be water retention from heat and extra fluid consumption." As 'Mrs. no thyroid', I'm used to watching my weight carefully and I am more than a little distressed.

"Well, you know, they always say muscle weighs more than fat, up to twice as much."

"Hey, you're right. I'd forgotten about that. Thanks, honey!"

We trudge on and finish our 20-mile day a few miles short of the Kansas border. We would like to make it to the border, but that isn't a realistic goal today. Fred drives us into St. Francis, Kansas, for the Memorial Day weekend.

Jerry

On Friday night, May 24, we stay with Alice and Harvey Lampe. We are instantly comfortable with them. Conversation flows freely and includes the topic of the need for rain for the wheat crops. Neither Cindy nor I object too much now when we have to walk in the rain, knowing our new friends need it for their wheat crop.

Saturday morning I awoke to the sound of Alice talking on the phone. Once in the kitchen, I found out that four young people had been in a serious car accident near the Kansas-Colorado border. Two teenagers were dead. It had happened Friday night. They failed to negotiate a long sweeping curve on a flat stretch of road, lost control, hit a low lying road approach and flipped twice. A witness said that they must have been going 100 miles per hour when they had passed him. This small town was abuzz with speculation of who was driving and all the other issues common to this type of breaking news. It was the week after high school graduation. The girl who was killed had graduated last week.

The rains were incessant; perhaps the heavens were crying. It meant we couldn't haul our luggage in Harvey's truck as planned, so he loaned us his car. We took our luggage to the donated motel room where we would spend the next two nights. Later in the day, Harvey and Alice called to arrange the switching of vehicles so they could have their car back and invited us to go get hamburgers with them. We eagerly agreed. House arrest in the midst of a deluge of near biblical proportions was not much fun. Going in and out of the motel got us soaked.

Sunday's weather was somewhat better. The main topic amongst the men at church was the rain. The subject of the recent tragic accident took a back seat. The men proffered their measurements of the rainfall until someone finally topped everyone else with five-

and-a-half inches at his place. Harvey could only come up with three-and-a-half inches at Alice's mother's place and soon dropped out of the bidding. We thought we had at least five inches at our motel right in town.

Today is Monday, Memorial Day. This former state employee and union shop steward has forgotten to schedule this holiday off. Alice and Harvey have driven us back the few miles into Colorado so that we can officially trek into Kansas. We drive past the scene of the recent accident. Fred and Ruth catch up with us later, and we complete our walk through Colorado early. The sky is heavy and downcast as if in response to the tragedy of Friday night. For some reason I am having trouble with this needless tragedy. It is as if I knew these young people. Everything appears gray. We walk by the accident site and see a few remnants of the vehicle and its tire tracks. The site itself looks innocent. Perhaps at a slower speed, they would have simply bumped over the road approach, come down hard and driven off, laughing at their mistake. Instead they were launched through the air. The thought of the tragedy stays with me. I keep thinking. Friday night four young people were together. For whatever reason, they drove too fast in an area they had to be familiar with. Tomorrow there will be funerals.

Tonight, Harvey and Alice take us to a Mexican restaurant for dinner and then we drive past the home of the boy that was killed. We see the vehicles of those converging on his family's home for the funeral.

Tuesday afternoon, the little drive-in restaurant closes at two o'clock so the young employees can attend the funeral. We stop so that I can buy a lemon yogurt cone before it closes. Tonight, we take a driving tour of the wheat crops and other places of interest with Harvey and Alice. The tour includes the cemetery. Fresh graves and flowers announce the termination of two young lives. Early Friday evening they were young and alive. Tuesday afternoon they are in the ground. The young driver faces charges. He will remember this all his life. On Wednesday we leave St. Francis and this tragedy and walk toward Atwood. It would be fruitless to try to explain why this affects me. Even I don't know.

During this time we found $1.04.

15

Double Dating

Day 110
Wednesday, May 29
Atwood, Kansas

Jerry

The soft green fields of wheat sway gently in the breeze along Highway 36 here in northwestern Kansas. They stretch beyond the limit of our vision, saturating the landscape. The lush wheat crop is approaching maturity. The farmers tell us they will harvest starting July 4. Unsightly coarse patches of intrusive vegetation occasionally interrupt the beauty of the blanket of green. Under overcast skies, these wheat field weeds are cast in a color resembling the outer skin of a cantaloupe. Their muted browns and greens are in rough contrast to the gently swaying green wheat stalks. Our journey today has rarely been interrupted by anything of interest, although we do pause long enough to take a photo of fence posts capped with old cowboy boots and ponder how and why this tradition began. The unbroken monotony of the landscape nearly hypnotizes us into a trance-like walk. It's kind of enjoyable really. I am alone with my thoughts for a while.

Highway 36 is the major route across northern Kansas. Surprisingly, traffic is not usually heavy and today the lack of traffic makes us feel isolated. Our rendezvous with Fred and Ruth is often our only contact with other people. Even the cow and horse population I often converse with are absent today. Bobwhites are plentiful though. I like to try to imitate their call.

They almost always reply. Cindy says it's cruel to get them all excited, thinking there's a "girlfriend" calling. I assure her they know the difference between a sweetheart and a weirdo walking across America.

We are walking through an area where towns are located about 20 miles apart. Kansas has 104 counties, so the larger towns are most likely to be county seats. Populations seldom exceed 1,000. St. Francis had a population of over 1,600 and we were excited to be in a larger city for the weekend. Perhaps, we have been on the road too long, for now a larger city means one with a Dairy Queen, a Pizza Hut or, if we are lucky, a McDonald's.

Atwood, Kansas, according to the sign at the outskirts of town is "Where People Care". Also, it is home of the Lakeside Motel, "worth waiting for" another sign tells us. Beyond the sign, the terrain changes to rolling mounds, some covered with wheat, others with native vegetation.

We are heading down hill, nearing a lake, when we are stunned by what rises before us. Unannounced, an ominously dark stealth fighter plane has emerged from behind one of these low mound areas, followed by its gleaming silver escort. We stand looking up at the bottoms of this sinister looking combination, dragging their shadows as they fly. We stand transfixed, unable to process our thoughts. We watch with both awe and a sense of evil. Finding no exact words, we improvise with our suddenly limited vocabulary before the pressure to move on extricates us from this frozen moment.

We hasten to finish this day. Although it is not a bad day, it needs to be ended. Down the hill we continue, past the well-advertised Lakeside Motel as we head into town. A car drives slowly and purposely by us. Four gray-haired ladies try to sneak glimpses of us without being caught staring. There are shy smiles as they ease by in their attempt to be unobtrusive. We wave, their smiles broaden and little hands rise barely above the car's door panels to acknowledge our gestures. These ladies were part of the group we spoke to last night at the church. They have come looking for us and they delight us with their timidity. This encounter gives us a moment of pleasure as we watch them continue a short ways, then turn back towards town. Moments like this are special. We don't forget them.

We walk past an abandoned drive-in theater. Wheat stalks now engulf the buildings and the old upright screen that were once surrounded by moviegoers in their vehicles. It is a strange dichotomy that amuses us. There is nothing flashy about Atwood. It fills our basic needs for bathroom and liquid refreshment. Before entering a mini-market, I take a photograph of the sign in the window: "Disabled Customers please honk for assistance with lottery products," it reads. I suppose if you need anything else, you can darn well get out of your vehicle and go inside.

A reader board, Kansas style.

We ignore the deli and head for the bathrooms, then return to the soda pop dispensers. Yes, we know that calorie free, nutrition free, Diet Coke with caffeine doesn't really slake one's thirst and isn't practical, but this is our walk, so we will eat and drink whatever we want. Anyway, if we were practical, would we be walking across the country for seven months? Once we down the large drinks, reality returns and we struggle briefly with the knowledge that we have loaded parched bodies with 64 ounces of caffeine-laden brown water and additives. Ah, but it was so good.

A hand-printed sign on a sandwich board placed in the middle of a downtown intersection amuses us. It announces our appearance at a church potluck tonight and invites the community at large.

Storm warnings follow us east this week. Dorothy Wolters, our hostess, gives us tonight's warning.

"If I holler at you to hurry to the basement, bring your pillow to protect your head, a blanket to keep warm and a flashlight to show the way."

At 1:30 a.m., we are awakened, not by Dorothy's voice, but by flashes of lightning followed by house-grabbing claps of thunder. We huddle together in front of our upstairs window and watch the show. The rain that follows looks like the backside of a waterfall. Fred and Ruth Hyde, our RV support team, are parked out in the yard in their motorhome. We watch and worry that the little motor home will be damaged.

The next morning they emerge unscathed and unbothered by the storm. When we ask them how they liked the storm, they both reply in honesty. "What storm?"

This week we stay with a new host family 20 miles further east each night, and each night we go to bed with some type of tornado warning. While at Kathy and Jay Holste's, we listen with intense interest as they recount their survival of a tornado that ripped through their little farmhouse. It is only because the back door blew open and equalized the air pressure inside and out that the house was not completely blown apart.

We have noticed that folks through this area of Kansas seem to always be on the watch for rain. The weather channel provides background noise to their lives because farmers are at the mercy of Mother Nature. This is a new concept to us. We soon learn to understand and accept it.

We sleep best while guests of Pastor Bob Raudemacher. We have been given a basement guest room. If the warning becomes a tornado, we will not have to go anywhere. We'll have to move over.

The following night, Cindy is up draining throbbing blisters at 3 a.m. when we again watch from the guest room window while a raging storm blows through Stuttgart. Gerald and Lela Bethke's home is our refuge tonight. Unlike the storms of the previous nights, this one devastates thousands of acres of crops, 60 miles east and south of here.

Today, we left Highway 36 at Phillipsburg and turned south to intersect with Highway 9 and once again head easterly. We have been walking the shoulders of Highway 36 for three weeks. We are walking through an area familiar to our friend, Ed Armbrust. Ed has been sending us interesting e-mails about Kansas. The one he sent yesterday explains the weather we have been having:

"...Please note that being east of the 100th meridian means enough rainfall to produce trees and enough water to create landscape that should protect you from the wind. I quote from Konza Prairie by O.J. Reichman.

'The prairie can be characterized by its weather extremes as much as its norms. The most consistently extreme weather

occurs in conjunction with spring and summer thunderstorms. Under specific conditions, intense clashes between warm and cool air masses spawn tornadoes. These terrifying cyclonic clouds produce winds higher than 400 miles per hour and generate tremendous gradations in air pressure between their center and their margins.'

Thought you would like to know. So air moves and this is called wind and you are probably not calling it Mariah."

Cindy

It is Friday, June 7 and we are in Gaylord, Kansas. This week ends with five new blisters. I thank God that it's Friday. Soon enough I thank him for our weekend hosts, the Dannenbergs. Patty Dannenberg and her granddaughter, Tember, meet us at our 18th mile this afternoon and walk into Gaylord with us. We've never had a host family do this so we're taken by their thoughtfulness right away.

When we get to their home, we meet Don, Patty's husband. Patty and Don are near our age and have similar values. They are blessed with a good marriage and show deep love and respect for each other and their family. We feel comfortable with them from the get go.

After dinner, Don asks us if we want to go "cruisin'." We're not sure where we'll cruise since Gaylord only has a population 52. It's a playful suggestion that conveys Don's sense of humor and pride so we're game. While we wait in front of their brick home with Patty, Don goes to get the car. He returns in a sea foam green 1950 Mercury sedan. He honks the horn and the three of us climb into the car and pretend to be 18 again. These two new friends then show us their town, their fertilizer business and their sons' homes. We ride by the school where they courted as teens. They point out their little post office. These everyday things are important to them. We appreciate being included in their lives. As a breathtaking sunset reflects off of the western prairie we return "home." This will be our first weekend in a host home instead of a motel. The daylight basement suite affords us plenty of room and privacy. We can't think of a better place to be.

With today being Saturday, we do the usual e-mailing, pay bills,

Patty and Don with their 1950 Mercury at their home in Gaylord, Kansas.

search for host families and do the laundry. Lots of laundry! We also get good news from Katie when she calls to say her parents-in-law, Suzie and Jim Bryan, have generously offered to fly her and little Logan out to meet us in Missouri. She is very excited about it. So are we! Suzie and Jim have been planning to come join us as support vehicle drivers since January. We have looked forward to their coming. Now we have even more to look forward to.

Tonight Don and Patty are taking us out on the town. This time we ride in Don's white Lincoln. Our destination is Smith Center, 12 miles from Gaylord. We first are treated to a special dinner at the Ingelboro Restaurant. It is a unique dining experience because the building is a renovated, turn-of-the-century hospital. The outstanding service and food are highlights of this special meal. We then go to a little movie house where "Twister" is playing. Don and Patty have been amused with our tornado warning stories from this week and they enjoy the idea of teasing us with this movie. This is the second time they have seen it. They can't wait to hear what we think of it. Basically, we think it was a good movie with a pretty predictable plot. The humorous parts were great though and we laugh when Helen Hunt is tied to a pipe with her belt, blown upside down and still ends up perfectly coiffed and dressed. The flying cows were entertaining too.

We end our date with a hot fudge sundae at the Jiffy Burger drive-in before driving back to Gaylord. We've had a wonderful time. The blisters are feeling better too.

We are not done dating, though. After church on Sunday the

four of us head out on another adventure. This time we drive to the geographic center of the contiguous United States, located near Lebanon. The little chapel there gives Jerry the opportunity to "preach" to the four of us. His sermon is anything but serious, however. We think this place is funky, but cool. It's the kind of place we would drive out of our way to, if we were traveling. We look forward to the world's biggest ball of twine in Cawker City next week!

Don drives us through Lebanon and we are struck by the feeling of hopelessness in yet another Kansas town. Like marshes that slowly transition into pastureland, many of the communities around here have begun reverting to nature. Skeletons of old businesses line the once robust streets. Exterior walls and windowpanes are now tombstone epitaphs of the businesses that struggled and died. It is sad to observe the carcasses of tourist facilities that have failed. It is the proverbial double-edged sword. Businesses fail for lack of customers. With no businesses, customers don't return.

Don then takes us past the area damaged most severely by the terrible storm we witnessed from Bethkes bedroom window while staying in Stuttgart Thursday night. There are grain elevators twisted into piles of metal rubbish. Leaves are stripped off one side of trees while the other side looks normal. Wheat stalks are lopped off near the ground like a giant lawn mower, with a dull blade, has passed through these fields. The devastation is overwhelming and sad. As we stare out the car windows, we are amazed to witness farmers and their friends out plowing the fields under and preparing to replant them. Don explains that they will plant Milo instead of wheat now. It is too late in the season to replant wheat.

The scene before us is eye-opening. We don't understand how farmers can face this storm season year after year and not give up. Don and Patty help us to understand. "Some do give up and move to town. Most manage to pull themselves up by their bootstraps and try again. We midwestern farmers are usually a determined bunch. We come from good stock and deep faith. It really isn't much different than you two, now is it?"

No, we guess it really isn't.

It's Monday morning as we are packing and preparing to leave our weekend home when a $100 bill floats down and lands on the stairs in front of me. What could this be about? I find out soon enough. Patty has already tried to give the money to Jerry, explaining that they had already sent a check to Habitat in support of our efforts. This is for our personal use, she insisted. Jerry feels extremely uncomfortable taking it. It is then that Patty tries the floating money technique. I see her pretty face peaking down with a smile. "Please accept it with our gratitude," she begs. She's making it hard to refuse.

We do not normally spend one penny of the money we are given for our own needs. Jerry's retirement check covers our expenses. Patty and Don know this and correctly assume that a little extra spending money might come in handy at some point along the route. I have no choice, but to accept the floating money with gratitude and an extra hug of appreciation to a couple of soul mates. They have reminded us this weekend that playing is a good thing, even if you are 50-something.

Both

It's almost four p.m. on Tuesday, June 11. We are near Cawker City. It has been warm since 7:30 a.m. We have talked to a multitude of bicyclists who are participating in the "Bike Across Kansas" event. We've had two media interviews. Cindy's got two new miserable blisters. Jerry's got a rock in his sock and bruised toes. It's 95 degrees now and other than that everything is fine!

Hey, things are turning around. Jerry just popped loose a dime from the melting asphalt.

A group of bicyclists passes by across the road from us. They ride in the same direction with traffic; we walk against it.

"Hey, you guys okay, need any help?" they shout.

"No thanks, we're walking across the country," we holler in return.

"Oh well, we're biking across Kansas, so we guess we have less to do," one guy laughs.

One of his buddies flips a parting shot as they ride on. "I sure hope you're happily married." He doesn't say it sincerely; it's more of a sneer.

His commentary on something we hold so dear irritates us. Why does our walk across America generate so many comments about our marriage? We really don't understand why people are amazed that a married couple can do something like this. The sarcastic biker accomplishes more than irritating us, though. Our ensuing conversation has taken our minds off of blisters, rocks and heat.

We do have a good marriage. Don and Patty get it, why can't everyone else? Loving each other really is not very complex. Jerry always describes it as being "twitterpated." It's that deep-down kind of love that still causes our hearts to skip a beat when we least expect it. Love is the glue that holds all good marriages together. What may be unusual in our Marriage is that we share the common characteristics of knowing how to work hard, play hard and dream big dreams, *and* we do it together. Our differences complement each other. We are energized by one another. Add to that, strong faith, an ability to communicate our needs and feelings to each other, and a deep commitment to our vows and each other. That's about it, we think.

Our son, Pat, thinks there's more. He says our marriage is like migrating salmon. He may have a point. There is immediacy, but not panic, there is purpose and compromise. He says we are wise, though childlike. We are independently connected, he says. His siblings agree. We like that.

Adventure appeals to our sense of playfulness so we work as a team, with a calm confidence and determination to make those adventures a reality. Where many couples look for excuses to not to do something, we look for reasons why we should. Call it luck, God's destiny or good genes. We think it's all three.

Okay, so maybe it's a little more complex than we thought. We continue on down the road, hand in hand.

During this time, we found $1.58.

Our Official Worrier

Walking the roadway along the shores of the Snake River in Oregon, Cindy and Jerry are playing a game of highway golf. They stop abruptly.

Jerry crosses the road to Cindy's side.

"Was that gunfire?" she whispers.

"Sure sounded like it. Came from across the river, I think, but I can't tell what they're shooting at," Jerry replies with an edge of concern.

"You don't think they are aiming at us, do you?"

"I don't think they would do that. They may just be shooting at something toward our direction. My concern is that they are lousy shots or just plain careless."

Suddenly Cindy's mother's words of warning, spoken back in January, come back to haunt her. One month before the walk was scheduled to begin, her mother had expressed strong concerns about Cindy and Jerry's safety on this walk.

Cindy had called her mom to inquire about her upcoming rotator cuff surgery. Her mom was far more concerned about the walk and Jerry and Cindy's upcoming departure.

"Oh, the surgery is scheduled for next Wednesday at two, but I'm not worried about that, it's the walk I'm worried about. I wish you would just forget the whole crazy idea," she had cried.

"Mom, we're not going to do that," Cindy had objected. " Jer and I WANT to walk across America. We want to spread the good news about Habitat for Humanity. Jer retired to do this. It's why we sold the preschool to Pat and Kim. It's not like we haven't planned carefully. We will have trained over 1,000 miles. We have already arranged some host families and support vehicle drivers and we have over $12,000 in pledges for Habitat. We can't cancel all of this now. Furthermore, we don't want to. You have to trust that God will protect us."

Undaunted, her mom had pressed on. "I don't trust anybody. Why can't you just stay home and be happy with normal things? You're going to wear yourselves out, and anyway, you don't know what kind of crazies are out there. They'll probably shoot you."

"I can't believe you said that," Cindy had stammered. "I wish so much that you were interested. You're usually supportive of the things I choose to do." Cindy was hurt and upset.

"Well, this is where I draw the line, honey. I just cannot support you this time."

In the days that followed, Cindy's mom's concerns lit the fire of concern in others, and soon there was a four-alarm blaze surrounding Jerry and Cindy. Cindy's dad supported her mom's view and he pleaded with Cindy to cancel the walk. While many family members were supportive, others were now beginning to question the wisdom of this undertaking.

Jerry, realizing Cindy's deflation and hurt, came up with a plan to get Cindy and her parents together just days before the walk was to begin. Her parents were refusing to join the rest of the family in attending the kick-off event. Cindy's father had softened and told his daughter that he truly was behind her, but her mom wouldn't budge.

The day finally came when Jerry and Cindy drove out to her parent's home. Her mother was already crying as Cindy bent to kiss her tear-streaked face.

"I'm still so worried about you," she sobbed quietly.

"I know, Mom, I know. We'll be okay. You'll see. I know you're going to worry no matter what I say, so how about you being the "Official Worrier of Habitrek' 96?" It will free up others to do more productive things and it will keep your mind occupied while we're gone. What do you think?" Cindy ventured, half-serious, half-kidding.

Cindy's mother laughed at the suggestion.

"By golly, that's a job for which I am truly qualified. I'll be proud to wear the title," she declared with a slight grin.

And so, Cindy's mom became the symbolic leader for many people who had unspoken fears for their safe return.

Now, back along the Snake River, gunshots are still ringing out.

Fortunately the support driver comes by at that moment. Instead of driving ahead as usual, Jerry asks Dotty Fehring to drive alongside them. A weird looking individual had been eying them as he drives by making them feel more uneasy. He drives back past them and stops ahead of them. With Dotty alongside them, they pass the ogler as they continue to study activity across the river. They can see men moving around, but they cannot discern what the shooting is about. Maybe they were shooting at rodents on the land located below the barren hills. The shooting stops as suddenly as it had begun. Their game of highway golf resumes. Now, if Cindy could just score a hole in one!

16

Walking Alone

Day 124
Wednesday, June 12
Asherville, Kansas

Jerry

Like most duos in history, we are together in this episode of
life, the George and Gracie of Habitat for Humanity,
walking across the country. We had talked about what we
would do if one of us couldn't walk. We said we could push the
other in a wheelbarrow.

You must know that when you are discussing these things,
that you are really hoping nothing will happen and that you won't
have to face the decision. I had always believed we would make
it. I realized that any number of things could happen along the
way to force one or both of us to quit. I didn't expect it to happen.
Call it faith, call it blind stupidity or ignorance (I prefer faith), we
would walk it together.

So here I am, walking the road without my partner. We have
walked together almost 2,000 miles. Now I am walking down the
shoulder of the two-lane road by myself. What I am feeling is
indescribable. I know that part of *us* is missing.

I hurry along, thinking that if I walk fast enough, I can reduce
the miles she will have to walk when she rejoins me. She is in the
motor home working on her blisters with Lela and Gerald Bethke,
our host family last week and support folks this week. The blisters

have been giving her a lot of difficulty these last few days. Lela thinks she might be able to run into a local pharmacy and find more Elastacon Tape that has helped minimize her blister discomfort. We haven't been able to find it for many weeks now. Cindy is the one who suggested I walk on without her. I couldn't make this decision on my own. Reluctantly, I agreed, only because I knew it would keep her off those blisters for a while. When I walked out of the RV, she was sitting there with two hot feet on blue ice packs.

My plan has merit. I will walk as fast as I can, not our usual 16-minutes-per-mile pace, and maybe I can get all the afternoon miles in for her.

I walk, feeling naked. We had always joked about doing the "naked mile." This wasn't the nakedness we had discussed. What is this feeling? I just keep walking. Cars drive past, people look, and I suddenly feel conspicuous. What could they be thinking as they pass a lone walker? No battling traffic together. No occasional comments about what we were hearing, seeing, or smelling. No chitchat about how we're doing or feeling. It's the traffic and me. She isn't positioned at my immediate left flank in our single-file positions. Life suddenly isn't the same.

After two miles of walking, the motor home pulls up across the road bringing my life-partner to join me. I am so intent in processing my thoughts that I am startled by the horn. I had hustled, I thought, but I saved her only two miles. She has hurried with the blister doctoring and, a half-hour later, we are two again. I tell her about the strangeness of walking alone. I can't fully convey my feelings. Perhaps there aren't adequate words for how the heart feels. George and Gracie are together and the two are one again. All is well.

Cindy

We felt an instant kinship with the Bethkes when we stayed in their home. When they agreed to come help us on the route, because we lacked a support vehicle this week, it was our good fortune. It turned out to be their misfortune.

We start this day in Miltonvale, as we start most days, by bandaging blisters. Before Jerry puts the bandages on, he suggests we take a photo of them. I am against it, because all photographs get mailed home to the kids. If they saw these they would either call a mental hospital or United Press International. No, I insist, this will be our little secret. After Jerry's two miles alone, we know we can trust them to help with the blisters without grossing out at the sight of my feet and nagging me to quit the walk, as many before them have done. They seem to understand my high threshold for pain and even higher degree of determination.

We begin walking (limping) at 6:50 a.m. Instead of eating breakfast, we graze from Lela's well-stocked refrigerator at each break. Today June 14, Jerry's beloved Flag Day. He has attached a flag he found along the road last month to his daypack.

After six miles, we approach the motor home with curiosity. There are extra cars parked on the road and people standing about. We do not notice the missing van.

"What's going on?" Jerry asks innocently.

Lela is momentarily speechless. She points across a green pasture to the beginning of a small ravine 30 feet away.

"The van," she stammers. "It rolled into that fence at the head of that ravine.

We see the teal-colored tailgate of their brand-new Ford Windstar sticking up in the air. The front end is tipped down into the ravine at a 30-degree angle. The only thing keeping it from rolling all the way to Oklahoma (with all of our belongings in it) is a barbed wire fence.

Temporarily speechless, we finally manage to stammer, "What happened?"

"Well," Lela explains, "I was driving the van ahead of Gerald in the motor home, and when we came to the mile marker where we agreed to meet you, I left the motor running and got out to show him where to park. I must have forgotten to put the van in park and set the brake. Next thing I knew it was rolling away. I tried to run and stop it, but I couldn't catch up."

"Thank God you didn't do that, Lela! You could have been killed!" we both exclaim.

Someone calls a tow truck and others offer their assistance. A deputy sheriff has stopped to investigate and help. It is getting late and warming up quickly, so we make ourselves peanut butter and jelly sandwiches and get back to the walk-limping.

After we leave, the extricated van is towed to Concordia,

where a badly bent left front wheel will be repaired. There are barbed wire scratches all the way up the hood that will need a good body and fender man also. Gerald and Lela will drive the motor home on to Kansas City and spend the weekend with their daughter before retrieving the van on their way home.

The damaged van is not the only problem on this day. My blisters are just too painful to continue. I object to the idea of Jerry walking alone again. We have already completed 15 miles and it is only 12:15 p.m. I have finally admitted that my determination to walk through the pain is fading. We could use the time this afternoon to seek medical advice about the condition of my feet. The Bethkes heave a collective sigh of relief and very enthusiastically agree with me. We will stop for the day.

The Bethkes offer to take us to lunch at the Cedar Court Restaurant in Clay Center, about 20 miles away. A half-hour after we arrive, Jerry has made it through the buffet line and returns with a nice plump chicken breast, a piece of Swiss steak and three fish sticks. When that is gone, he goes back for his fruit and dairy servings. He returns this time with one serving of apple crisp and one of cherry crisp. Each is topped with vanilla soft freeze! In the meantime, I have gone outside to use the phone booth. Failing to contact a doctor by phone, we decide to drive the 45 miles to Manhattan, our lodging city for the weekend, and go to a sports medicine clinic in hope that it may see me without an appointment. My hopes are high that I may finally get some relief.

Arriving at the clinic, I limp into the receptionist's desk in my socks. I am sweaty and covered in road grime. Glamorous I am not. I figure I'd better explain real fast.

"Hi. I know what I'm about to tell you is a little unusual. Hopefully, you can help me with my dilemma." I give her the condensed version. She seems sympathetic and says she'll have to go talk to her supervisor before she can let me see a doctor. I feel hopeful and say a silent prayer for compassion while she is gone. She returns with her supervisor who looks at me like I have just landed from Mars with a less-than-credible story. She rattles off their rules for seeing new patients.

There can be no exceptions; the wait is six weeks. I am welcome to make an appointment for July 31 at 12:45 p.m. Her demeanor is stern. Her face is devoid of any softness. Her hair is as black as my mood. I'm sinking fast. I explain that I will have walked to Memphis by then and doubt I could keep the appointment. Can there be no exceptions?

None. I am welcome to go to the emergency room if I can't wait.

I am crushed. I begin to cry out of sheer frustration. Jerry tries to intervene and stresses my plight to the stern woman. She remains unyielding and he too, is unsuccessful. He puts his arms around me and we walk out the door, across the parking lot and into the air-conditioned motor home. Gerald and Lela are waiting expectantly. They are sympathetic to my plight and as frustrated as we are. They need to be on their way to Kansas City so they drive us to Ronnie and Tom Walen's home and help us get settled and then leave. We have become very close in our short time together and it is difficult to say goodbye. I shed more tears.

The next 24 hours are spent with many special activities meeting wonderful folks from a town with a great Habitat affiliate and a big heart. It is here that the largest pledge per mile was made to Habitat through Habitrek '96. A couple we don't know and never have the pleasure of meeting, pledges $3,000. It is a significant boost to our sagging morale. Always in the back of my mind though, is what to do about the blisters. Ronnie and Tom try to think of a solution. I call Dr. Horsman, our podiatrist back home. He says he will send a 10% formaldehyde solution and some heavily padded adhesive foam in the mail. He believes I need to toughen up the skin on the bottoms of my feet. I will follow his directions to swab it on twice a day and I should see a difference in three to four weeks. It sounds a little strange, but if it's good enough to preserve dead frogs, it's good enough for me.

The next morning, Tom suggests we go to a pharmacy that may carry foot dressings. They have nothing there that we don't already have. They suggest we drive over to Olsen's Shoe Service in Aggieville, near Kansas State University. We're willing to try anything.

We push open the glass door to this quaint little shoe shop and are greeted by a pretty young woman named Jamie. We are surrounded by displays of Birkenstocks and she is wearing a pair. This is a good sign.

"May I help you?" she asks in a way that makes me believe she really wants to.

"I sure hope so," I reply hesitantly. "No one has been able to help so far. Let me explain what's going on and we'll see what you think."

She is surprised by my story and interested in how she can help make the next 1,200 miles more comfortable. She thinks, first of all, that our choice of footwear is a wise one. This is refreshing, given most folks' reaction. She asks me to walk and then watches each step intently. She then assesses the situation quickly and with a high degree of knowledge.

"As you know, the great thing about Birkenstocks is the way they strengthen your foot muscles. Unfortunately for you, your arch muscle has become so strong that the ball of your foot is striking with too much force. That contributes to blister formation. The unpadded leather insoles aren't helping because your skin is very soft. I agree with your podiatrist. The formaldehyde solution should help that. I would like to add arch and metatarsal pads to your sandals and pound out the leather ridge a bit to see if we can't cut down on the friction on your heels. I'll cover the insoles with Pasizoid. It's a tough foam pad that will mold to your foot. We usually put it in diabetics' shoes, but I think it will serve you well, also. How many pairs will we need to fix up?

"I rotate three different pairs, so all three need to be done. I have them all in the car because our host, Tom here, is taking us to the Holidome Hotel for the weekend.

"Great. Bring them in. I'll fix up one pair for you right now and drop them off at the hotel front desk on my way home. You'll have to wear the same pair all next week. If you'll give me the address of your host family for a week from now, I will ship them directly."

I don't even know how to begin to thank Jamie for her knowledge, care and compassion. She has been a real blessing. I may have come face-to-face with a real angel. A blister angel it seems.

Sunday is Father's Day. As they did for me on Mother's Day, Pat and Kim have called and made plans for us to have brunch. After a wonderful brunch in the hotel restaurant, we return to our room and call my Dad with wishes for a special day. He says that Mom, the official worrier, wants to talk to me. She gets on the phone.

"Hi Sis, how's it going?"

"Oh, the walk is great," I say truthfully. I avoid the part about the blister problems. If she knew about my recent woes, she'd be more worried than ever.

"How's everything with you? Did you get your shoulder sling off?" I ask.

"Yes, my rotator cuff is healing well. That's not what I wanted to talk to you about. I've been thinking a lot about this worrying stuff. It's no fun at all. The walk seems to be going well from all reports. I want to resign as head worrier. I thought you would be happy to hear that."

"Mom, that is great news! I am happily accepting your resignation as of this very moment. You've made my day. Jerry will be thrilled to hear it also. Between this and a special angel I met this week, it's going to be a great week."

We found only 50 cents during this time.

Believe

Believe in yourself, what you think, what you feel,
Believe in the truth, in the good, the ideal.
Believe that your dreams can someday become real...
Forever and always, believe.
Believe in yourself and in what you can do,
Believe in the goals that you strive to pursue,
Believe in your friends, who believe in you too,
Forever and always, believe.
Hold fast to dreams for if dreams die,
Life is a broken winged bird that cannot fly.
Hold fast to dreams for if you let go,
Life is a barren field
Covered with snow.

Langston Hughes

17

Birkenstocks Lost

Day 136
Monday, June 24
Topeka, Kansas

Jerry

The pickup is headed straight for us. I feel like I am watching an action video that has slowed to show one frame at a time. What happened to all our preconceived escape plans? Why are we frozen in the moment? This isn't real. My prolonged stare at the driver's face reveals nothing. He appears to have checked out of reality. It's nothing personal on his part, just a random meeting with two walkers in the path of his errant vehicle. Our paths are about to intersect at the edge of Highway 32 between Topeka and Lawrence, Kansas. They say your past flashes before your eyes at a moment like this, I see only the present.

We had a very refreshing weekend in Lawrence. The hotel setting was wonderful. We were thrilled to find a fruit basket and a bottle of sparkling cider as we entered our room Friday afternoon after a long hard walk to Topeka. We had come to Lawrence for the weekend because the Habitat affiliate in Topeka had no special events planned with us and the Lawrence affiliate did. We spent Saturday with them, visiting their Habitat homes and speaking at a potluck. Cindy finally got help for a throbbing blister when a walk-in medical clinic agreed to see her. Dr. Burt was amazed that her blood pressure was only 88/56 until she explained what we have been doing for the last four months. He drained and cultured the site and said a callous had formed over a blister, trapping germs. She must now take medication for a staph infection. The fiasco at the sports medicine clinic in Manhattan had meant walking another week before we could get another chance for medical help. Now with the immediate treatment and the medication, her feet are slowly on their way to improving. Thank the Lord for Dr. Burt.

This Monday morning, we have been driven back where we stopped on Friday in Topeka, her feet better and with a new support team, Jean and Curtis Wilkerson. They live in Texas during the winter and spend most summers building houses with the Habitat Care-A-Vanners. It is rush hour, both directions. People from the west hurrying east, people from the east hurrying west. If they would just swap houses or jobs, there might not be a need for all this scurrying. The highway is full of tailgaters commuting to jobs, or wherever, unable to slow down for two intruders on the side of the highway. Large dump trucks join the melee. As they rush to and fro, we are nothing more than a roadside nuisance.

We have been very careful to not impede or challenge traffic as we have walked. We knew there could be low tolerance for walkers, especially if a motorist's routine was upset. Although we have encountered many large trucks on this walk, we find ourselves most wary of dump trucks. Other long-haul truckers seem to get used to us over time or to have passed the word to others truckers that we are out here. Dump truck drivers are in different situations. Their routes are short and purposeful–move their loads from one place to another, then return for more. Beelines are not to be interrupted, and if we venture into their paths, we will be more than stung. If we shared the road long enough, they might get used to us, but usually we encounter each other for only a short time. Today, we hope we will be out of their way soon.

Road conditions have deteriorated before us. The shoulder has narrowed and the grassy back slope rises from the edge of the narrow shoulder at a steep angle. As we walk, I note that it would be extremely difficult to climb the slope, if we should have to. Moreover, we have no clear escape route for much of the way. All our senses are tense as we continue to recognize the increasing potential for harm. It has been impossible to relax for much of the morning. Relaxation will not come until traffic volume finally diminishes.

Suddenly, there is a break in the traffic. It comes as a surprise. The frenzy has momentarily ceased. I look ahead and see cars slowly veering into the other lane to avoid a dead raccoon in the lane adjacent to us.

And then SHE appears. She is driving a minivan. The windows are tinted, so I can't see if she has children with her. I quickly realize she has no intentions of swerving. She will hit the partially shredded road kill. I quickly turn to tell Cindy to stop. She has already seen what's coming. We might have enough distance to save us from the bloody splatter.

The woman has her wheels aligned perfectly, and she hits the raccoon, flipping flesh and innards through the air, falling just short of our feet. I look into the van at the driver, but there is no glimpse our way. Was this an accident, or inattention? I hope it was not malice. In disgust, I watch as the van continues a short distance past us, then turns to the right up a side road. Still dismayed by what we have seen, we return to walking past the scattered remnants, placing our feet very carefully.

Rush hour has ended for good now. We let ourselves relax a little, but we still must walk single file. Facing traffic, we continue onward, and again are unprepared for what happens. Though our senses are keen to traffic noises and conditions, we have never mastered the sound of a vehicle passing another from behind us. On a two-lane road, the passing car approaches in the lane next to us. It is unnerving because we are not prepared for it to happen and we are not used to a vehicle being that close to us traveling in the same direction. We have had large trucks do it and it has never ceased to be startling and unsettling. Rarely can we anticipate or prepare for it. The wind from the passing car rustles my sleeve as the car hurries by before moving into its proper lane. On this narrow shoulder, Cindy has been walking behind me and on my right, near the edge of the traveled lane. The car nearly clipped her as it scampered by.

At last we have passed the dump truck drivers hive of activity, located off the road to our right. The volume of traffic is getting lighter and cars come by more often in packs, rather than as individual speedsters.

We are once again back in the potential disaster video.

"Mar, do you see this silver pickup?" I shout.

"Yes, I see him!"

We both know we are about to be hit. There are no options for escape. We can't move. Where could we go? We see the open area to our left that was hidden by the terrain moments ago. It offers refuge, but the truck will take us before we can run far enough. Eyes fixated on the driver, I watch and wait for him to hit us. Cindy stands tight behind me. Does she think I can save her? I prepare to take the hit for her.

Suddenly, I see the driver's body jerk, as if he is returning from sleep. He jolts out of his trance. His eyes are large. Miraculously, he corrects his divergent course by steering to his left, but not so much that he overcorrects. I watch as he goes by. He does not look at us. We heave huge sighs of relief. We have been spared.

It is at that moment that I realize if we hadn't been here with our reflective vests on, he may have run off the road. He may have been the one in danger after all. Perhaps we were here for him, and that's why we had no sensation of fear. We are observers. We briefly ponder the moment, and then move on.

As we continue our walk to Lawrence, we meet a newspaper photographer who thinks he has found a scoop. He takes our photos and revels in his coup; then he drives off. At the end of the day, we meet Jean and Curtis at their fifth wheel RV on a side road. Another newspaper reporter is waiting with them, as are people from the Lawrence Habitat affiliate. This reporter takes photos and interviews us more extensively than the last one did. This done, we ride in to our host family's home in Lawrence for the night.

We were expecting our repaired Birkenstocks from Manhattan to be there, waiting for us. Cindy's feet are in desperate need of them. When we get to Van and Sally's home, Cindy inquires if we have gotten a package. They tell her no.

Van drifts off to his room, and Cindy goes to shower and get ready to go out for dinner this evening. I am left in the living room with Jean Wilkerson and Sally. I had briefly overheard Sally's conversation with Van about returning a package that they hadn't ordered when we first arrived. We had just completed a tiring day, so my mind didn't comprehend much at the time.

Things are quiet as I kill time waiting for my turn in the shower. Offhandedly, I mention how surprised I am that our sandals didn't come. Sally then mentions that they *had* gotten a box with sandals in it. I ask, "Where is it?"

She replies, "Oh, we returned them to the post office. We didn't order any sandals; we thought it was a senior citizen scam. It had Jerry written on the box after our name and address, but I just never thought of you."

Remarkably staying composed, I try to piece together what has happened while I begin hatching a plan to retrieve the box. I ask about the nearest post office and quickly call it. It is nearing six o'clock. Jeff answers. I tell Jeff about us, and why we need the box. He does not seem surprised to hear that we are walking across America, and asks to which post office the box was returned. I ask Sally. She does not know. Controlling an urge to raise my voice, I encourage her to go ask her husband. Quickly! She goes down the hall to find him.

She returns to say, "He's taking a little nap. I don't want to disturb him."

I resist the urge to tell her to wake him up, as I tell Jeff that I don't know which post office. Sally thinks she knows. Jeff tells me it might be too late, that mail may have already gone back to Manhattan. He offers to look and call me back. I hang up the phone, trying to figure out what Jamie the "blister angel" in Manhattan, will think when she gets the package back, marked "Refused."

Cindy is still in the bathroom, oblivious to the events unfolding in the living room.

The phone rings within what seems like seconds. Jeff has found the box. He asks if I would like him to mail it back to our host family's address. I blurt out, "NO, I will come get it!"

Sally has now gone back down the hall, this time, to roust Van from his nap.

He walks into the living room with a yawn.

"Van, I need you to take me to the main post office. That package you returned was our sandals!"

He tells me again about their concern that it was a senior citizen scam. I don't really care. He tells me that they had opened the box, seen the repair tags on the sandals, and noted that the box had their name written on it followed by Cindy's. He said hey didn't know our names. When we had arrived, they had shown us a newspaper article about us, which our mutual friends, Mountain Mama and Walter Nelson, had sent to them.

Van drives up to the post office and I jump from the car, not waiting for him to come with me. I follow Jeff's directions, cross the parking lot and head for the loading dock. Although we have never seen each other, Jeff sees me coming and holds the box up for me to see. I thank him profusely for his perseverance and willingness to help, with thoughts of the uncooperative woman at the Manhatten sports medicine clinic still in my mind. Van and I make the return trip silently back to his house.

Thanking God for Jeff, I tell Cindy the story. She had no idea what had been taking place. Jean had filled her in on with the details when she emerged from the bathroom. The box did have the Van Tassel's name on it; followed by "Jerry/Cindy," the same names listed in the newspaper article they had shown us on our arrival.

After the many events of this day, I am look forward to talking to my wife and shedding the frustrations and concerns we shared. Eight of us go out to dinner, and someone suggests that Cindy and I not sit together, since we have been together all day. I respond so quickly with a no, that I shock even myself. I explain that we haven't talked much to each other all day and that I would like to sit by my wife.

I apologize for my bluntness, but I am truly not sorry. We sit side by side at the table. Frustrations and traffic hazards now behind us, all is well.

During this time we found $12.26, which included the majority of a $10 bill that had been cut into pieces by a lawn mower.

Jerry's Road Rules

There were five thousand, four hundred and twelve pedestrians struck and killed by vehicles in 1996. Three thousand, seven hundred and fifty eight of them were male!

Cindy can explain this huge discrepancy in statistics. If those males were anything like her man, they came to this planet with clear directions to protect their women at all cost. These are the rules Jerry operated under during Habitrek '96. They were generally unspoken, but well understood.

Rule number 1 . . .

Always walk in front of Cindy when forced to walk single file facing traffic. During interviews, he would always joke that he did this because he had the most life insurance. It was good for his sought-after laugh but not the whole truth. In reality, he did it so he could alert Cindy to impending harm. He felt he needed to be in front to see the situation first and then to be able to push her out of harm's way if necessary. This is not rational when a 175-pound man is faced with an out-of-control car traveling at 65 miles per hour, but then, love is seldom rational. Cindy liked the thought behind this notion even if it would never stand up to scientific proof.

Rule number 2 . . .

This is the same as rule number 1, with a positional twist. When they were lucky enough to have shoulders wide enough to walk side by side he insisted on walking on Cindy's right side, closest to the lane of traffic. With him always on the outside, he was once again in the position to offer protection. Jerry takes his husbandly job to protect seriously. Cindy has come to understand and appreciate this point of view and does not see it as a commentary on inequality, for Jerry certainly does not intend it that way.

Rule Number 3 . . .

It was also his self-determined rule to clear the shoulder of obstacles for Cindy. Yes, he was a human minesweeper of sorts. Without missing a step, he used the ball of his right foot to make a sweeping motion towards the ditch, effectively clearing the road of debris for her. Now, sometimes his timing was off and the object hit her left foot in mid-stride. Momentarily irritated, she reminded herself that it was just his way of rolling out the red carpet for her.

Rule Number 4 . . .

When they were navigating a curve with no shoulder and poor sight distance, they would abandon their normal walking position "against traffic" and cross the road to walk "with" traffic. Being on either side of the road could, at times, be dangerous, but being invisible to a car rounding a curve was a bigger risk. To cross straight over would have put Cindy on the outside, a definite breach of the rules, so they would change positions like a well-rehearsed drill team. He would step forward and to the outside while she dropped back and to the inside without ever missing a beat. It was amazingly choreographed!

Jerry and Cindy were always aware that they were vulnerable walking alongside traffic. Every day they thanked God for safely completing another 20 miles. They knew it was a true blessing to not be included in the car pedestrian statistics. Cindy also recognized that Jerry would be one of those males killed in a pedestrian accident before he would ever have let anything happen to her.

18

Habitat Hoopla

Day 140
Friday, June 28
Kansas City, Missouri

Cindy

After exactly one month and 400 horizontal miles of walking across Kansas, we put our footprints on Missouri soil and our seventh state.

We have begun spraying our ankles with tick repellent now that we walk mostly on grassy shoulders. Once in awhile we have to pick one of the pesky insects off our socks. For the most part, they avoid us.

Speaking of grass, big lawns and their maintenance are as much a part of home ownership here as washing windows is at home. There is lawn pride in these parts. We often notice that it is women who mow these spacious lawns. They also create beautiful front porches furnished with wooden rockers, country baskets, flowers, flags and a variety of other ornaments. We wonder aloud if there is a little friendly competition among neighbors concerning these things. We'll have to research this possibility when we get a chance.

Now that we have finished walking across Kansas, we have built up a defensive attitude about the state. We have heard the state maligned so often that we find ourselves defending it when people suggest that our month there must have been a real bore. We are offended by a newspaper article that says Kansas is ranked 50th in the nation as a tourist destination. We have developed an unexplainable fondness for Kansas and the people we have met.

Lawn observation aside, Jerry suddenly asks a rather strange question.

"Today isn't June 28 is it?"

I think for a moment and reply, "Well, it must be. Tomorrow's Saturday and we are meeting Linda and Millard in Kansas City for the big event. Why do you ask?"

"Mmmmm, well then, you're right. (He speaks those two little words women love to hear!) I have a news bulletin for you from the guy who tracks our schedule. Today was supposed to be a day off."

Flashes of wasting a perfectly good "sleep late and have a leisurely breakfast morning" zoom through my mind before I respond.

"Oops, now what?" I ask with restraint.

A "pro" and "con" conversation ensues. We decide to finish 10 miles this morning. It never hurts to have a few extra miles in the bank. We'll knock off early, have lunch and get settled in where we will be staying before a busy day tomorrow.

A newspaper reporter is waiting for us back at Bev and Don Knutson's, our current and very much appreciated host family. Once the interview is over, I excuse myself to make some phone calls.

The end result of a long and frustrating conversation is the confirmation that the apartment where we are scheduled to stay with a woman tonight is not large enough for her, our luggage and us. To add to that frustration, the lady who has committed to getting us a complimentary hotel room for Saturday and Sunday tells me she has dropped the ball. We discuss the possibility of staying here another night, but decide we should get closer to the weekend activities. We put this current dilemma in our prayer pocket, pack up and say goodbye to Bev and Don. With only 19 miles to drive, we should be settled soon. We load our tired bodies into Wilkerson's pickup, fifth wheel trailer in tow, and head towards Independence, Missouri.

One-and-a-half-hours later, we emerge from a huge traffic jam. We have not gone far, but at least we have been able to pass the time by talking to strangers who roll down their windows to ask us questions about the walk after they read the banner tied to the back of the trailer.

The Wilkersons get settled at the RV park. We still have no place to stay tonight.

Jerry makes several phone calls during the next hour while I hang out in the trailer. It is discouraging, because a year's worth of planning is being undone and there is nothing much we can do about it.

It is finally decided that we will stay at the Olive Branch Inn for the entire weekend. It is close to the banquet event we will attend tomorrow night and the RV Park where Jean and Curtis are parked.

Once there, we go through our customary ritual of moving the twin beds together and nightstands aside. The coffee table becomes our office space. I have a lot of work to do in this room because we have no host families for next week. It is good to have some furniture moving to do. It helps dissipate stress that has built up during a frustrating day. It is not always easy to be flexible, patient and…what is that third one again?

The Saturday morning sun is bright and it is already warm. Our energy is renewed. We drive through Kansas City to look for the Mission Methodist Church where we are to meet Linda and Millard Fuller.

We have been looking forward to this day for almost a year. We hop out of the pickup and trot across the tree-lined street in this beautiful part of Kansas City. We see them standing in the churchyard talking to the founders of the KC affiliate, John and Mary Pritchard. Millard, tall and slender with graying hair and glasses, always seems to have a smile on his face. Linda stands next to him, her twinkling eyes and demure smile showing as much interest in the current conversation as she has shown in our walk for over a year. It is so good to see them.

Millard rushes up with greetings and hugs.

"Y'all don't even look tired!" he exclaims with characteristic enthusiasm.

"How many miles has it been now? How's it going?"

"Close to 2,000 now. It's going well. We've not lost any walking days to illness or injury. God has blessed us every mile of the way. Some minor frustrations, but nothing we can't forget about at the next turn of the road. We really appreciate you taking time out of your busy travel schedule to be with us."

Lacking the crowd we were expecting to join us in the eight-mile walk to the three-house dedication across town, we begin walking. Linda and I carry the banner between us. We chat about her upcoming trip to Europe with her mom and sister, of how she will meet Millard in Hungary for the Jimmy Carter Work Project in August. We talk about the joys of grandchildren and Linda's busy travel schedule. I have new appreciation for her need for "girl time" while on the road. Finding time to shave our legs, do our nails and curl our hair are "girly" things neither of us seem to have enough time to do when traveling.

Meanwhile, the guys are chatting about details of the walk. Millard offers to send a copy of his latest book to each host family who has so generously helped us to make the walk a reality. Walking past an FAO Schwartz toy store, we duck in for a quick look-see with grandchildren in mind.

At the halfway point, a television crew intercepts us. Millard clowns around with my umbrella hat while the crew interviews us.

"Hey, Linda," he drawls, "I think I better get me one of these things!"

Millard and his gracious mate defer the entire interview to us. They are internationally known and loved. To not intercede in an interview is a generous gesture. It is not lost on us.

A mile and a half before we reach the dedication sight, we

Linda Fuller, seated, laughs at Millard wearing Cindy's umbrella hat in Kansas City.

meet 30 folks who will walk the rest of the way with us. Linda is not feeling well and drops to the back of the crowd. One little girl is having serious doubts about being able to walk so far in this sweltering heat. If we weren't in a large city, this would be the perfect day for the naked mile!

"Oh, come on and help me carry this banner. My friend isn't feeling very good." I cajole. "My name's Cindy, What's yours?"

She grabs one end of the banner with her dainty little ebony hand.

"Keasha," she says, sweetly but shyly.

"That is a beautiful name," I reply. " So, how old are you?"

"Eight," she replies with a grin.

"Wow, that's old. So what do you want to be when you grow up?"

"A ballerina!" she enthuses.

I have clearly hit on a subject for which she has much passion. We're a team now, and there is no holding us back. We move to the front of the group.

"Well Keasha, you hold onto that dream. There will be people all along your path who may tell you that your dreams aren't rational or practical. You just keep your eyes on the prize. Work hard and follow your heart. Achieving your dreams will bring you much contentment. You can begin today by hanging in there and finishing this walk. That will help you realize that you can do anything you set out in life to do. It's an important first step, literally."

Thirty minutes later, the crowd of waiting people cheer wildly as we arrive. Keasha has made it. The moment of triumph is not lost on this beautiful little girl. She has accomplished a small goal. I give her a hug and hope she remembers this day whenever life throws her a curve.

It is Monday, July 1. Another week is dawning. Just before we leave the room at the inn, I check our phone messages. Mark and Mary Nash live near here and have worked miracles while we slept. They have managed to get us host families for the rest of the week. They join an ever-growing list of walk angels.

The blisters have improved about 75% since Jamie remodeled my sandals. As the Formilin continues to toughen the soles of my feet, I expect the blisters to disappear altogether. For now, I treat one or two small ones each week and continue aggressive preventive measures.

Out on Highway 7 near Peculiar, Missouri, Mr. Eagle-Eyes spots something on the shoulder. As we approach it, we and realize that it is a woman's purse. A black leather, basket-shaped purse with two shorthandles. It appears to have been placed there rather than lost. Jerry picks it up and immediately looks inside for identification so we can return it to its rightful owner. A wallet inside contains photos of two adorable children and the driver's license of a 32-year-old woman. A wad of envelopes is underneath the wallet. Some have addresses on them, but none have postage. Below them are syringes. Jerry stops his search. It appears highly possible that the mother of those cute kids is somehow connected to drug activities. We already know that methamphetamine production is rampant in these parts. We decide that we have no choice but to deliver the purse to the Clinton Police Department, instead of to her. Hopefully, if it represents what we suspect, she will get help and turn her life around. Until we can catch up to Curtis and Jean in their pickup, we take turns carrying the purse. Seeing Jerry swinging a purse is the only comic relief in a situation that is profoundly sad.

The next day, Jean and Curtis must leave us. After two weeks as our wonderful and compassionate support people, the Millard Fuller look-alike and his pretty, dark-haired wife with slowly mending broken ribs, need to be on their way to a Habitat building project in Michigan. Our friends, the Hardestys, from the fire ant experience, have driven up from Texas to spend the day with us. Pam will walk. Denny will drive ahead.

The three of us have walked two miles when we catch up to Denny. He is kneeling on the grassy shoulder of the road, connecting the rope of the Habitrek '96 banner underneath the trunk of their car. He completes the job and stands up to admire the nice smooth banner carefully aligned on the back of their Chevy Lumina Sport. The three of us attack the legs of his blue jeans with rapidly moving palms. He looks down to see the objects of our attention– hundreds of tiny blood sucking TICKS! If any one of them had any intention of taking a drink from Denny's veins, they quickly changed their minds. He is free of any hangers-on. It is then that we all laugh at a strong friendship that appears to be based on bugs. Fire ants in Texas. Ticks here. Who knows what kind of bugs will crawl into our future years of friendship adventures?

During this time, we found 77 cents.

Author's note:

Four years later, the four of us are helping build a house at the Jimmy Carter Work Project in Americus, Georgia. This time, we are "bugged" by gnats! Lots of them. They are particularly attracted to the moisture in our noses and mouths, which is infuriating, and a real distraction from the hammering and sawing we are intent on. At the suggestion of many, we tie dryer sheets to the earpieces of our glasses and become experts at blowing the little monsters away from our faces with sideways puffs of air from our contorted mouths. We look like weirdoes, but it works.

When we comment on our continuing buggy friendship, Pam is finally able to explain the whole strange phenomenon. They used to own a pest control business!

"Fulfillment of dreams do not come easy. It is with struggle that we appreciate the accomplishment."

Anonymous

19

The Dogwood Bunch

Day 153
Thursday, July 11
Springfield, Missouri

Cindy

W e're walking on Highway J, just east of Springfield, this morning. A pleasant-looking woman with a big smile pulls her car alongside us and lowers her window.

"You two look like you could use a nice cold Pepsi," she offers.

"We can always use a cold drink," I reply, gratefully reaching for the cans. "But really, do you always drive around Springfield handing out sodas?"

"No, actually I saw the story about you in the newspaper. I recognized you just now, as I was turning into our housing development. I am Linda Courtsy. I can't believe I actually got to meet you."

Linda is anxious to ask questions about the walk that weren't answered to her satisfaction in the newspaper. Then an inquiry about our route for the rest of the day prompts a suggestion from Linda.

"If you have time for a slight detour, I recommend you take a few minutes to discover Turners. It's about a mile from here but not on the main road. If you decide to stop there, you will need to turn to your right off the highway and walk down a steep slope and across railroad tracks. It will be on your right. Actually, I could give you a ride. I promise not to tell a soul. It's only a little ways."

Discovering the "town" of Turners, Missouri.

"Thank you for the offer. We really don't take rides. It can be difficult for people to understand this but we really like walking, even though it is warm today. We are determined to walk the entire distance, one slow step at a time. You've been wonderful, though. Thank you for your generosity," Jerry replies.

We are intrigued enough to take the suggested detour. It's nearly time for lunch anyway.

We stop by our support vehicle to tell them to meet us there, and then we follow Linda's directions to Turners.

"Are you sure this is where we are supposed to be? I thought we were going to a town," I ask Jerry. I answer my own question when I read the signs above the door: "Turners Station Mercantile. General Merchandise. Groceries. Gas. Feed. Dry Goods. Turners, MO. Since 1889. United States Post Office. 65765."

We have arrived.

The support team exits the van as Jerry opens the store door. We all follow him into an authentic general store, one like we would associate with generations past. To our right, standing behind the counter, is a gray-haired woman with a kind face. It only takes an instant for her to recognize us.

"Well, I'll be! Aren't you the couple I saw on television last night?" she proclaims.

"Yes, we are the Schultzes, just out for a little walk," Jerry teases.

"Oh, and this is the rest of our gang," He quickly interjects. This is our daughter, Katie and our youngest grandson, Logan. These are his other grandparents, Jim and Suzie Bryan. They all came here from Olympia, Washington to be our support people for the week. We're having a great time."

"Well, my gracious, get in out of that heat. Welcome to Turners, Missouri–population five. I'm Josephine." She smiles as she extends her hand to each of us.

"Jill! Jill, come up here," Josephine hollers. "There's some folks here you've got to meet."

A pretty woman with long blonde hair walks to the front of the store.

"This is my daughter, Jill. She moved out here to help run the lunch counter. And while we are making introductions, the postmistress over there behind the mail counter is my cousin. This little "town" is all in the family. Has been for three generations," Josephine concludes.

Jill is as friendly as her mom. She quickly invites us to order complimentary sandwiches from the deli and to take sodas and chips from the wooden store shelves. As I wait in line to order, I savor my surroundings. Under my feet are the store's original wood floors. Above our heads are ornate ceiling fans. Adding to the atmosphere are the wonderful aromas of pungent deli meats, sauerkraut, mustards, dill pickles and a variety of breads. A sign proclaims: Today's Special. Corned Beef Sandwich, $1.75.

Alongside the sign are little cans of pork and beans with a plastic fork rubber banded to each the side of each can. They are stacked in pyramids next to the cans of cocktail wieners. Sitting next to them is a gallon jar of pickled eggs. These are things we would not see in Olympia and I am intrigued.

This has been one more special stop during a morning when the people of Springfield have reached out to us in love. It's been a pleasant surprise because the days leading up to this have had some frustration mixed in with the love.

Jim and Suzie had originally met up with us in Clinton, Missouri last Saturday. They couldn't have come at a better time. We have been friends ever since Katie and Curtis started dating in 1990 and we were thrilled that they had volunteered as support drivers for this week. In the beginning, we enjoyed showing them how kind people were to us. They, in turn, were great at engaging folks in conversation and finding us places to rest.

Things started to go south when the staph infection in my foot flared up Monday. Getting a refill for a prescription originally written by Dr. Burt in Lawrence, Kansas (200 miles back) had proven frustrating, but we had eventually been successful. That same day, a host family that came to us by way of a third party, turned out to be in turmoil over a death of a friend and not much interested in our cause or our comfort. When we asked the man of the house about their plans for supper, he suggested that the four of us "just go find a restaurant," without him or his wife. We were also having a hard time making connections and plans with the Springfield Habitat office or the Regional Center, also based in Springfield. Consequently, we had no host families for the next two nights.

Jerry had vocalized his frustrations to a guy and the man had replied,

"Well, the problem is, folks around here want to know more about you. They don't know if you are gay, "colored" or even married. There's a reason why Missouri is called 'The Show Me State.' You have to *show* most of them."

"Well, just tell those people that we are married, just not to each other. That'll get 'em talking'! Jeez, what bone-headed questions!" Jerry had huffed. "And if they need people to 'show' them, I'll show them something they don't want to see!"

Just as we were about ready to give up on finding a host family in the Springfield area, we received a voice mail from our friend, Pam Hardesty. Her friend, Cindy Baker, lived there and would be happy to host all six of us for two nights! She was renting a crib and planning a dinner party for 30 of her friends and family to meet us. She was also organizing a news conference to coincide with our arrival in Springfield. And she wasn't involved with Habitat, nor was she connected to any other groups that had come to our aid in the past!

After our walk day on Tuesday, and before going to Cindy's home, we drove back to the Kansas City airport to pick up Katie and Logan. We were obviously very excited. It had been three months since our tearful farewell in Utah. On the other hand, we were apprehensive about whether nine-month-old Logan would recognize a couple of strangers who just happened to be his very tan grandparents.

Our hearts leaped with joy when we saw him and Katie appear before us. She was pushing him in a stroller and they both were wearing big grins. A baby blue hat, that matched his plaid shortalls, set off Logan's bright blue eyes. He was kicking his legs excitedly and smiling–right past us. He was smiling at Jim and Suzie, the grandparents he recognized. He then looked curiously at us. Was there a moment of recognition? We could not be sure. A long, warm hug from Katie went a long way toward putting our "absent grandparents'" guilt to rest. We knew we had brought this on ourselves by what we are doing. At what cost does one follow their dreams? Had we pushed it too far? We didn't know, but we looked forward to the opportunity over the next five days to make up for time lost.

Except for Logan getting an ear infection, the next two days were wonderful. Not only was it great to be surrounded by family, Cindy Baker had proven that her motto was, "Show me strangers, I'll show you love." Her party was a big success.

So, with hugs of appreciation to Cindy, we left her home this morning and have been enjoying the enthusiasm of all the people who learned about our walk because of the news conference. As we walked down Sunshine Street, people were honking their horns and shouting good wishes to us. It felt real good.

"Can I get you a cup of coffee?" one man had shouted as he ran out his front door and down the sidewalk.

"That is really generous of you but I don't drink coffee," I had replied.

"Oh, neither do I," he smiled. "Haven't touched the stuff in 20 years!"

Later, Jerry had walked out of a restroom at a service station and was followed by a teenager named Lewis. "Can I have your autograph?" He asked, thrusting a newspaper under Jerry's nose. We had not seen the photo of us holding Logan that appeared on the front page this morning. It was taken yesterday during interviews with the largest gathering of media we have had to date.

Lewis has one last comment.

"I don't know how you do it," Lewis puzzled. "I don't even like to walk to school."

Sunday, July 14

After the lunch in Turners on Thursday, we finished our 20 miles and drove down to Branson for the weekend. Friday was not a scheduled walk-day; it was to be used as a makeup day if we had to take a day off along the way due to illness or injuries. Since that had not happened, we now had a free day. The six of us got motel rooms and spent two days exploring this great tourist area. Although not our first time here, it was everyone else's. A restful weekend with family has been good for our souls. Logan warmed up to us quickly and we loved having this time with him and Katie. This morning, they all returned to Olympia. Logan had gotten real comfortable with us, and watching his little hand wave bye-bye was a heartbreaker. As with the other family departures, tears flowed once again although I have gotten better at hiding them.

This evening, we are hunkered down in our motel room and in a funk. We are lacking enthusiasm for walking the last 700 miles of Habitrek '96.

We have major concerns about our lack of host families, which makes finalizing our itinerary difficult. We try to let go and let God, because we are weary of the hunt. Jerry is napping after a poor night's sleep. I plop onto the bed beside him, pull out my devotional, and begin to read today's reading. As is often the case, the words I need to hear are on the page in front of me. Yes, I agree, God does not require more of us than we can accomplish. And yes, I remember that all things are possible through Him. Uh huh. Yep. When I finally feel like I've gotten a much-needed kick in the pants, I finish this quiet time with a very specific prayer.

"Lord, please grant us the gift of enthusiasm for the remaining seven weeks of this magnificent venture. We would appreciate help finding host families too. Amen."

Eighteen hours later, my prayers are answered in the form of Margie Hazelton and the Dogwood Bunch. It is Monday morning, July 15. Margie has stopped near the Dogwood cemetery to ask our new support drivers, Bob and Norma Olsen, if they are having vehicle problems. They explain their presence to her. They have come from Pennsylvania to assist us. Margie is amazed. Bob tells her that he is 82 years young and he and Norma have been married seven years. They originally thought they were coming to help build houses, but

Being greeted by the Dogwood Bunch.

once they found out people are walking instead of building, they are happy to help. Bob's story infuses Margie with a mission.

When we arrive at the motor home one half-hour later, we are greeted by a cheering and enthusiastic band of locals that Margie has rounded up. It's a little hard to maintain a funk with this kind of zealousness before us. We find ourselves smiling again as we answer questions and jump into photos. These folks are the epitome of why we wanted to do this walk in the first place. We hoped people like the Dogwood Bunch existed. Now we *know* they do!

Margie is relatively new to the Missouri Ozarks. This little dynamo may be short in stature, but she is long on energy and enthusiasm. She has made many friends in these parts. Her stylish gray hair and artistically applied makeup are topped off with a white cowboy hat. Wrangler jeans and brown leather cowboy boots complete her ensemble.

We are enjoying this chance meeting but, unfortunately, we must get back on the road. We begin to say goodbye to everyone when Margie interrupts.

"Do you have plans for lunch?"

"No, we don't."

"Well then, can I throw a little somethin' together at my house?" Margie proclaims.

"That sounds great. Our planned lunch of cold baked beans and cottage cheese can wait for another day. We'll get back out and finish our 15 miles for the morning and you can give the Olsen's directions. We'll see you about noon then."

At noon, we stop walking at Honey Creek Road and hop into the mini-motor home to ride to Margie's ranch. As we drive under the big timber archway over her long driveway, the carved wood sign proclaims:

"Teeny Weeny Ranch Two, Home of the Frog Hook Brand with Margie Hazelton."

The four of us are warmly welcomed into her home and given a quick tour of this all-wood ranch house. We look at many interesting mementos of her years as a horse trainer with the rich and famous and enjoy the opportunity to ask her questions about them. There is also a lot of hustle and bustle going on around the long pine table in the big ranch-style dining room. In addition to the friends we met at the cemetery, there are three more here. Miraculously, these friends have put together a fabulous feast in honor of our presence. Before us on the table, are big bowls of chips and fruit surrounded by salads and grilled cheese sandwiches. Blue enamelware bowls of soup arrive from the kitchen, along with pitchers of ice tea and bottles of crisp wine. As if this weren't enough, ice cream and cookies are served up for dessert. Accompanying all of this are huge portions of entertaining local stories.

The big clock hands soon move past 2 p.m. We must disengage ourselves from this wonderful moment and head back out into the 92-degree heat with humidity to match, away from this marvelous group of people. Lydia Maack hands us a piece of paper with her phone number on it.

"If you need anything as you pass through Ava tomorrow, please do not hesitate to call," she says.

Back at Honey Creek Road, yet another group of enthusiastic creatures greets us as we emerge from the motor home. This time, it is beautiful black butterflies, flitting from one orange wildflower to the next. As soon as they spot our orange vests, they gently dance around us and finally land, first on the orange mesh fabric and later dipping their soft feet into the sweat on our arms. Are their touches really the touch of God? We believe so. Their presence is an added burst of beauty to our already elated feelings.

Blessings continue to flow from the Dogwood Bunch this evening when our previously arranged motel plans fall through.

Rather than deal with the rude manager in Ava, we pull out the wrinkled piece of sweat-dampened paper and call Lydia Maack. We need a place to stay tonight. Does she have any ideas? Of course she does, we must come and stay at her house!

Once again the magic of friendship produces an evening full of pleasant events and stories. There's a barbecued hamburger supper with all the trimmings. Lee, Lydia's husband, calls the Assumption Abbey, near Gentryville, and makes arrangements for us to stay there tomorrow night. Margie comes by for a final visit and Lee, an amateur silversmith, gives us a demonstration of his craftsmanship. Lydia shares a poignant story of battle against cancer. We all roar, when nine-year-old Sienna tells us that she really likes Raisin Bran, except for the raisins! The day has renewed our spirits and given us deep respect for the people of this amazing little valley southeast of Springfield.

Jerry

A struggle a day keeps the boredom away. This week, for sure, we would not be bored.

It is Tuesday and the road we are walking is hilly with lots of curves and little or no shoulders. There is very little traffic and we are grateful, because sight distance for automobiles– and for us– is very limited at times. We had not scouted this route when we drove through in 1995, but had driven Highway 76 to the north instead. I had sent a letter to the West Plains affiliate asking about the route, but never heard from them, so we are making the best of the unknown. I had to pull the mileages for this route off of a computer program, so I did not have any physical references other than road intersections. Bob, out of concern for us, thinks we are walking too far today. We understand his concern but we have to stick with my reference points if we are to end up where we expect to be by the coming weekend.

Our Styrofoam cooler that transports our drinks and fruit during the week has just slid off the motor home bench seat and broken into pieces. Ice is everywhere and we all dive in to help clean up the mess. The refrigerator doesn't work in this little Toyota Dolphin, so Norma graciously gives us their cooler until ours can be replaced. Food sources are scarce between Ava and West Plains, so we have to do make do with what we have stored in the cooler for snacks and lunches.

There are a lot of little box turtles on the road in this area. Many have been run over by vehicles. We attempt to save those that have not, by first lecturing them about the dangers of crossing the road without a crosswalk. When we pick each one up, their heads retreat into the safety of their shell while their legs flail about. As we place them in the grass away from the road, we admonish them to stay out of the road and then we move on until we come to more turtles to save.

The rest of the afternoon is a struggle for us. We have to walk further than planned between water bottle refills when there is some confusion about where we intended to have Bob and Norma wait for us. We pass the extra time with a mind game we call "recall every host family we have stayed with in chronological order of appearance and in what city." We recall every one. Cindy can even describe the bedrooms where we slept.

Since we started walking at 6 a.m. on a new walking schedule (designed to minimize the impact of these hot days) our bodies are a little out of synch. The upside is that we finish our 20 miles by 1:35 p.m. We then climb into the motor home to backtrack two miles before heading south toward the Catholic monastery.

The paved access road ends after about a half-mile. We travel the next four and a half miles on a washboarded dirt and gravel road leading to our destination for the night. Not long after passing over a beautiful river, we see a brick building in the wilderness as the austere walls of Assumption Abbey appear before us. We hesitate before exiting the vehicle and approaching the door.

A young man, who introduces himself as one of the brothers, greets us at the door of the abbey.

"You must be the married couple," he announces.

"Yes, we are."

"Come, I'll show you where you will be sleeping."

We follow him into the building, through the entry room, and down a long hall on our right.

"This is your room," he says to Cindy, and a few steps later,

"This is your room," he says to me. He walks in with us and seems to see some humor in our reaction to our separate rooms as he explains that we *do* share a common bathroom. He explains a few details about meals and we exchange other questions and comments before he departs. Cindy is surprised by our rooming arrangements, but I assure her it will work out. I am surprised only because I thought they might put us in separate areas of the building. This can be worked out. Once we are alone, we make our own room assignments based on the "Jerry and Cindy's Rules for Cohabitation". Monastery or not, we will sleep together in one twin bed. We have not often slept apart in our 32 years of marriage, and we are not going to do it tonight. In fact, we have other ideas about things that probably don't happen too often in an abbey.

I put my suitcases in "my" room to at least make it look like I am occupying it, then set up the computer to make entries in my journal while Cindy works on correspondence and paying the bills back home. We shower and feel better after washing the day off. We lock the doors and enjoy our moment alone.

Six-thirty p.m. is dinnertime, so we amble down the hall toward the eating area. The room is drab. There are a couple of tables and two other guests. Dinner is split pea soup and white bread with Peter Pan crunchy peanut butter, some cookies and drinks– not a lot to replenish the calories we have burned today. The peas apparently had split after the soup was made, so it's watery and there isn't a lot of nourishment in the bowl.

After finishing our repast, we tour the parts of the Abbey accessible to us. We are shown into a room with literature, postcards, and some of the fruitcakes that Assumption Abbey is famous for. (They ship 22,000 fruitcakes a year, apparently to people who have grown weary of zucchini.) We ponder buying a fruitcake, but decide we aren't that hungry or desperate yet. Cindy buys some post cards and we return to our room.

We are glad for this opportunity to relax without interruption. We love staying with host families and visiting, but there are the times when it is nice to just kick back and not have to think about things to say, or to remain attentive.

We manage to share the twin bed in "her" room and sleep well until the bells ring at 3:30 a.m., 4 a.m. and 4:30 a.m., calling the 16 monks who live here to prayer and whatever else they do at those early hours. I wake up once more before our alarm goes off at 5:30 a.m. I wonder what happened to the night.

We get everything packed and take some things down the hall

to be ready to load into the motor home after we finish breakfast. Breakfast is a bowl of bran flakes and instant coffee. There is no juice or other options. This is no "continental" breakfast in a hotel; this was a "Model T Ford" breakfast in an abbey. Cindy has a bowl of cereal, but she does not drink coffee, so her only option is water. This is not a good way to start another walk day. We visit briefly with the brother and the two guests, thank him, load up our luggage, and head back north for a 20 minute ride on the bumpy road to Highway 14. We are thankful for the restful afternoon and evening, but struggling from the lack of sleep and energizing food. Tonight we will drive beyond our walk route into West Plains, have a regular dinner, replenish our food and drink supplies and hopefully share a room with a full-size bed.

During this time, we found $1.50.

HFHI's Quilt of Dreams

Everyone's quilt of dreams looks different, depending on its creator. The organization for which Jerry and Cindy walk was founded on a dream, but its owners were very wealthy so their quilt blocks were made of satin and velvet and other fancy fabrics. The problem was, the owners of that quilt were discovering that money was not buying them happiness. Their fancy quilt was in shambles.

Their names are Linda and Millard Fuller and they thought their quilt was complete in 1965. In fact, it has since been torn apart and reconstructed. It is a much more beautiful quilt now that it is based on helping low income families realize their dream of home ownership.

As a young married couple living in Alabama, Millard was making $100,000 a year. A natural entrepreneur, at age 29, he had acquired his first million. In order to make this much money, this young attorney was spending more time with his business partner than his family and didn't seem to know how to change until Linda decided she had had enough and left him. Broken-hearted, he followed her to New York City where, with the help of a trusted pastor, the two of them made the decision to come back to the Lord and to discover His plan for them. In preparation for beginning a new quilt, they sold all their assets and gave away all their money. Eventually, they moved their children to Koinonia Farm, a cooperative Christian community near Americus, Georgia. There they met one of the founders, Clarence Jordan. They enjoyed a very close friendship based on deep faith and respect. After working with other Christian endeavors away from Koinonia for two and a half years, they returned in 1968 and, along with Clarence, helped found Partnership Housing. They worked steadily until 1973 when the Fullers accepted a call to be missionaries and moved, with their four children, to Zaire. Their quilt was growing larger, but the squares were of a much more modest fabric in rich colors, like the people they now worked with.

For three years, they worked to help people in Zaire build their own homes. Then they returned to southwest Georgia. In the fall of that year, based on their experience and dreams of the previous seven years, they founded Habitat for Humanity® International.

During the next 25 years, that quilt has grown to gigantic proportions, thanks in no small part to Jimmy and Rosalynn Carter. Over 130,000 homes have been built and millions of lives changed, with the help of partner families and volunteers from all over the world. Habitat is on target to build additional 100,000 homes in the next five years.

The basic principles of Habitat have not changed since its founding. It is a partnership with all people. The affluent and poor, high school students and senior citizens, conservatives and liberals and most religious, racial and ethnic groups. Humans may disagree on all kinds of things, but thank goodness we can all pick up a hammer and begin to build houses together for the good of our fellow man.

Still based in Americus, Georgia, there are local "affiliates" of the international organization in over 2,000 communities in 87 countries around the world. Families are selected based on their inadequate living conditions, their ability to repay the no-profit, no-interest mortgage and their willingness to partner with Habitat. Individuals, corporations and groups donate money to the affiliates that initially build the houses. That money keeps on building houses forever through the revolving Fund for Humanity. As homeowner partners pay their mortgages back to the affiliates, that money goes to build more homes. It is an ingenious plan and it works!

Millard is president and head spokesperson, speaking hundreds of times a year on behalf of Habitat and the partner families whose voices would be lost were it not for he and Linda's dedication to their dream of eliminating substandard housing from the face of the earth. Linda works tirelessly, too. In addition to a rigorous travel and speaking schedule she helps establish programs that involve special groups. Women, migrants and mental health communities have all benefited from her work.

The Fullers dream will not be realized in their lifetime and it won't happen without the help of many student groups, churches, corporations and individuals. It will happen, though, and all because two people redirected their lives and dared to dream of a world where everyone could have a safe, secure home in which to begin their own quilt of dreams.

20

Go Home, Dog

Day 159
Wednesday, July 17
Gentry, Missouri

Jerry

The day is hot and humid as we continue walking along Highway 14 through the Missouri Ozarks. As we leave the east perimeter of Ava, a dog eagerly runs out to greet us, as many others have along our way. Unlike the others, this dog soon let us know that he intends to walk with us in spite of our repeated efforts to send him back. We repeatedly tell him to "Go home," and throw sticks and rocks in the direction from which he came, hoping he will chase them. He dutifully retrieves some of them and returns them to us. We cannot get out of his sight, and finally, we have resigned ourselves to the fact that he will be with us for a while. He is smaller than a collie and appears to be of a mixed breed. He black coat is long, with white markings.

We have neither the time nor the desire to walk this dog back to the place he came from, so we continue walking. We think maybe Bob can take him back when we meet up with him about three miles ahead.

The dog has proved to be an entertaining companion. We wish we had some of his energy as we watch him dart into a ditch, nose low to the ground, then return to us with a beer can in his mouth. There is no doubt that this dog thinks we need him. He rambles about both sides of the road, then returns to check on us periodically. We've had no formal introduction, don't even know each other's names, but he has displayed an immediate loyalty to us.

We know he should go home, yet we are enjoying the diversion of his companionship and his entertaining personality. He comes when called and parks his rump at our feet while looking up at us awaiting further instructions. Other dogs have come out to challenge "our dog," but he's never very concerned. Each occasion ends with his display of indifference and four determined paws moving on to the next event.

The dog has voluntarily heeled on my left. The roadway shoulders are narrow, and we must walk single file. Sometimes when we have to do this, Cindy stations herself so close behind me that we collide if I stop suddenly.

The loyal and faithful dog is making a feint to pass me and I glance over and down as it does. My mind is rushing to comprehend what I am seeing. Processing what I see, I spin around to tell Cindy to stop. It is too late. Her left foot is on its downward glide and inches from stepping on a snake. In milli-microseconds I decide that the process cannot be stopped. I say nothing for the moment and the dog continues on unimpressed by what we have encountered.

Finally I calmly say, "You just stepped on a snake."

She begins hopping down the road on one foot, repeating,

 "I can't believe I did that! I can't believe I stepped on a snake!"

She did.

The snake, low-profiled and wide-bodied, lying there in an "S" shape, never had a chance. Two people and a large black dog have randomly wandered into its life and a Birkenstock sandal tried to leave an imprint on its back.

Cindy is now far down the road as the dog and I return to examine the snake. She does not return. I want to take a photo, but immediately interpret the words from Cindy's mouth to mean that I probably wouldn't want to. Since neither the dog nor I are herpetologists, we have little idea of what we are looking at. We both conclude that it is some type of snake. It is definitely not happy. It seems to fit the description of a juvenile cotton mouth, but I don't take the time to look inside the now gaping mouth. It is definitely not rattling. The dog is disinterested with my study of the irritated snake, whose compact and solid body, now coiled and erect, is turning with the dog's every movement. I, however, am making mental notes. A mottled brown back, I note, head slightly triangular. There is no visible forked tongue, so I know it's not a politician. Cindy is still hopping on one foot, unwilling to put the other down. Her Birkenstock sole is contaminated.

"She has a long way to hop. I hope she makes it," I say to myself.

My snake-study is now over as I watch the snake crawl into the grass. As it crawls away, it still seems to look miffed as it slithers away. I wonder what it will tell the other snakes.

By now, Cindy is gingerly placing her left foot on the ground and almost back to walking instead of hopping.

"I thought it was a stick," she says.

"I didn't have time to warn you," I say.

The dog says nothing, but its actions indicate that it is ready to move on.

Nearing a bridge, we must walk the shoulder on the inside of a curve. We hear the squealing of tires, and our now-refined hearing tells us that trouble could be on the way. The squeal tenses my shoulders, as I yell to Cindy to cross the road so we'll have better visibility. We cross quickly, and then the three of us await the oncoming vehicle. There is a risk in what we have done. The car's speed and lack of control could send it toward our side of the roadway. My calculated hope is that once the driver has seen us, he will correct his careening and veer toward the other shoulder.

The car squeals past, tires barely gripping the pavement. We are safe, and I was correct as I watch the lone male driver fighting his stupor and the road to maintain stability. His eyes appear glazed, and he looks startled to see us as he now rockets past us and out of sight.

We cross back over to the other shoulder and continue on our way. The dog seems to have approved of our decision and agrees to continue with us.

As we near the Gentryville General Store, we can see the RV waiting for us in the gravel parking area. This will finally give us an opportunity to send the dog back to its home, although we are not totally convinced that it actually has a home, since it has been so willing to stay with us.

Inside, Cindy eagerly asks the proprietor if he knows whose

dog it is. He has an idea. She asks him if he will call the people. His silence is his refusal.

"If you don't want the dog to follow you, just hit it with a club," he says without feeling.

"We're not going to hit that dog. It's a nice dog. It just needs to go home," she replies.

Cindy perceives the direction the conversation is going with the proprietor's attitude and hastens to exit the store as I engaged in idle conversation with the two men sitting at a table. The conversation turns, like conversations between strangers often do, until we finally find something in common between one of the men and us. He has been to Chehalis, Washington and knows where the cannery is located. Not wanting to face the proprietor again, I search for additional things to discuss as I seek to ease the tension in the room.

Eventually, we use up our words and the conversation ends. The proprietor has been waiting and quickly turns the conversation back to the dog. Unwittingly and unwisely I wade deeper into the subject, only to be caught in a mumbling quagmire. I mention that this is the second dog that has joined us on this walk. I proffer an opinion that it is sad dog owners don't take care to see that they are tended to while they are away. The trap is now set. I venture forth with words I quickly regret.

"Sometimes we get half-a-notion to keep the dog with us," I say in passing, Birkenstock clad foot now firmly planted in my mouth.

From behind the counter he verbally pounces. "You'd steal a man's dog!" he barks.

"NO!" I quickly respond, not knowing what has hit me. "I didn't say I'd steal a man's dog. I said I have half-a-notion. That doesn't mean I'd actually take the dog."

It is too late. I have violated the dog code of the Ozarks.

"Well, if you don't want the dog to follow you, club it!"

"I'm not going to club that dog!" I respond, voice now rising.

"I can't believe you'd steal a man's dog," he repeats in disbelief and disgust.

"I didn't say I would. Half-a-notion means you really

wouldn't do it!" I say, now trying to extricate myself from the conversational mess I have created. Somehow, I ease out of the store. I walk toward Cindy, Bob and Norma, with my shoulders sagging in defeat and utterly dismayed by what has occurred.

"What happened after I left?" Cindy asks.

"You won't believe the conversation I just had," I mumble. I repeat it as best I can and they are all amazed. The code says you can club a man's dog, but you can't steal it. The dog watches us without sharing his opinion. We leave him with Bob and Norma and walk on. It is up to them whether they want to take it back or leave it at the store for the proprietor to club. We suggest they take it back. Humbled and defeated, I suggest we move on down the road. We will miss "our" dog, but I no longer have half-a-notion to keep it. Maybe I should have given the dog a club and let him take care of the proprietor.

Lament to an Apathetic Reporter

I think I've just heard
an uncommon word;
two peripatetics, did you say?
Yes, that just might be us,
since we have wanderlust
and our journey is well underway.

With your pencil in hand,
try to understand,
the thoughts that we carry within.
In your notebook, please write
what we tell you this night,
our story's about to begin.

It is noteworthy now,
so envision somehow,
though bewildered you look, as we talk.
As you've noticed this night
we're not struck with stage fright,
for our journey's been more than a walk.

From sea foam in Budd Bay,
near our home far away,
we've come trotting across this vast land.
And we're happy to state
it's copacetic to date,
the people have all been so grand!

Putting procrastination aside,
we calculated each stride,
our equation 'cross each latitude.
While the fearful would warn,
that we'd come to great harm,
but our feelings have been gratitude.

"They're bananas!" they'd say,
wrinkled brows they'd display,

"They'll shoot you and ransack your gear!"
But try as they might,
to intimidate with fright,
we refused to succumb to their fear.

Generally it's been fine,
as we've followed our line,
a smattering of dogs posed no threat.
Oh,.....blind we can't be,
we use caution you see,
and nothing has harmed us as yet.

Briefly homesick in spring,
we missed most everything,
even crocuses erupting through soil.
Family had now gone home,
we were walking alone,
inner feelings more burden our toil.

Then in April we'd see
our first buds on a tree,
an evolution; soon blossoms would appear.
In the scrapbook of mind,
we pasted in this new sign,
and birds' songs grew once again clear.

God's creation again,
transformed burdens within,
with beauty and wonders, so bold.
Therefore, understand now,
what we tell you somehow,
as our message to you does unfold.

Perhaps, I assume,
'round the circumference of this room,
Our story will prod some to action.
But, in faces we see,
What was, still will be,
dismayed, we now end this transaction.

For our bodies are tired,
too, our spirits, once inspired,
and a bathtub beckons us, "come renew".
Thank you now for your heed,
what you write, we will read,
in hopes that you capture our view.

But, before we depart,
did you hear with your heart?
Your dreams may be calling, you see.
If you chance to decide,
don't let fear override,
and regrets become your legacy.

This poem is a summation of a number of encounters with individuals, reporters and groups, who realized they would never make the decision to do something they longed to do, like we had. It was painful to hear them and know that they spoke the truth.

Jerry Schultz

21

Sneaking into the ICU

Day 159
Wednesday, July 17
West Plains, Missouri

Cindy

Walking through the Ozarks these past few days has been awe-inspiring. Rolling hills and vivid green trees surround us. There are few houses and fewer cars. The green fields are dotted with wildflowers and in turn, the flowers attract butterflies like the ones that first found us past Dogwood. We have not understood why we do not see them before 11 a.m. until a storeowner explains that they must wait for the dew on their wings to dry before they can fly. These beautiful creatures continue to land and ride on our shoulders. They ride along on our bare arms, drinking our salty sweat, as we watch in amazement. Their hitchhiking record is two miles during one stretch of particularly peaceful roadway.

The trees do not grow close to the road for shade and there are no clouds floating overhead to give us reprieve from the scorching rays today. We stop on a bridge to peer into the creek flowing gently below. We like watching the turtles paddle around. From the first day forward, every bridge has warranted a "stop and look" moment. Sometimes we have seen snakes below a bridge, and other times, nothing more than cottonwood fluff. No matter, Jerry always spits into the water to see if he can get a fish to rise before we move on.

Since we have become strong enough to walk four miles between stops now, we tell Bob to drive ahead and meet us at the corresponding milepost. I remove three bottles of ice-cold beverage from our cooler, two full of water and one of PowerAde. Two of them go into the bottle holders in my waist pack. I hold one to drink immediately. Jerry does the same.

As we trudge along, the penetrating heat makes me wish I were walking in my swimsuit. Our son-in-law, Curtis's question, posed 2,200 miles ago (when he was trying to add levity to our tearful farewell) comes back to me.

"Hey, Jer…It's hot, there's no cars and no people. This just may be the time for the naked mile. What do you think?" I tease.

"I think there isn't enough sunscreen in this county for the two of us to walk a mile in the buff!" He laughs.

"I think you're right." And my mind moves on to other diversionary thoughts.

I have a lot of time to think in any 20-mile day. Today I'm thinking of the good news that happens every day we are on this walk. Sometimes the smallest things give us a boost, like the construction workers who just stopped paving a church parking lot long enough to offer us ice water refills. Even just a word of encouragement or a wave reminds us that there are so many good people in America that we never hear about. I begin to daydream about a national newspaper or television network that only reports good news. People would have a choice about whether they wanted to read or watch the latest murders, rapes, robberies and car crashes, or if they would rather see the good news that happens each day. Even on days when there are big national tragedies, folks would have someplace to turn to escape the hours of gloom and doom coverage. They could find out about volunteers, Good Samaritans and other good people accomplishing great things. I get excited thinking about how wonderful it would be for children to see this on the six o'clock news instead of the usual, and how it might change the way they see the future. When we stop to rest, I tell Jerry of my thoughts. He agrees, but believes the people who could make it happen would not be interested. He's right, of course, and I dismiss it as the heat messing with my addled brain. But still, I wonder…

We are heading down the road with the goal of completing 13 miles before lunch.

"Honey, let's sing. I am thinking that Christmas songs might cool us down. You know that mental stuff that usually works? You start."

"Okay, I'll play your silly game. How about *Winter Wonderland*?"

"…we sing a love song as we go along, walkin' in a winter wonderland."

We are drinking more water than normal and we are grateful for the refill back there. We soon pass the mile marker that confirms we have walked three miles. I realize we haven't seen Bob drive by yet. He's probably engrossed in a good book. I'm sure they will be along in the next 15 minutes. I start my last bottle of water. It is 10:30 a.m. and already 80 degrees. Sixteen minutes later, we have completed four miles and I have run out of water just as we had calculated. Where are Bob and Norma? The thermometer on Jerry's pack is climbing rapidly. The humidity is oppressive. Jerry has half a bottle of water left. There is no breeze. The sun does not relinquish its grip on us. We feel like we are its prey and it is trying to wear us down before the final assault. Bob and Norma have still not driven by to meet us.

After months of being covered in sweat during the warm walking hours, I realize now that my skin is dry. Should I be alarmed? I begin a silent review of the signs of heat stroke, but I do not tell Jerry. It is not until I become lightheaded and begin to stumble that he realizes there is something very wrong.

"Mar, what's going on with you?" he asks, now concerned.

"I'm not sure. I've been out of water for 15 minutes now. You don't suppose this is the beginning of heat stroke, do you?"

"Yes, I do. Here, drink the rest of my water. "

"I can't take your water. You need it, Jer," I protest.

"Mar, you and I both know you need more fluids than I do. Please, just drink it!"

I know he's right. I guzzle the now-warm liquid in one big gulp. We slow our pace and continue walking, glancing over our shoulders. Where could they be?

Finally, the little Toyota Dolphin slows as it drives by. Jerry motions for Bob to stop and we cross the road.

"Where have you been? We have walked over five miles. We've been out of water for the last mile and a half. We need to get in out of this heat fast. Pull over right here. Even though it is only 11:15 a.m., we're going to eat lunch early. The corn flakes for breakfast didn't last."

When we get in the motor home, Norma apologizes for them being so late.

"Bob just doesn't listen well sometimes, and then wants to argue about what's been decided. Please know that it won't happen again. I will guarantee that!"

"Thanks, Norma. We really appreciate all the time you two are giving to us, we really do. It just that we get very tense when we think our safety is being jeopardized." I try to explain as gently as possible.

Bob mumbles a weak apology as we chug-a-lug Gatorade.

The smell of hot asphalt ushers us into the last two miles of the day. A highway worker greets us with questions about what we are doing and then agrees to let us walk through the repaving zone as long as we stay far away from the equipment. As we walk along, Jerry reminisces about his early days with the department of transportation as a paving inspector. I notice that my Birkenstock soles are becoming thick with a mixture of gravel and hot tar. By the time we complete today's miles, we have inadvertently accumulated a half-inch of asphalt on the soles of our sandals. We find ourselves amused by this and talk about how it will make our soles last longer.

While we are riding into West Plains, I realize that my contacts feel very scratchy. I assume they are just dirty and remove them immediately. We make a quick stop for groceries, then we stop to pick up the key for tonight's accommodations. We will be occupying a dorm room at Southern Missouri State University. After unloading our luggage, Bob and Norma depart because they will be staying at an RV park tonight.

We unlock the dorm room door and are pleased to see a living room. Jerry needs to use the bathroom and passes through the bedroom on his way.

"Hey Mar, guess what?" he says in a strange tone.

"What?"

"We have twin beds again!" Arrrghhhh!

We remind ourselves, again, to be flexible, then shower and walk across the lawn to a complimentary supper at The Yellow House Restaurant. It is quiet and cool inside, and the owner is gracious and welcoming. The meal is sumptuous and the respite appreciated. We look forward to an early bedtime and a better tomorrow.

My eye is still bugging me so I leave Jerry sending e-mails in the living room and climb into the bed we have chosen to share. My eye feels like there is something in it, but I convince myself that all I need is a good night's sleep. I close my eyes. They immediately pop back open. The pain is searing when the lid is down. I try again. There is no way I can keep my eye closed. There is something scraping across the eyeball. I get out of bed and try irrigating my eye. No luck. Jerry gets involved. With a Q-Tip and eye ointment, he gently tries everything he can to get rid of the intruder. He cannot see anything, but hopes it will be better. It is not. Now, we are both frustrated. The pain heightens my frustration as I peer into a mirror in search of the elusive invader. The eye is so swollen and red now, it's clear that we are going to have to seek medical help. But where and how?

It is 10 p.m. and our only source of transportation is at an RV park, located somewhere on the outskirts of town.

It is then that Jerry remembers the business card Father Justin, president of the local Habitat affiliate, handed us after we met him to pick up the room key this afternoon.

"If you need anything at all, don't hesitate to call me," he had said.

"Jer, *do* you think we should call Father Justin?"

"I hate to bother him, but he said to call him if we needed anything and I really can't think of another solution."

"Hand me the cell phone and I'll see what he thinks," I suggest.

After I explain the situation to Father Justin, he says he will see what he can do and will call me back. Ten minutes later, the phone rings.

"Hi, Cindy. Okay, this is the deal. I will pick you both up in front of the dorm in 10 minutes. I'll be driving a burgundy-colored Ford Taurus. See you then."

It is still very warm and muggy outside when Father Justin

drives up to the curb. His kind face is set off by his clerical collar. I do not give him a chance to greet us as I slide across the seat. I feel an apology is necessary.

"I am really sorry to bother you," I say. "I deeply appreciate your doing this, though."

"No problem. After all you are doing to help Habitat, this is the least I can do for you. Now here's the plan. I have a friend who is a charge nurse in the ICU unit at the local hospital. As luck would have it, she's on duty. She wants me to sneak you into the intensive care unit and she will irrigate your eye. She will not sign you in. That way you can avoid the cost to be seen in the emergency room. I put my collar on so the security guard will think I'm accompanying a distraught couple to visit a critically ill family member. How does that sound?"

"Well, to be honest, a little deceitful, but since we are with a man of God and you think we'll be forgiven, let's go for it. We certainly don't want to get anyone in trouble, though."

He changes the subject. "This hospital made national headlines a few years ago. You may remember the story. A guy owned a chimpanzee and it became ill on a weekend. He took it to a vet, but the vet said there was nothing he could do. Since the guy thought of the chimp as his child, he took it to the emergency room for treatment and they treated the animal. Caused quite a fuss because people thought the doctors were putting the treatment of animals ahead of humans."

He is finishing the story as we arrive and he parks near the emergency room doors. We speak in hushed tones as we enter the hospital through heavy glass doors. The hallways are dimly lit and look abandoned. I feel a little like a cat burglar.

"Shhhh," Father Justin motions with his index finger to his lips. All conversation stops and we follow him down the corridors that lead to the ICU. I am relieved to reach the unit without anyone stopping us to ask why we are there. Sneaking isn't something I do very well.

A pretty young woman with a big smile greets us.

"Father Justin, it's good to see you," she declares enthusiastically.

"Good to see you too, Mary Ann. This is Cindy and Jerry Schultz. They are the folks walking across America for Habitat."

"It's great to meet you. Read all about the walk in the

newspaper yesterday. You're doing a great thing. Let's see if we can take care of this and get you on your way. You're lucky it's relatively quiet in here tonight. Follow me."

She grabs a bag of saline solution and a syringe and ushers us into a private room. She motions me toward the gurney, raises the head up, pulls the light up close and gets to work. She asks me questions as she works. What do I think might be in my eye? What's it like to be *walking* across this country? She pauses frequently and asks me to do test blinks. Each time, I must report the interloper is still there. If anything, the eye feels worse because the salt water stings.

"Well, that's not going to work. All I have accomplished is to make the eye worse. It's so swollen it is going to be very difficult to find whatever is in there. Here, hold this ice pack on your eye and I'll go see if one of the ER doctors will see you for free. Hang out in here and watch TV. I'll be back."

The black hands on the hospital clock now reads 10:45 p.m. There is breaking news coming across the television screen. News that is stunning and puts my present situation in perspective. TWA flight 800, bound for our beloved Paris, has exploded over Long Island Sound just 20 minutes after take-off. All 229 passengers are presumed dead. The three of us say a prayer and watch in stunned silence.

Mary Ann returns with a smile.

"Well, I have good news and bad news. I found a doctor committed to helping you for free, but you'll have to wait an additional 45 minutes. They are swamped down there in ER."

"Beggars can't be choosers, we'll be happy to wait," we agree.

Mary Ann leads me down a new corridor. Jerry and Father Justin go to the ER waiting room. At 11:30 p.m. Doctor Laird greets me and goes right to work. He first numbs the eye with drops and then searches with some fine tipped tweezers. He sees nothing, but I still can't blink my eye without the sensation of scratching. He drops in some yellow dye and uses a very intense light to look more carefully. It is then that he sees the clear, pointed base of a seedpod imbedded in my upper eyelid. He tweezes it out easily and shows me the minuscule monster that has made the last several hours a trial. It is a relief to finally blink without pain. Dr. Laird sees many scratches on my eyeball. He directs me to pick up a prescription for eye drops tomorrow and tells me to use them for 10 days. He'll call the prescription in to a local pharmacy and we will be able to pick it up after we get off the road tomorrow.

We offer profuse thanks to everyone who has helped us tonight and arrive back at the dorm at 12:15 a.m. As we crawl into our cozy bed, we realize that we have been awake for 21 hours. Sleep comes quickly.

The alarm clock rudely wakes us from deep sleep at 5:30 a.m. We need to get enthused about walking today. My eye is crusted shut, so Jerry soaks a washcloth with warm water and brings it in to me. A tomato-red eyeball emerges from behind the green crust once I finally get the eye opened. We are ready for pick-up by 6 a.m. when Bob and Norma drive up. They are surprised to hear how our evening had gone and sorry they could not be here to help. We appreciate their concern and believe the day will go well once we stop for a fast-food breakfast with lots of caffeinated drinks. While we eat, Bob drives us 17 miles west of West Plains to begin where we stopped yesterday. We will walk into West Plains this afternoon. It's always interesting to stay in a town before we walk into it, but that is how it often goes.

We encounter lots of big rigs as soon as we start walking. Each time one approaches, we must move off the roadway and into the tall grass of the shoulders. Usually, this is no big deal. Today it takes more energy than we have and we begin to struggle. It is warm again. We drink wisely and graze on high carbohydrate foods at each break. The bagels, yogurt and bananas begin to kick in. At mile 11, we are relieved to reach Highway 63. It is a multi-laned highway with wide shoulders. It gives us the opportunity to walk in "autopilot" for the six miles we will travel before lunch. We will have only three miles to walk after lunch today. We are relaxed and enjoying walking through this pretty little college town with its tree-lined streets and quaint houses.

Once back in the cool dorm room, we shower and take a much-needed nap before a 3 p.m. telephone interview. We then take a short walk over to the Medicine Shoppe Pharmacy and prepare to pay for my prescription.

The pharmacist interrupts. "Oh, there is no charge for this, Father Justin already paid for this."

We are deeply touched by Father Justin's many kindnesses. We are once again reminded of how privileged we are to live in a country where so many kind people reside. Now, can we begin planning the first edition of the *Good News Daily Chronicle*?

During this time, we found $4.10.

Road Games of Habitrek'96

Jerry and Cindy had no plans for games to play as they walked. They had laminated song sheets and brought bubbles for blowing, but they had brought nothing else for entertainment. After all, they thought, could walking day in and day out really be that boring?

The answer is, sometimes, yes!

It wasn't until Jerry found a little bouncy ball along the road on day three of the walk that they began inventing road games. Besides many more bouncy balls, they also found many tennis and golf balls even though they seldom walked past tennis courts or golf courses.

The rules for highway golf were simple and the only goal was to get a hole in one. Using the road's centerline as a target, a hole in one was declared when the ball stayed on the centerline stripe. Other than that, there was only one rule. If someone's toss landed the ball near the centerline, it was expected that a debate would ensue regarding the placement. Of course, a round ball doesn't stay on a sloping roadway very easily. If it did, Jerry had usually been the one throwing it. That didn't keep Cindy from trying, although they most often celebrated her determination, not her skill! This activity came from two people who don't play golf, except for the miniature version. Our highway golf game turned into a cross-country tournament of sorts. When folks walked with Jerry and Cindy from time to time, they were encouraged to join in the challenge, often with impressive results.

Highway Bowling began from a different set of circumstances, and since they only found one bowling ball in 3,000 miles, it had a short history with Habitrek '96. It happened in western Idaho on a brisk, sunny March day. Glenn and Dorothy Johnson, Paul and Ruth LaRue and Margaret Bosela all were walking with them for three days that week. Jerry spied the bright blue bowling ball down a 12-foot embankment. Margaret, the youthful member of their entourage, scampered down the steep slope to retrieve it. Then they found 10 empty beverage cans and lined them up, bowling pin style, on the centerline of the seldom-driven road they were walking on that day. A bowling game ensued amidst riotous laughter. When they resumed walking, they took turns carrying the bowling ball while making up wild tales of how the bowling ball got tossed over the embankment. Engraved with two names, one located over the other, they wondered why the first owner's name, Linda, was blacked out. And where was the second owner, Sharon? Had Sharon been upset when her man gave her Linda's old bowling ball with both names on it? Another scenario was that it had rolled out of a truck on its way to the dump, but that wasn't nearly as intriguing or entertaining.

The bowling ball with a past got moved each day, along with Jerry and Cindy's luggage, until Pat and Kim took it back to Olympia after joining the walk in Idaho, then heading home from Utah. The old blue ball, with its hidden story, has a permanent home under the desk in Jerry and Cindy's guestroom.

Road games turned out to be a great way to pass the time. Those games and the bantering that went with them were also representative of a marriage that has always enjoyed a lot of fun and games.

22

Low And Beholden

**Day 161
Friday, July 19
Thayer, Missouri**

Jerry

It has been an extremely difficult day. We feel like the sun has cooked us in our own perspiration.

We made an unwise decision regarding the clothing we chose to wear because our Sun Precautions clothes were dirty. We both put on tank tops and shorts and applied sunscreen liberally throughout the day. It clogged up our pores when it mixed with our sweat. Underneath this layer, a red, itchy rash slowly developed. Cindy thinks it is sun poisoning.

There were few respites this day, although I almost got a sampling of cinnamon schnapps from a storeowner for consumption later. He and his wife gave us a check for $25 for Habitat. For some reason known only to her, she didn't think it was appropriate for him to provide me with alcohol.

At last, another taxing walk day is over and we climb into the little motor home to travel to a radio station in Thayer for a scheduled interview. We will be staying in a motel in Thayer for the weekend because the singer, Ricky Skaggs, is in West Plains and there are no motel rooms available there.

As Bob drives south, I note that we traveling through a very sparsely inhabited rural area. Cindy is seated in the back engaged in conversation with Norma while I ride in the passenger seat in front, scanning both sides of the road. Then, right next to nowhere, I see a motel sign on my right. I tell myself to not believe what I see. That cannot be our lodging site for the weekend; I must be looking in the wrong place. I say nothing to Cindy and she fails to see the isolated motel as we pass by.

Bob pulls the RV into the parking lot at the radio station and the three of us get out and go into the air-conditioned building. The folks there are very friendly, and our radio interview goes all too quickly. We hesitate to go back out into the heat.

Bob and Norma are scheduled to leave us after today, and if that is our motel, we will be three miles from the nearest town without any transportation. I think it is now time to tell Cindy about the motel. I describe what I glimpsed as we rode by and tell her how far away it is from town. She shares my concern about its remoteness so we ask the receptionist at the radio station about options for other motels and explain our situation. She phones the only motel in Thayer. They have no room for us. Eventually, after we run out of options, she offers us her car so we can go into town later and get food for the weekend. She needs it back tomorrow morning, so we will be without any transportation then.

Bob drives back to the dreaded motel. We exit the borrowed car with reluctance. The woman who owns the motel greets us and is pleased to announce her benevolence.

"Ain't I generous?" she asks with a toothless grin.

She is, and we try hard to appreciate her donation of a free room for these three nights. She shows us to our room on the far end of the small complex. If we need anything, just let her know. Only one other room is occupied. Bob and Norma back the Dolphin Motorhome up to the corner of the building and hook up to the electrical outlet located in the outside wall opposite the head of our bed. It seems inconsequential at this time.

The dark paneled room is tiny. Most of the space is occupied by the double bed. After we unload our luggage, we have a small path remaining, leading from the bed to the room's door and into the bathroom. The one window is small and the TV, located near the ceiling to our upper right, receives one and a half channels. By now we have stayed a lot of places on our walk and have become fairly flexible and adaptable to most situations. We stayed at the plush Hyatt in Beaver Creek, Colorado and now view this as the "Low-at" in Missouri. Cindy asks if I think this is the low point of the walk. I tell her that I hope so.

This week has been such a struggle, that it has been hard to remember to appreciate the good moments and the good people we have met. We both are hot, tired, itchy, in sleep deficit and mentally worn down from coping with some of challenges we have encountered this past week. My e-mails reflect our mental situation when I tell the folks back home that we are in "Nadir," Missouri. We try to make light of our situation and do a reasonable job, but this really does seem to be the low point of the walk. We are in the middle of nowhere, with nowhere to go.

After carelessly dumping all our gear in the room, we lock the door. Bob has a tendency to walk in while he is knocking, giving us little time to react, should we be partially clad, or worse. We quickly shower in the pink tub surrounded by moldy walls, scrubbing off the layers of sunscreen and sweat and trying to ignore the irritating itching that has developed under the residue. Our towels are as thin as cheesecloth, but we manage to dry off before the humidity dampens us again. At last, we are ready to escape to dinner in the borrowed car.

Cindy and I have been waiting for a year to go back to Fred's Fish House for dinner in Mammoth Springs, Arkansas, across the state line from Thayer. We had eaten there when we were scouting the route in 1995 and I couldn't wait to go back for catfish, hush puppies and peanut butter pie.

The rear window of the station wagon is missing and the car is stifling hot when we get in. We roll the other windows down to create 60-mile-per-hour air conditioning and start to drive across the motel's gravel parking lot.

Bob sees us as we are driving away and yells for us to stop. We have planned this to be a special evening for the two of us, so I briefly consider not hearing him. From the passenger seat I get encouragement to ignore what I hear and to drive on. I can't do it.

I stop and Bob asks where we are going and if they can ride along. They have been our support vehicle people for a week, what can I say? Even though we wanted this to be a special evening for the two of us, I didn't want to sound ungrateful to them. We tell them that we are going to Fred's Fish House in Mammoth. It sounds fine to them, so off we drive.

We are seated at a large table near the front of this small, but very popular restaurant. They are busy this Friday night, but the waitress soon arrives at our table. I order the all-you-can-eat catfish special with hush puppies and Cindy orders a shrimp salad. I then ask the young waitress if the owner is around. She tells me that Junior, the owner, is in the next room eating. I don't want to bother him. She insists that I go talk to him and leads me to his table. He is with three other people, but he quickly turns his attention to me. I tell him who we are, what we are doing and how excited we are to be back. He is most congenial and shows genuine interest in our endeavor. Not wishing to take up too much of his time, and feeling a little self-conscious, I end the conversation and head back to our table. Our dinner orders have arrived. Before we can dive in, Junior arrives at our table, greets everyone and checks out our orders. I have more catfish than I need to be eating, so he is fine with that. Cindy's shrimp are too small for his satisfaction and he tells the waitress to take the salad back and get larger shrimp. He intends to have us fed well, which would never have been a problem, even if he had not intervened. He wants our meals to be just right.

Bob and Norma can't believe the service and the amount of food we are served for the price. I barely have enough room for the $1 slice of peanut butter pie, but I manage to squeeze it in. The waitress then announces that all our meals are on the house. We protest, but Junior has sent her with his message. There will be no arguing. I leave her a generous tip. Sated, I return to the car.

We drive back to the Wal*Mart in Thayer. The store looks like it has been around awhile and timeworn. We are surprised how limited the inventory is, since we have been frequenting Super Wal*Marts in other towns. We purchase food to keep in our little foam cooler to eat for breakfast and lunch this weekend.

Cindy and I are not eager to get back, so I drive past the motel to look for the restaurant that is rumored to be over the hill and around the corner within walking distance of our motel. We find the building, but is deserted and appears to have been closed for a very long time.

When we get back to the motel, there is a message for us from the lady who has loaned us the car, saying she has to come by to pick it up by eight o'clock tonight instead of tomorrow morning. Now we are really trapped. We are not excited by the thought of walking three miles into Thayer for dinner and three miles back here everyday. With the food we have purchased, we will be all right for breakfast and we can make decent lunches. With no way to cook, we have little that will suffice for supper. We get in bed early, both struggling with our itching arms. We vow to wear our *Sun Precautions* clothing Monday morning. The motel owner has generously offered to let us use her washer so we will be able to do our laundry.

The opening ceremony for the Summer Olympics is on TV and the "half" channel comes in well enough that we can make out the happenings through the "snow". We are lying there on the saggy mattress watching TV and feeling patriotic when an ant bites Cindy on the back! This might be the last straw.

I found a clock radio along the road this week, dried it out and got it to working. Unfortunately all we can get is country western and we don't need any sad music. With no newspaper and no radio, our TV is our only source of outside news. I spend a lot of time in creative communication with family and friends via e-mail. The message below gave them an overview of my *true* feelings of our present predicament:

"...O.K. here we are in the middle of no place with no car. We are concerned that this room is starting to look normal. We love dark paneling, poor TV reception, noisy air conditioning, dim lighting and bugs. And those are the good qualities.

"...Our only hope for reality this weekend is e-mail from all of you. We are headed into Arkansas Monday without our passports and the TV channel we get best doesn't even have sports, just golf. We don't want to watch it because we don't want to get over stimulated. At first we thought we were watching a program about walking. They showed a guy walking all the way from the tee area to the golf cart. That was after he had his caddy take a shot for him. Golfing has really become advanced. They now have designated drivers! Oops, I'm sorry, that was a chip shot!

"We borrowed insect spray to keep the ants away from us. We are so remote here we are starting to talk to the ants. They tell us that if you live here long enough the motel doesn't seem too bad. They crawled here from Mammoth Spring, Arkansas and find taxes in Missouri less taxing. I have

befriended an ant named Emmet from Pismire, Missouri. They all get good TV reception because they have antennae. They live in an anthill just outside that they have named Anita Hill. The flies do tend to bug them though. Emmet just tells them to bug off. They said the flies moved from Texas. The cockroaches seem to be native to the area.

"Katie says sometimes people don't believe what I write. Do you think I would make this all up? Like the newspapers, I only print the truth. Speaking of that, I read Bob Dole's doctor said he was in excellent health and his health is improving each day. What is above excellent?

"The argument in town on Saturday was whether it was 98 degrees or 102 degrees. Who the h*ll cares about four degrees when it's this hot?

"The good news is, I got an Olympic "Watch and Win" thing from McDonald's for Greco/Roman mud wrestling. The bad news is that the Greeks were penalized two strokes for dirty fighting. There goes the free coffee I would have won.

"We are now 2,600 miles from home and we have walked every step of the way. And that is no joke!"

The owner's generosity continues. She gives me coffee each morning. She lets us have ice to keep our food cold and loaned us some bug spray. There are no amenities with the room except the TV and a phone. She tells us that she wants to sell the place. I can't convince Cindy to buy it.

On Saturday morning I bum a ride into Thayer with Bob and Norma to scout out a few yard sales. There is not much exciting to find. I do manage to purchase a few books to bring back to read. I even resort to purchasing a couple of children's books in my desperation for reading materials.

For Saturday dinner, we ride back into Thayer with Bob and Norma to eat dinner

Bob and Norma generously offer to stay with us through part of next week because that support person cancelled. We are concerned that we are wearing them out and messing up their plans. We humbly accept their offer and tell them that we will continue to work on getting vehicle support from the Jonesboro Habitat affiliate so they can leave by Wednesday.

Sunday morning, we are awakened early by a loud "thunk" at the head of our bed. It is Bob jerking the plug out of the outlet in the outside wall. Later we learn that they went to Mass at the Catholic Church in Thayer. We wish we could have gone with them. It will be a very long Sunday in this dark abode. For breakfast, we eat our yogurt, bananas and bagels with peanut butter.

I resort to writing a few more creative e-mails and manufacturing fractured fairy tales to send home to our nieces. I even fabricate more of the story about the ant we found in our bed. The family at home thinks I have finally snapped.

Sunday evening finally arrives and we ride with Bob and Norma into Thayer to eat at McDonald's.

We have steadily come to realize that this isolation has come at a good time for us. We have had more down time than we ever would think we needed. It reminds Cindy of the similar situation in Meeker, Colorado. We have read, written and phoned. We have gone to bed early and slept until about seven in the morning in spite of the electrical cord getting pulled out of the wall plug earlier each morning. I have read everything I purchased, and Cindy has read her *Good Housekeeping* magazine cover to cover. We will leave our literature here for anyone else who stops by and needs some activity. Cindy has also looked at our little photo album brought from home. She says she can hardly remember what home is like and is ready to find out.

We are no longer the ingrates who arrived here Friday afternoon. We have come to realize that we were put in this situation to reflect on what we had become. We have not always been appreciative this past week as we let the tough times overshadow the good times. We have tended to focus on the negative. The heat and occasions of poor diet have contributed to our emotional letdown and our batteries needed to be recharged.

We also reflect on these luxurious accommodations, compared to millions of families who live in much worse conditions all their lives. It is good to be reminded of our Habitat for Humanity "cause" and how much worse things could be for us.

Bob jerks the cord out of the outside wall socket one last time. It is 5 a.m. Monday morning.

We are not ready to be up, so we stall for a while before getting ready for the day. Our route starts one mile back and gives us one last opportunity to view our weekend home away from home. It's McDonald's for breakfast. I use my new "free-refill" cup; then we head up the hill as we officially enter one more state.

We take a moment for the standard photograph session at the state line, and then we are on our way. It is cooler today and there are a few clouds moving in. We are well rested. We look forward to a good week. Thinking back as we walk, we both wonder if the weekend was as bad as we thought. Was it?

"As a rule, a man's a fool.
When it's hot he wants it cool,
When it's not he wants it hot,
Always wanting what is not."

Anonymous

23

Frightening Lightning

Day 164
Monday, July 22
Mammoth Spring, Arkansas

Jerry

We crossed into Arkansas this morning, 25 days after we entered Missouri. This is our eighth state and we have walked 2,250 miles. We are becoming so used to accumulating miles on foot that we no longer recognize the accomplishment as unusual until someone points it out. Even then, we tend to downplay it.

I read somewhere that lightning strikes Earth 100 times each second. Twice in two minutes was more than we ever care to see again. The morning had already presented a challenge. A storm has taken its time passing through and forced us to retreat to the confines of the small motor home several times. Each time we got in, we listened as Bob counted off the seconds between the flash of lightning and the thunder report, and then announced the distance we were from the bolt.

I have had no fear, (or is it appreciation?) of the power of lightning. I dismissed this fear while staying at my brother's house in Northern California when I was 12 years old. A midsummer storm hit in the hills around us. Where we lived in Washington State, we rarely had lightning storms in the summer. When we did, we called it "heat lightning," and it seemingly always occurred as flashes of light in the distance followed by a summer shower. In the redwood-covered hills in California the flashes became more frequent and startling. My sister-in-law retrieved me from the bedroom where I had sought refuge and imparted her logic to me that if lightning was going to strike you, it would find you no matter where you hid, including under a bed. Somehow this made sense to me, and this rationale lasted for 40-plus years. In fact, I would be careless about it at times.

As we walk together along the edge of this insufferable road, I have become increasingly irritated with the narrow, sharply sloping shoulders, the rain, and the road construction that has already forced us to ride about a half-mile. The flagger warns us that they have tack-coated the southbound land with emulsified asphalt, and that the rain will wash it toward the side of the road we are walking on.

When we planned our route, we knew that we had selected a course that would require an occasional ride for various reasons, and those areas were factored into the total distance we would walk. We accounted for those areas by adding extra miles on other roads to make up the difference. Unplanned interruptions, however, have never sat well with me. When someone told us we would have to ride through an area, I've never gone willingly. This is no exception.

My first instinct was to walk the road anyway. Perhaps a flashback to my decision-making at the Columbia River crossing caused me to give in to the three people with me and the flagger. As we rode, I looked out the steamy window and saw that the storm water runoff was going toward the opposite shoulder. We could have walked through here! Why did I give in to the naysayers? We had been plagued with people telling us where we shouldn't walk and why, and we almost always ignored them and found they were wrong anyway.

Trapped in the motor home while the rain increased in intensity, all I can think about is how soon we can get out and get back to walking. I feel like a racehorse waiting for the gate to open. After a few minutes that seem like hours, the storm breaks and I am quick to say, "Let's go!"

The clouds have passed and the sun is trying to regain territory lost to the storm. We cross in front of a long line of traffic waiting to be led through the construction area and note people staring at us through their rain-speckled windows as we pass onto the narrow shoulder and up a slight grade.

"Looks like the storm clouds have moved on." I comment to Cindy.

"Hopefully, we're done with them for the day."

Without warning, the first bolt strikes. No smell of ozone, no hair rising on our wet scalps, nothing. An ambush we didn't see and that we naïve Northwesterners did not expect. If we had been counting the time between flash and retort, we wouldn't have gotten past zero. Flash and sound are so simultaneous we are bewildered by what we have just witnessed. We are too far from the motor home to seek refuge by this time. We expect them soon, though, because we told them we didn't trust the weather.

We spin toward each other with faces betraying our fright, our hearts pounding with rushes of adrenalin. We ask each other the same question.

"Where did *that* come from?"

We are near panic. The clouds are beyond us to the east. The sky above is fairly clear. The sun has regained the day and is giving us reprieve from the rain. We can't go back to the motor home. We have no place else to go. We must walk on, or stand here wasting a good adrenalin rush. Nearby is the only driveway to the only residence that we have seen in many miles. Numerous posted signs warn us of the owner's sentiment toward trespassers.

With a consensus of two, we walk on for perhaps 100 feet when the second bolt arrives. There are utility poles to our left and the bolt hits nearly vertical to the left of a pole. This one we see and hear. The artillery is getting our range. The bolt sizzles its threat. Again, there had been no warning. The sky above is clear and blue.

"RUN!" I yell to Cindy. She needs no further instructions. Two as one, with the same instinct, we are immediately running toward the forbidding driveway, both of us wondering what to do when we get there. The second bolt has short-circuited our reasoning. Reaching the driveway, we finally speak. My words are blunt.

"Where the hell is Bob?"

I no sooner finish the question than the motor home pulls slowly into the driveway. We both excitedly blurt out that lightning had nearly hit us.

Bob says slowly and carefully, "I just timed that last one, and it was a half-mile away."

"No, Bob. It almost hit us," I try to say calmly, but firmly as I struggle with the two rushes of adrenalin.

"I just timed it," he declares firmly. "It was a half-mile off."

Finally, Norma intercedes, perhaps sensing that we are scared beyond wanting to debate this issue further. In a slow, calm voice, she says, "Bob, we *were* a half-mile away from Jerry and Cindy."

This conversation is over.

We get into the motor home again, not knowing what else to do, hoping that this is not a rolling casket for four, and Bob drives part way up the driveway. The number of "no trespassing" signs increases, as does the severity of their messages. It may be better to risk the lightning, I think, as we head back toward the road and sit there, waiting for courage to come out of our metal hiding place.

Still stunned, with trepidation and little trust in the weather, we finally emerge and hesitantly take the steps leading us past the point of the last lightning strike. We have to force ourselves to do this. The site is foreboding. I feel like the next artillery shot could come at any moment.

I have lost something in Arkansas to two lightning bolts. I have regained a fear that I never wanted in the first place. I have had respect for what lightning could do, but had I not taken it seriously enough. I will be tainted by this day for a long time.

We continue under sunny skies with no further storm activity. The storm just wanted to leave us with two parting shots. After all my grumbling about it, the storm got the last words.

"How appropriate," I think to myself. "Many spectacular events end with a display of fireworks, so why not this storm?" Well, I'll admit it—I was also afraid of fireworks when I was young.

Bladder Matters and
Other Incidental Musings

It is an inescapable fact that being a female and walking across this vast land requires some creative and unusual bathroom strategies. As with other life skills Cindy has acquired, new ones take practice, practice, and practice. So it was when she had to learn how to use a "FUD".

Cindy and Jerry's son Mark had done a fair amount of rock and mountain climbing and recommended the use of a Feminine Urinary Director. He based this recommendation on the enthusiastic endorsement of women who had climbed with him. Cindy ordered one from Campmor catalog. It never occurred to her to test this contraption after it arrived in the mail. She just packed the little blue plastic device (resembling a flattened funnel, and about the size of her outstretched hand) into a Ziploc bag and tossed it into her daypack to await the day she would need to use it.

The first two days of the walk, she managed to find bathrooms along the way. On the third day, however, she needed to use a bathroom and there were none. Surveying the area where they were walking, she saw nothing but evergreen trees and pastureland. Mount. St. Helens watched discreetly from a distance. So did Jerry.

Cindy would have to use the "FUD". The process wasn't smooth because Cindy wasn't quite sure how to urinate while standing. The veteran with whom she walked offered no advice. (He had learned his lesson long ago when he tried to teach her to drive a stick shift car).

Over time, though, Cindy became adept at using it and actually came to appreciate the convenience and modesty that the little odd looking device offered her.

There were some bladder matters that didn't quite go as planned, however.

During the first week of Habitrek '96, during a desperate bathroom need, Cindy was excited to see a police substation as they walked near Battleground, Washington. Surely they would let her use their restroom. Under normal circumstances, maybe. This day was not normal though. She was suddenly the center of attention when she walked in on a federal Alcohol, Tobacco and Firearms training alert. Being sternly denied her request, she slowly backed out of the building only to discover she was completely surrounded by police vehicles from many surrounding precincts. Fortunately, their guns were not drawn.

Another day, just before entering the "state of confusion" via the Interstate 82 bridge, Jerry and Cindy left their daypacks in the support vehicle while a photographer took some shots for a local paper. The motor home was late in rejoining them and Cindy's bladder needed relief. The "FUD" was in her pack so she began looking for a place to hide and squat. Without any trees in the area, this was no easy task. Finally she spotted an outcropping of large, beige boulders across the road. She hurried over and hid behind one.

It wasn't until she heard a train whistle that she realized her mistake. She had been well hidden from the traffic zooming by in front of her but not at all hidden from the railroad tracks behind her. She assumed that the Burlington Northern engineer blew the train whistle out of coincidence, but maybe not.

By the time Jerry and Cindy reached their 11th state, Cindy was a pro at using the "FUD". So much so, that she did not always pay much attention to where she was standing. One particular time, she looked down, and to her astonishment, saw her left foot planted right in the middle of an anthill. As ants scurried up her leg in protest, she quickly reacted to her predicament, only in the wrong direction. Her right foot was suddenly in the wrong place at the wrong time!

Bathroom challenges were most often Cindy's. After all, Jerry had many years' experience. However, there were occasions when even he needed a little help finding even the most elemental place to hide from traffic. The first time he lamented about having to go with nothing to hide behind, Cindy suggested that she could just ask for a little divine intervention. Jerry figured, why not?

And so, with apologies to God for such a minor request in the face of serious world problems, she prayed:

"Lord, could you just give Jer a minute or two to relieve himself along this fence line without any cars passing by?"

That simple little request was granted that day and every other time it was requested for the rest of the walk!

If anyone is ever looking for a good cause, Jerry and Cindy know of some areas that could use some strategic tree planting.

24

Susie's Blue House

Day 168
Friday, July 26
Jonesboro, Arkansas

Cindy

The sun reflects a burnished glow through the lace curtains of this Victorian guest room. It is 5:30 a.m. and returning to consciousness is a struggle. My foggy brain does manage to register that I am in Traci and Mark Perrin's home and that it is our 74th host home since we left home. I stumble into the bathroom and plunge into my typical morning routine. I finally ditch the grogginess of a too-deep sleep when tantalizing smells drift from the breakfast buffet. That entices me to hurry through my routine and join Traci and her mom Delores in the kitchen. They have laid out English muffins, fresh fruit and homemade miniature fruit strudels.

"I would be happy to fix you anything at all," our hostess drawls. "There's Captain Crunch or grits, scrambled eggs and bacon. Anything sound good to you?"

I choose the grits. One of the many perks of being a visitor in someone's home each day is having all these wonderful regional foods prepared. I intend to experience as many as possible and I do believe Jonesboro, Arkansas is close to the epicenter for grits!

A copy of the *Jonesboro Sun* is on the table. Traci has opened it to the article by Hazel Ashcraft written after our one-and-a-half-hour interview last night. Burned out by the never-ending flow of negative news she must report, she is energized by our story. She writes eloquently about the walk and our relationship. We count her among the top reporters we have talked to and are pleased with the story. A quick glance at the sports page also assures us that our Seattle Mariners baseball team won last night.

"Ready for another 20-mile production?" Jerry asks as I finish stuffing my daypack with an umbrella for use during the predicted thundershowers.

Traci and Delores aren't so sure. They are concerned for our safety today because we won't have a support vehicle. Like many people we have met, they worry that our lives could be in jeopardy while walking in heavy traffic. We, on the other hand, have had abundant blessings in almost 2,300 miles, leaving us with a false sense of security. Really though, it can't be time for our final exit yet, can it?

Traci drops us off in downtown Jonesboro on her way to work. This area is a little rough around the edges. Perhaps this is why they are concerned for our safety? Merchants are already out sweeping sidewalks and hung-over street people give us strange looks. We don't let them bother us. We just smile and say good morning, reminding ourselves that these are all faces of the America we walk. Although traffic is heavy and we are walking against it, we make good progress in the relative cool of this day. We look forward to only walking 15 miles today because we will be participating in a Habitat fund-raising walk tomorrow.

David Mason, the son of our hosts from two nights ago, just drove up in his little gray pick up. We couldn't imagine why he was here, then we saw a big grin on his face. He had a great surprise for Jerry.

Two days ago we were walking over the Black River Bridge near Portia when Jerry's white baseball hat, with the Habitat for Humanity logo on it, was blown off his head by the wind of a passing truck. (He usually tethers his hat to his shirt collar but had neglected to do it on Wednesday.) With a few choice words for the wind, Jerry watched as the lightweight hat floated down about 50 feet into the black muck of a marshy riverbed, turned soybean field. We talked about trying to retrieve it and then realized that would be impossible. It was gone. He'd worn the hat all summer and it had lots of pins on it from communities we have walked through. Those, he could live without. The one pin he was very upset about losing was from our son Patrick. He had given it to his dad just before we left home, as a token of his love and for good luck. Tokens like those mean a lot to Jerry and he was understandably upset about losing it.

That night, Jerry told the lost hat story to the Masons as we were gathered around their dining room table. Unbeknownst to us, they began making plans for the hat's retrieval.

Now, David is here and anxious to tell us how they actually got the hat.

"When you told us how upset you were about losing the pin your son had given you, Dad and I just had to attempt a recovery. We drove around until we found a little farm road that lead down to the soybean field. Once there, we started walking through the black mucky soil and the soybean plants. At the same time we were keeping an eye on the bridge. We tried to calculate which direction the wind would have taken the hat. Once we thought we were in the right area, we started searching. The fact that it was white really helped. After a few false finds of white litter, we found it lying amongst the plants. It was pretty dirty so we took it home and mom took it from there. She took all the pins and the clip off and tossed it in the wash. It came out real nice, don't you think?"

"It sure did!" Jerry says gratefully, as he places it back on his head *and* clips the tether on to his collar. "I can't believe you guys went to all that trouble for my hat. You are great! Please tell your dad thank you for me."

David drives off with a wave. Southern hospitality is very much apparent to us at this moment.

It continues when Diane Thomas and Sheridan Cole pick us up for lunch. These two women from Jonesboro Habitat engage us in lively conversation during lunch and then chauffeur us to television station KAIT for our first talk show interview of the walk. Coming straight from the road, we are sweaty and coated with road grime. No one seems to mind, or at least they are polite enough to not comment. We are met by security folks at the front desk and hurriedly escorted to the set where we meet the show's anchor, Miss Grovernell Grisham, an attractive blonde woman in her thirties with the mannerisms and speech of an authentic Southern belle. We find Grovernell to be delightful, with excellent questions and an intense interest in the walk. The three of us click immediately and only wish we could have had more time to talk with her. Her co-host is a match for Jer's quick wit when he suggests, "If God had intended for people to walk 2,500 miles, he would have given us hooves!"

This afternoon Traci takes me to a complimentary eye doctor appointment that Delores has arranged. The eye infection from last week's road debris has not improved. The bloodshot eye is not getting better, and I still have to wipe green matter from it all day long. The doctor is able to quickly discern that I am experiencing an allergic reaction to the very medication I have been faithfully placing in my eye twice a day! He writes a new prescription and assures me that the infection should clear up now. I thank him for his donation of time and make a mental note about another kind act towards our cause and us. We stop at the pharmacy to pick up my new prescription and I pay for it with a crisp $100 bill–the one Patty Danenberg had floated down the stairs to me seven weeks ago. Then back to Traci's house for homemade ice cream and a refreshing shower before leaving for a reception in our honor at 7 p.m. It has been a pretty typical day in this quixotic adventure.

Today is Saturday. As we walk with the local folks, I strike up a conversation with Suzie and am delighted to discover that she is one of this Habitat affiliate's partner families. She wants to talk about our walk. I answer a few of her questions, but I really want to hear her story. Having been chairman of our local affiliate's Family Selection Committee for three years, I love hearing homeowner stories. Suzie senses my sincere interest and readily tells me her story.

When Susie's husband divorced her, she and her two kids had to move to a public-housing apartment with only two bedrooms. It wouldn't have been right for her 13-year-old daughter to share a room with her younger brother, so Susie slept on the couch and gave each of the kids their own room. She had little money and no hope of ever owning a home for her family. Her hopelessness eventually gave way to prayer. She began to pray that God would help her find a house. She felt God telling her that she would get a blue house. She answered an ad for a blue house and felt hopeful that her prayers would be answered. When she applied for a conventional mortgage, however, she was turned down. The blue house would not be hers after all. This event thrust her into a deep depression.

One day she heard a radio advertisement. Habitat for Humanity of Greater Jonesboro was accepting applications from families interested in owning a home. Susie didn't know much about Habitat, but she figured it wouldn't hurt to call. The person who answered the phone encouraged her to apply. She finally did. After two interviews by the family selection committee, they came to her one last time.

"We just have two more questions for you," they said with twinkles in their eyes.

"What color carpet and siding will you want in your new house?"

Susie couldn't believe what she was hearing. She was going to own her blue house at last! The volunteers requested that she meet them the following Saturday out at the site where her house would be built. She could hardly wait to see her new neighborhood.

She followed their directions to the site, got out of her car, and walked up to the folks she had met when they came to tell her she had been selected.

"Hi, Susie. Well, this is where your house will be built. Do you like the property?"

Susie was devastated at what she saw next door, but did not want to seem ungrateful. She stammered,

"I love the property but, but..."

"What is it? Feel free to tell us what is bothering you."

She told them about the prayer and that God had told her she would get a blue house. And then she looked over to the house right next door.

"But I see the neighbor already has a blue house. I assume you won't put two houses of the same color right next to each other," she said dejectedly.

"Oh, but you are making the wrong assumption. This house built here will be your house. You will help build it and take care of it for many years to come. If you want a blue house, a blue house you will have!" Susie wept with joy at the news.

Our walk ends today at Susie's three-bedroom house. It is impeccable. She beams with pride as she gives us a tour through it. It is the most beautiful blue house we have ever seen.

During this time we found $6.91.

*"Somehow I can't believe there are many heights
that can't be scaled by one who knows the secret
of making dreams come true.This special secret can
be summarized in four "Cs:"*
Curiosity
Confidence
Courage
Constancy
The greatest of these is confidence."

Walt Disney

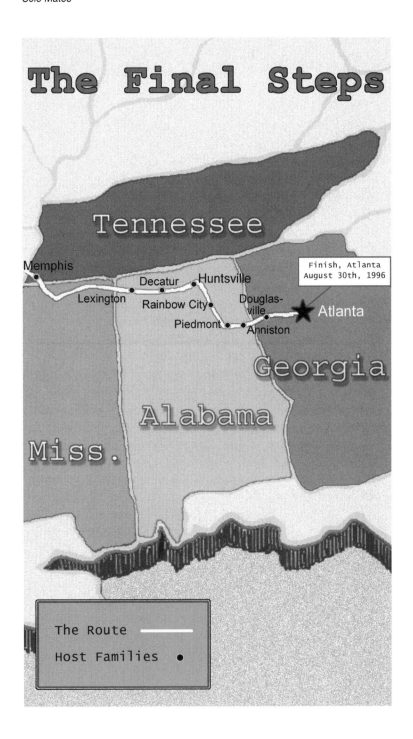

The Final Steps

Tennessee

Memphis

Decatur Huntsville

Lexington

Rainbow City

Piedmont

Douglas-
ville

Anniston

Finish, Atlanta
August 30th, 1996

Atlanta

Georgia

Alabama

Miss.

The Route ———

Host Families ●

Chapter 25

Walking in Memphis

Day 173
Wednesday, July 31
Memphis, Tennessee

Cindy

We are staying in a condo belonging to Jan and Joe Franks. Jan is an interior designer and the room reflects her skills in creating a warm and inviting environment. The bed looks especially good to me tonight. Flopped across the bedspread of warm colors and rich fabrics, I have just begun to recap the day in her journal when Jerry walks in.

"Whatcha doin', Mar?" he asks.

"I'm trying to put into words what this day was like. It was really cool, and I'm not referring to the weather. Far from it!"

"It *was* hot, wasn't it? In two words or less, I think southern hospitality would sum up the day, don't you?" Jerry muses.

"That pretty well does it, although I think 'long' describes the day, too. I'm beat. How about you?"

"Considering that we've been up since five o'clock this morning and didn't get off the road until 5:30 p.m., I'd say so. I'm going down to talk to the Franks for a little longer, then I'll be up to join you," he says as he departs

"Okay, honey. I'll finish this and get ready for bed."

This day started with an interview and live telecast on the Morning Show on Memphis Channel 3, although we were in Marion, Tennessee. Upbeat reporters and excellent questions kept the interview lively. After the interview we walked to the junction of Interstate 40. Al Stokes, our support vehicle driver from Huntsville, Alabama, drove us across the Mississippi River Bridge into Memphis. Foot traffic is not allowed on the bridge, and there are no alternative routes that we can walk from Marion. Once in Memphis, local members of the Habitat for Humanity affiliate greeted us before we began walking east on Poplar Street. We would have two more television interviews and three newspaper interviews before the walk day ended at Germantown City Hall. Along the way, we had our hearts warmed by businesses that welcomed us to this beautiful city by putting "Welcome Jerry and Cindy Schultz" signs on their reader boards.

We were amused by a group of summer school children standing along the sidewalk, obviously watching for someone. When we crowded behind them and in front of teachers, one of the adults had read our vests and proclaimed,

"Here they are, children! Here are the walkers we've been watching for on the other side of the street."

They squealed with delight as they all started to explain why they had been watching for us on the other side of the street. We gleefully accepted their invitation into the cool basement of their Episcopal Church, and then spent time answering their thought-provoking questions. We both love children and have not had the opportunity to spend time with a school group since we left Idaho.

The morning passed quickly and the day had been invigorating. We walked only eight miles before lunch. We were scheduled to have a potluck event with the local Habitat affiliate. When we arrived, many of their volunteers greeted us, not only with an impressive spread of food, but with balloons and signs of encouragement. Rose Klemick presented us with prayer bracelets made by her Sunday school class. She explained, that when we see them on our wrists each day, we will be reminded of all the prayers being said for our safety until the walk ends. We loved receiving them and know that they will be an important part of our apparel each day.

We emerged from the lunch gathering to do another live television interview before we began whittling away at our mileage deficit.

Back on Poplar Street, a woman, wearing pink, feathery, high-heeled slippers emerged from her front door and ran down the sidewalk.

"Are you the people I saw on television who are walking across America?" she called out.

"Yes, that's us," we replied, somewhat stunned by her exuberance.

She continued, "It is such an honor to meet you. My name is Ruby Wilson. What you are doing is real special. Do you know who BB King is?"

"Of course," we replied, smiling and squinting into the bright sun.

She added more information to this chance meeting and ended with a question. "My husband is his manager and I sing down at his club three nights a week. You simply must go down to Beale Street while you are here and be my guest at the club. Can you come tonight?"

"Unfortunately," we responded, "we won't be free to go until Friday night. By then Cindy's brother will have joined us. He's a huge blues fan, so he would enjoy it, also."

"Alright," she continued, somewhat disappointed. "Neither BB nor I will be there Friday night, but you take this business card and show it to the girls at the door. Tell them I said to let you in with no cover charge. Thank you so much for giving me the opportunity to meet you and God watch over you all the way to Atlanta."

As she trotted back into her beautiful brick Tudor home, she left us feeling very welcomed and looking forward to Friday night.

The thermometer had reached 95 degrees by the time we met up with the Germantown Police Department and prepared for an escort into their City Hall. Jerry tried to object to an escort during rush hour traffic because it would create a commuter traffic nightmare. However, the officer would not hear of us walking unassisted. His "boss" (the mayor) said we were to have an escort. Reluctantly, we crossed the street to walk in the same direction traffic was flowing. We were soon embarrassed by the rubbernecking we were causing and the traffic jams that resulted. Jerry's Birkenstock buckle suddenly broke, causing another delay while he tried to repair it. By clenching his toes and altering his step, he was able to keep the sandal from falling from his foot as we walked. When we finally arrived at City Hall at 5:30 p.m., our efforts and exhaustion were rewarded with beautiful cut glass steins bearing the city seal, and filled with finest ice water we have ever tasted! Walking in Memphis has been an unforgettable day. Our hearts have been as warm as the outside temperature.

Today is Thursday, our last walking day for the week. Tomorrow is another planned day off, our recompense for our healthy and injury-free ways.

This morning, we enjoy the results of yesterday's media blitz. Past Germantown now and still walking along Highway 72 through Collierville, we enter Mississippi, at Sladen, and stop to pose for our traditional photo. People honk and wave at us all day long. We love returning their hospitality with a wave and a smile. A Hostess truck driver stops us and suggests that anyone walking across America should have his or her pick of any snack cake on his truck. He cannot carry my favorite, chocolate-coated Donettes, he explains, because the heat melts the chocolate. I choose Twinkies and Jerry chooses a berry pie and we thank him for his generosity.

Two sisters, having recognized us from television, stop to give us some money for Habitat. They explained that they had seen us earlier, drove their old car to the bank, withdrew $10 and drove back out to find us. We are amazed at their tenacity and generosity. Another woman gives us three dollars for the cause. All have asked questions and given us encouragement. Southern hospitality is everywhere and it feels mighty fine!

At noon, a reporter stops us for an interview while Al goes to buy us some lunch. A Collierville alderman stops to present us with a souvenir pin to his city. They all are amused when they see our pleased reaction to our first authentic pulled pork, barbecue sandwiches topped with coleslaw that Al has returned with. They are melt-in-your-mouth fabulous and we enjoy every delectable bite.

We end this day at Janis, Ron and Jennifer Risley's home after returning to a suburb of Memphis. We must say a grateful goodbye to Al Stokes now, but look forward to our time with him and his wife, Elouisa, in Huntsville, Alabama in two weeks. As is my usual end-of—the-walk week ritual, I get the laundry going as soon as we have our showers. While I move clothes from the washer to the dryer, I lament, to Janis, on the awful color of our road-grimed socks. She says she has heard that boiling them in water with lemons will make stained socks white again. Out comes a big jelly making pot and in goes the ingredients for whiter, brighter socks…water, lemons cut in half and socks. Lots of socks! When Jennifer comes home from cheer leading practice, she casually walks over to see what fabulous entrée her mom is stirring up for the potluck to be held here in a few hours.

"Whatcha' cookin' there, mom?" Jennifer asks as she wanders over and peers into the pot.

"Oh, gross out mom, you've gone off the deep end this time!" she proclaims in disgust.

The three of us roar at a teenager's proverbial disgust at anything a mom would do. It is a little weird, but it is supreme proof of how far a person will go with their southern hospitality.

Later that night, we are guests of honor at the fabulous potluck dinner. While visiting with guests seated across the table from us, the phone rings. It is for us.

"Hi, Poppa, this is Drew."

"Hey, Sparky, how 'ya doin'?" his Poppa replies with a rapidly melting heart.

"I'm good," our four-year-old eldest grandson replies.

It has been four months since we have seen him and he sounds mature.

"We need to have Gramma on the phone too."

"Okay, wait while we get her on another phone."

"Are you there, Gramma?"

"Yes, sweetheart, I'm here. How are you?"

"Hey, guess what? Mommy's going to have a baby!"

Tears of joy well up in both our eyes. A constant din of conversation swirls around us, but we are alone with our loved ones and the good news of another life that will be welcomed into our family. Pat and Kim get on the phone to give us details of the impending birth. The baby is due on April 9, my birthday. Tonight we fall asleep with a feeling of deep contentment about the child to come for there is no doubt in our minds that children and grandbabies are a blessing from God.

Waking up to a "vacation" day this morning makes us feel like a couple of kids anticipating a day at the beach. We can hardly wait to get going! Knowing that my younger brother, Paul, will join us today is even better. It has been one month since any family members have been with us. We are excited to see him and to hear about things back home. Paul was widowed very suddenly last May when his wife Mimi died during an asthma attack. It has been a rough year for him. His time with us will be the first time he has gotten away, and comes just before he leaves for a six-month professorship exchange in Japan.

We are surprised to see him at 10 a.m. this morning, however. We know he drove 600 miles yesterday to get here from a visit in Nebraska with Mimi's sister.

After hugs and introductions, Paul (always one to enjoy telling a good story on himself) tells us that he left the hotel a little early today in hopes that no one would recognize him after what had happened last night. What did happen last night could best be told with an e-mail Paul sent home to our family after Jerry prepared them for the story with his own *slightly* distorted version.

Therefore, in Paul's own words, (tongue in cheek) this is what *really* happened!

"The smoke was caused by a defective microwave. Clearly, the timer and heat adjustment was way off or I never would have fried the popcorn. I was extremely tired having driven from Omaha, NE that day. As you would expect after a drive of 14 hours over hellish highways my attention was not 100%. Yes, the smoke did fill my room causing the alarm to go off. I casually dressed myself appropriately, and attempted to vent the room using windows and vent fans. Had the room been properly vented I would have had no further problem, however, in the end I opened the door to my room and allowed smoke to exit into the hallway of the hotel. Much to my surprise, this sensible procedure activated the hotel alarm system in the entire hotel. People were overly cautious and immediately left their rooms. Some stood dazed and blurry eyed in the hallway waiting for the all-clear signal. Unfortunately, the signal didn't come for quite some time. In fact the fire department arrived first. I had tried to call the front desk to inform them that everything was all right. It just so happens that everyone else in the hotel was trying to call them at the same time to see if it was a real fire. My call did not get through until too late. As I entered the lobby, the firemen

were trying bravely to deactivate the alarm system and find the source of the fire. They did look somewhat surprised when I walked boldly up to them and told them I knew the origin of their trouble and had fixed it myself. 'Hmmm, popcorn!' said Mister Fireman. 'Yes!' said I, mister microwave man. Upon returning to my room with a fan to help vent the air out a window, I was sorry to see a young couple sitting on the curb of the parking lot with their luggage stacked around them. I guess they had an early bus to catch, as it was midnight. I also was happy to hear others in the smoke-filled hallway say they too had burned popcorn in the past.

The worst slight of all came the next morning when I was forced, due to schedule, to leave my room.

I no sooner opened the door, than a guy said,

'Hey, had any popcorn this morning?'

I think it showed remarkable courage to show my face in the lobby breakfast nook that morning.

I had a long blond wig and heavy coat on but I did walk upright among the light sleepers and grumblers. No one dared say anything even though I reeked of burned popcorn.

So, now you know the whole story, sordid as it may be.

Well, now, if Jerry will just give me reasonable directions, we may actually make it to Atlanta one of these days. ('Turn left right here' is not very helpful)'."

Yours in Truth,
Paul

The e-mail exemplifies the good-natured ribbing Paul and Jerry have always enjoyed. It will continue during his time with us, much to their mutual delight.

While planning our upcoming three weeks with Paul, we unfold a USA map. I stare in disbelief.

"Jer, we only have an inch to walk!" I blurt.

Everyone laughs at my dumb reaction. This is the first time I have looked at the full country map since we left ours hanging on the planning room wall at home. For me, it is shocking to see how far we have come and how few miles we have left. It is a distance of only 365 miles between here and Atlanta. Even a slow driver could be there by sundown. It will take us 18 walk days and a calendar month to make our triumphant entrance. We will make it won't we? It will be triumphant, won't it?

With our lemon-whitened sparkling socks packed in our luggage, we say goodbye to the Risleys.

At the suggestion of everyone we have met in these parts, we head to Corky's Barbeque Restaurant for lunch. A Memphis landmark, it is a new experience for three northwesterners. The smoky barbecue smell of this place is enough to set our noses twitching before we taste the food. The pulled pork, smoked to perfection and topped with a tantalizing tomato based sauce, is no less amazing than we have been told it would be. Baked beans, coleslaw and homemade dinner rolls accompany it. To be southern, we even chase it with iced tea. We haven't quite developed an appreciation for the taste of sweet tea yet, but we are working at it.

Paul has been talking about visiting "Graceland" for months. He jests about his late wife, Mimi, agreeing to meet him there, and keeps trying to convince Jerry that it will be great. Jerry is not going for it. Nonetheless, Paul drives us out for a firsthand look at Elvis Presley's famous home. Jerry's attitude begins to change soon after we enter the visitor's center. Maybe this will not be so glitzy after all. Is it possible that Elvis was a semi-normal guy blown out of all proportion by an exploitive media and an adulating fan base?

By the time our self-guided audio tour of the mansion is complete, we now see that a man blessed with an incredible voice, also had a big heart and a great sense of humor, qualities Jerry holds high. He confesses that he has enjoyed what he originally thought was just a tourist trap. We have both altered our attitudes about Memphis' favorite son, and we are glad we came. Paul did not see Mimi, though. They must have had their schedules crossed.

Tonight we head to Beale Street and another new experience for three who lean toward soft rock and a little bluegrass. Memphis is a hot spot for blues, and Beale Street is the place to be. Closed to cars, it is crowded with street acts and reveling folks of every age and background. In the darkness of this warm summer night, the myriad of neon signs infuses our enthusiasm. Among the clubs, specialty stores and souvenir shops, we are, of course, watching for BB King's Blues Club. Once we find it, we flash Ruby's business card to the young woman at the door and follow that action with a lengthy explanation. Her acceptance is signaled by the slap of a rubber stamp on each of our hands, allowing us easy exit and reentry. We hesitantly enter the unfamiliar atmosphere. It is dark, smoky and loud. Not wanting to look like rookies, we hoist our fannies up onto high stools around a similarly tall, round table. The guys order a Bud and an O'Doul's and some catfish strips and dip. This is where the guise must stop for me. I order a Diet Coke.

Jer slips his arm around my back and we listen to the words of the performers and watch people dancing and having a wonderful time. We have entered a place where their souls feel at home. Ours can understand.

During this time we found $ 2.03.

By the way, Emmet, the ant, left Jerry's creative processes today with this one last e-mail home.

It's over! Emmet the ant from Pismire, MO had an ant-i-climax. He turned on me Sunday night and bit me on the foot while I was brushing my teeth, so I squashed the little bugger. Elvis says he thinks Emmet was having an ant-i-body experience and forgot where he was. I felt terrible about it, but he was becoming very ant-agonistic. After his ant farm failed he wanted us to give him the money to fly to Antwerp, Belgium. Anyway, Elvis is happier now. He doesn't like all this walking and Paul won't let him ride much. When he does, Elvis is quick to say, "thank yuh, thank yuh, thank yuh very much."

Encouraging Words

There were many factors that kept Jerry and Cindy moving steadily, albeit slowly, eastward. Encouragement from others was an important one and would come in many forms.

One form they looked forward to was by way of voice mail. Each Sunday night Jerry or Cindy would update the outgoing message on their toll free voice mail that Habitat for Humanity® International had provided them. Then friends and family and people they met along the route would call in to hear an update on their progress. Many folks, after hearing the latest progress report, would leave a message for Jerry and Cindy. Long time friend, Melania Elias's voice was often there, as were Kay Harris's and Lucile Torgerson's. It was the next best thing to actually having them there. Averaging eight to 10 messages on most evenings, these uplifting and inspiring messages infused them with energy for the next day.

They also receive hundreds of cards, letters and e-mails from their family, friends and church family. These words reminded them that no matter how difficult the task, there were always people thinking about, and praying for them.

Some words were serious; many were comical.

David Steen, their pastor and group's Bible study leader (who led the drive to raise ten thousand dollars in pledges) sent this e-mail.

Fourteen weeks! Remind me to introduce myself when you return.

This is an epoch in the making . . . . just walking and loving each other will never do . . . . except with us.

They may never tell you–being good Lutherans–but we are all very proud of you.

Poppa Steen

Pastor Rob Hofstad sent this "snail mail" letter.

Greetings to the Lord's Foot Soldiers!
I don't mean to be callous, nor put my foot in my mouth,
but for some reason I have been thinking about you two
particular soles. I hope while you are away, you will continue
to toe the mark!
(I know that last sentence was quite a feet!)
I pray for you each day...for your safety, your health and
most of all your sanity in the midst of an insane adventure.
I admire your courage and am very proud of you.

All my Love,
Rob

Michael Fennerty was just nine years old when he created this
drawing and sentiment. It was included in one of three books Jerry
and Cindy received from their church congregation. Each book of
wishes was hand-carried to Jerry and Cindy when anyone from
Olympia traveled to meet up with them.

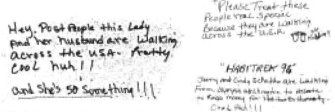

Cindy's sister, Kay, would send packages on special occasions.
She wrote these sentiments on the outside of each package. Jerry
and Cindy don't know if the postal employees read the words but
they were certainly entertained upon each package's arrival!

26

Slug Burgers and
Other Southern Delicacies

Day 178
Monday, August 5
Holly Springs, Mississippi

Cindy

When we asked Paul to consider coming to support us during the walk, we carefully selected the last three weeks of the walk as our optimum choice of times for him to be with us. We thought by now we would be physically exhausted and emotionally fragile. We also imagined we would be edgy and hard to get along with. Because he's a psychology professor, we imagined he would combine his love for adventure, and for us with his profession to gently prod us toward the finish line. In our minds, we would stagger into Atlanta like a couple in the desert that finally reaches a long sought water source.

We imagined wrong. With three weeks to go, we are energized and having the time of our lives! We find humor in everyday things.

Kudzu, that invasive, bountiful weed that was brought to the south from the orient decades ago, is a real challenge for folks in these parts. It grows over everything in its path and eventually sucks the life out of brush and trees. Its fragrant purple flower is in full bloom right now. We feel guilty for admiring it, knowing what a scourge it is to the residents of the south, but we can't help being fascinated by it. It's broad, bright green leaves climb over everything in its path, creating gigantic green sculptures. Some folks tell us that it grows at a rate of 12 inches a day. We set up photos to make it look like Paul and the red rental mini van are being swallowed by Kudzu. We think it's funny. That's because we can leave it behind!

After walking three miles, we meet up with Paul at Bolden's Country Store. He has already been inside. He won't tell us much about it. He simply warns,

"Wait 'til you see this place." His grin is accompanied by rolling eyes.

With more than a little curiosity and thoughts of ice-cold soda pop dancing in our heads, we push open the old screen door. There is only one clear path through an entire room full of clutter. It leads from the front door to the cash register. On each side of the path is a combination of garbage, flea market items and snack foods, all overlapping and disorderly piled. Everything is covered with country-road dust.

As we make our way to the front counter, we finally see a woman peering out from behind more clutter piled on the counter. Only Addie Bolden's shoulders and head are visible. Boxes of junk mail, haphazardly stacked on her right, surround this short, gray-haired woman who appears to be in her mid-sixties. To her left are jars of candy mixed in with boxes of salt and old melted candles leaning out of little sauce dishes. There are cartons of stuff and more junk mail stacked on top of this. A half-filled gallon jar of pickles holds a prominent spot on the very edge of the counter. On the top of one candy container are lollipops stuck into holes like porcupine quills. On the shelves behind her are family photos surrounded by cans of corn and old plastic flowers. Rows of cigarette packs are the most organized things in the place. As if a collage, there is a bulletin board hung in front of these and a lantern hung on that and a beehive hung on the lantern. We think some of the plants are alive. It's hard to tell.

We are simultaneously amazed and intrigued. We introduce ourselves while trying not to stare. Jerry feels a need to give her a sale. He reaches into an old metal Coca-Cola cooler and chooses a glass bottle of Diet Coke. He then chooses a package of his favorite cream-filled oatmeal cookies and pays for it all as he tries to make conversation with the shy woman. We take a photo of Paul talking to her. She smiles faintly, but seems a little nonplussed.

Once outside, Jerry rips open the cookie package and takes a bite. It is too stale to enjoy. He spits out the bite, which attracts a very skinny dog and cat from underneath the van. They are extremely undernourished and devour his cookie contribution.

We walk into the town square of Holly Springs and are greeted by several friendly residents who recognize us from the Memphis media blitz and welcome us to their unique little town in Northwestern Mississippi. Nine-year-old Jervis is a precocious young man. He blurts out,

"Hey, I saw you on TV! I recognize your sandals!"

He asks us some very mature questions. We love talking to him and are in no hurry to move on. All of a sudden he says, "Ya'll better git walkin'."

Okay, then, the conversation is done.

We explore Booker's Hardware Store, an old-fashioned store with worn wooden floors and hundreds of tiny little drawers in wooden cabinets that contain every kind of nut and bolt a person might ever want. The three of us love building materials and find our souls right at home amongst the hammers and saws that line the walls.

A few blocks from town, we stop at Philips Grocery Café. Housed in an old brothel by the railroad tracks, this historic joint has bragging rights to serving the third-best hamburger in America. We sidle up to the locals and order one for each of us. We also order our first fried green tomatoes and fried apple pies. As the temperature continues to rise outside, we wait, impatiently, for 45 minutes to receive our food. The antiques crammed in every nook and cranny keep our attention for a while. Jerry is thrilled to find old Grapette and Lemonette soda bottles. He snaps photos to prove their existence to doubters back home. The still-filled bottles bring back memories of his days of sorting bottles for two cents a case at a soft drink bottling plant in Centralia.

We finally get our food and eat quickly as the thermometer on the porch post outside reaches 94. We rate the burgers as great, the tomatoes, good and the fried pies, well...cooked greasy apples. We take our now well-greased joints out the door and waddle on down Highway 7 and into the humid heat of a dog day afternoon on the back roads of Mississippi.

We find ourselves talking a lot about how we feel now that

the walk is close to ending. We are both retrospective and nostalgic about all that we have experienced in the last six months. We feel pride in what we have accomplished and wonderment in the many miracles that have come our way. There is a part of each of us that is not ready for it to end. Maybe we could keep going?

At the same time, we are anxious to see our family, friends and many of our support vehicle folks at the 20th Anniversary Celebration in Atlanta. We are wondering what the future holds for us. For the first time in our married life, we do not have a clue. In planning for and executing the walk, we have forgotten to plan beyond. As we walk along today, we talk about that. We know we are not ready to go home to rocking chairs and a sedentary life. Many have asked us if we plan to write a book about this experience and we always say no; we are convinced no book will be coming out of us.

As we are talking about what the perfect job might look like, a guy stops us to ask if we need assistance. We explain our presence. He is fascinated with our explanation and we enter a lengthy conversation. We discover that he is a Disney Merchandise Representative. Jerry is fascinated with that. After the guy drives away, he thinks maybe that would be a good job for him. After all, he has collected Disney memorabilia for 20 years. We buy 10 shares of Disney stock for each grandchild as they turn age one, and we have been to every Disney theme park except Tokyo. Yes, we are a Disney family.

The job wouldn't fit all our criteria, however. Our idea of a perfect job would be one where we could work together, preferably out of a home office. We would like to travel in connection with our job and we have always liked the special event planning we did as volunteers with many organizations throughout our lives. If we could combine these things and work for Habitat for Humanity, we feel like we would have the best of all worlds. We believe this is a job that only exists in our dreams.

Our miles for the day completed, we end our conversation with our traditional kiss and a high-five. Whatever is in our future, we're in it together.

Tuesday, August 6
Corinth, Mississippi

Emy Bollard, an energetic young woman with the Corinth Alliance, has made all arrangements for us in this area. We now meet her for an interview for the Corinth Daily Journal. She presents each of us with a "Slug Burger Festival" T-shirt.

"Where we come from, slugs are slimy little creatures that eat our flowers. You don't really eat them, do you?' the ever-naïve Cindy asks.

"No!" Emy assures the three of us. "They are a hamburger patty. They were paid for with a little coin called a five-cent slug during the depression, and the beef was stretched with cornmeal filler. Y'all will have to try one before you leave town."

We adjust the prayer bead bracelets, slurp Diet Coke and contemplate the questions reporter, Jane Clark Summers is asking. We hold hands during interviews, partly because we are used to holding hands but also because we have a signal system worked out. If Jerry wants me to answer a question, he squeezes my hand. If I want him to answer one, I squeeze his. Sometimes there's a "squeeze-o-war", but not often. After all these months we generally know what the other will say and we usually agree with what's being said. If we don't, the other one adds their opinion.

"What will you miss the most about the walk, now that you are nearing the end?" Jane asks.

I squeeze Jerry's hand.

"The people and the energy each new person brings to us. This has been a life changing experience. Take away religion and politics and we have discovered that people are more alike than different. It's an awesome realization," he replies for both of us."What will you miss the least about the walk?" she says.

I don't wait for a hand squeeze.

"Packing and unpacking!" I blurt out. "Living out of a suitcase for seven months is a challenge that I won't miss for a moment."

Feeling adventurous after the interview, Paul takes directions in hand and heads for the White Trolley Café, where slug burgers are made, while we get our last two miles of the day in.

Paul returns and waits for us to finish. We enter the van and begin to drive toward Shiloh National Military Park for a little tourist activity. We are famished and ready for our slug burgers. We remove them from their white paper wrappings and take a bite. The taste and texture is interesting. The greasy burgers have had an opportunity to cool in the air-conditioned van while Paul waited for us.

"A little dry. Did you get any ketchup?"

"Yeah, here you go."

He is amused with how they are made and between mouthfuls, explains the process.

"I don't know if their preparation would pass food inspectors in the Northwest. They precook the patties and stack them around the grill. There are huge stacks of them everywhere. When a customer orders one, they pick one up with a slotted metal spatula and run it through the hot grease and then slap it on a bun. That's it. And these little buggers with no condiments cost 69 cents now."

We think the first bite tastes okay, albeit greasy. By the time Paul finishes telling us how they are made, we've each had more than we can enjoy. The guys finish theirs and then begin asking if the *Tums* are handy. We cut our visit to Shiloh National Miliary Park short, partly because of the heat, mainly because none of us feel well. We have tried a local custom, in our minds, an important part of this adventure. Our final analysis? Three thumbs down.

During this time we found $3.77.

"Choose your own path in life.
Follow it fully, walking gently,
lightly and joyfully toward your goal."
Anonymous

27

Close Encounters of Another Kind

Day 184
Sunday, August 11
Florence, Alabama

Jerry

We are staying at the Comfort Inn on a rare day of rest. No church. No interviews. No speeches. No special events. When we awake at 6:20 a.m., we know we should not go back to sleep. If we do, we will not be sleepy early tonight, and with a 5:30 a.m. wake-up call Monday morning, we need to get to bed early. We decide to go into low voltage awake. We click on the television and watch an old black-and-white movie starring Blondie and Dagwood. We read the Sunday paper.

Cindy eventually gets down to paying bills. We have been living on my retirement wages since Cindy sold our pre-school last year and so far we are doing okay. We were irritated last week when a grouchy (or was it envious?) woman suggested we must be wealthy in order to be taking seven months to pursue a dream. We tried to explain to her that we are rich in lots of things; money isn't one of them. We wanted to explain that following dreams couldn't wait for the "perfect" time. That time may never come. Our explanation was in vain. She had her mind set and nothing we could say would change her thoughts.

It's 3 p.m. when Paul comes by our room and the three of us go for dinner at Logan's Road House. We throw peanut shells on the floor with the locals and order barbecue like they do too. To complete our rather mundane, although much appreciated day, we stop to purchase groceries. We buy mostly beverages–Blue Raspberry PowerAde, Diet Coke, bottled water– and, of course, ice. We each drink two and a half gallons of fluids a day now. We purchase lunch items, too– baked beans in little tins with pop-top lids, cottage cheese, tuna salad lunch kits, string cheese, baby carrots in single size servings, bananas, oranges and bagels. We still have peanut butter for the bagels. That is what we will eat this week. It is what we ate last week and probably what we will eat next week. Egg McMuffins and Diet Coke supplement this in the morning followed by ice cream treats at the end of most days. Then there is supper with our hosts, or at a restaurant.

With bodies and souls sufficiently rested now, we get to bed early in anticipation of another week of walking. Our motive has always been to see things along the way and to meet people we would not otherwise know. Our curiosity about what lies around the next corner and over the next rise has not changed, either. When we began our trek, we were concentrating on raising money and awareness for Habitat for Humanity and we still work to do that often. Slowly, though, we were getting a message to pay attention to the little things, to those things that led us to pursue this dream in the first place–the people–the adventure–the challenge. Those things remain as important to us today as they were early on.

When Paul returns us to our route this morning, the four-foot-wide paved shoulders are a pleasant surprise. This means we don't have to watch for ticks on our socks. It also means we get to walk side by side and hold hands. We are increasingly aware of how few days we have left on the road. It means that we now treasure each day a little bit more. This walk has caught our hearts and right now we can't bear the thought of having it end.

THUD! We look up to see a pickup truck towing a horse trailer hit a large bird. Feathers shower around and upon us. It's another hazard of spending our days on the road. Compared to the raccoon guts in Topeka, feathers are better.

The litter thingamajig hanging from "Habimobile's" rear view mirror is a work in progress. This shrine to the back roads of America gets increasingly gaudy as we make one "exciting" discovery after another. Paul receives these treasures with much fake aplomb and then proceeds to string them up along with the existing items. The little toys from kid's meals are particularly coveted. Pocahontas and Barbie take front and center. A little samurai doll is perfect for Paul's upcoming trip to Japan and seems somehow prophetic. A plastic rose adds a touch of class. A Washington State Lottery pencil, found along the road here in Alabama, gets a special place of honor. Is it possible that this collection of itty-bitty "sacred" road junk is in fact guiding us on our journey through these perilous last weeks? No, we never lose sight of who's in charge. This shrine is all in jest, adding to the frivolity of these last precious days.

A dog rushes us. Cindy takes her usual shielded stance behind me. I square my shoulders and try to sound very firm as I see the bared teeth and hear the dog growl and bark.

"Go home! Go on–get outta here!"

We have been extremely fortunate not to be bitten so far. We brought two pepper spray canisters with us for protection, but we have been increasingly determined not to use them. There was only one time when we felt seriously threatened. A big black dog of mixed parentage was quietly slinking towards us, teeth bared and growling. Its owner hollered for him just as he was within 10 feet of taking a chunk out of one of our legs. I chastised that dog also, and can still remember the sound of its toe nails scraping the pavement as it came to an abrupt stop. That was the closest we've come, and that was after only 500 miles of walking.

We stop at a mini-mart for morning break. There's a scruffy-looking guy propped on a stool behind the counter. He asks what we're up to.

"We two are walking across America. Paul is driving a support vehicle for us."

"Do y'all ever get a rest?" Cindy understands him to say.

"Oh, yes, we're resting right now," she replies.

"No, arrest!" He yells as if saying it louder will somehow make us understand him better.

Cindy shrugs and gives up so I jump in.

"No, we've never been arrested. Police officers have been real friendly to us."

The guy is getting visibly frustrated with us, but he doesn't give up.

"I said, ARRASSED," he shouts again.

We are both embarrassed that our northwest ears cannot understand his southern accent, so we look to Paul for help.

"Harassed?" Paul queries hesitantly.

"Yeah, do folks ever stop and bother you or anythang?" he drawls.

"Nope, people treat us real well. They often stop to offer us a ride or ask us if we are on some kind of litter patrol because of our vests. Thoughtless drivers sometimes pass one another along side us, putting us in jeopardy. It's not out of meanness. They don't realize how close they come to us."

The man accepts my explanation with a nod. I pay for my Sun Drop Soda and Cindy's and Paul's Diet Cokes.

"Thanks y'all. Nice ta meetcha."

It is hard to believe that it is now Tuesday, August 20. It has been 193 unforgettable days since we left Olympia.

Right now, though, the walk seems to take more energy than we have remaining in us as we sit slowly down at the picnic table in the park along the Gadsden River in the town sharing the name of this meandering stream. This has been another one of those days that is hard on our bodies mentally and physically. Spirits low, I wonder how much longer our bodies will be forgiving. We are fortunate to have good weather now. Sometimes, a blessing comes with consequences. Warm weather, though better than wind, rain and cold, brings different kinds of struggles. Coping with the heat and humidity takes persistence and makes some days seem longer than others.

Last night, amidst laughter and gracious hosts, we had no foreboding of the day to come. From the house on the hill, we peered out into the night, letting the vastness of the sky surround us. Sparkling starlight poked through the darkening sky, partially diminished by the distant city lights and reflections in the glass.

We felt privileged to meet Cary Guffey, child star of one of my favorite movies, *Close Encounters of The Third Kind*. Though filmed 20 years ago, it was startling to see how much he resembles the four-year-old in blue pajamas who watched out the kitchen door as the spaceship landed in his backyard.

We engaged in lively conversation as we exchange autographs and discuss our brief moments of fame.

Though wanting the moment to last, conversation soon turned

"Close Encounter..." child star, Cary Guffey, helping map tomorrow's route.

to essential details as we gathered at the breakfast bar to discuss the map of the next day's walk. Steve Scharfenberg, our host, had worked with the city to develop a 20-mile walk route in and around Gadsden. The walk was broken into two parts, and planned so that we would arrive at City Hall before lunch to be acknowledged and received by the mayor and city council.

This morning we were up at 5:30 a.m. Paul in the "Habimobile" soon arrived. After our typical morning repast of breakfast sandwiches, coffee for me, large Diet Coke for Cindy, we arrive at the park, our starting point for the day. Breakfasts are always light and simple now, no heavy food to weigh us down and make us sluggish.

Leaving the van, we adjust clothing, daypacks, sandals and attitudes as we anticipate the day before us. We must walk 14 miles before 11 a.m. It is now 6:30 a.m. If we can maintain a four-mile-an-hour walking pace, we should have more than enough time, including breaks and traffic interruptions.

Unlike some urban mornings, this one is relatively calm, with a show-stopping sunrise thrown in. The traffic is behaving for now. It doesn't last.

The walk route exposes us to a variety of terrain and scenery as we wend our way through and around this city of over 40,000 people. It's like moving from room to room in a large house with each door revealing a different setting and atmosphere. Stately homes with groomed lawns and regally erect flowers are left to memory as we move through this dwelling without walls. Beauty turns to drab, thriving turns to desolation, large supermarkets, with displays of apples, oranges and other produce beaming under bright lights and glistening water drops are left behind as we pass small unassuming corner grocery stores.

We are unable to see inside the stores because the windows are cluttered with multitudes of paper signs written on with red, blue and black paint, listing specials of the week. Even the quality of the signs varies, sometimes looking professionally lettered and neat, more often, looking messy and amateurish.

We have now come to the hill leading up to Noccalula Falls Park. We have wandered off course a bit having been fooled by the map and we are now separated from Paul and our support vehicle. There is concern that we have lost him, since opportunities to use bathrooms are rare and challenging.

We chug up the hill, battling tall grass and the uneven, unkempt dirt shoulders. We cannot find a suitable place to walk, and it is not safe to walk in the roadway. Traffic is incessant and motorists seem impatient, so we must stay alert with every step we take. There are no sidewalks anywhere along this road, a point I will be sure to make later when we meet the mayor. This reasonably short climb becomes very challenging as we struggle and forge our way to the top.

Once at the park, we check our watches, look for Paul and note that we have no time to be tourists. A bathroom break is critical, so we take time for that and emerge to find Paul has rejoined us. He had been lost. He knew we would be coming up here, so he decided to try to catch up with us. We are tense as we begin our descent, knowing what we will face. We have to walk the opposite side of the road to face traffic this time. We cannot walk down the side we came up since it would put our backs to traffic and further endanger us.

The walk down proves more unpleasant than our ascent. Rock outcrops and other obstacles impede sight distance for motorists and us. No one expects to round a corner and encounter two walkers in orange and yellow vests. Our bodies and minds tense with each near disaster. I decide we should go boldly. If we flinch, we might further anger drivers, for to flinch would imply that we knew we shouldn't be there.

Once down, we have no time to relax. We must move fast to be at city hall on time. Our route takes us through urban fringes with no particular attractions or distractions. Time is the focus now, not surroundings. We are rote walking, trying to make a deadline. Head down, long-range guidance system locked in, I notice something unique to my left. Through the chain link fence I see headstones arranged like vertical piano keys. My interest is piqued by one headstone in particular. It is shaped like a cartoon mouse and I tell Cindy to stop and look.

A worker emerges and tells me that if I don't see what I like, they can order others. I wonder if our appearance prompts him to make this offer.

Encouraged by the humor of this moment, we lift out of our "Noccalula" funks and walk on. As we near the end of our morning walk, we are momentarily forced off the sidewalk and into the street to avoid kudzu that has encroached from a vacant lot to claim the sidewalk. Beyond, we meet up with Paul with barely minutes to spare. The map fails us and we can't find city hall where the map indicates it should be. Circling around unfamiliar streets, we finally locate it and are greeted by two anxious hosts. We are hustled inside, sweaty and very dirty.

We stand in the back of the room to minimize our aromatic intrusion, made worse by Cindy's day-old hair permanent. We listen to the mayor issue a proclamation honoring long-haul truckers. We are soon called forward and join the mayor at the microphone. The mayor praises us and the work Gadsden-Etowah Habitat for Humanity has done in Gadsden and Rainbow City and then allows us a chance to speak. I thank him, note the goals of our walk and the work of the Habitat affiliate, and then mention the need for sidewalks going up toward Noccalula Falls. Someone later thanks me for this comment. It wasn't the mayor.

Once dismissed, we join our hosts, the Scharfenbergs, for a delicious lunch at "The Warehouse" restaurant. While there, we are introduced to David Commer, pastor of the church we spoke at on Sunday, who was absent when we were there. He is leaving as we finish our meal. Instead of bringing us a bill, the waitress comes to say that David has paid for all five lunches! We never had the chance to thank him, so we ask our host to pass on our thanks when they next see him.

Paul returns us to our morning stopping point to begin our after-lunch walk. Although we have only six miles to go to complete the day, the temperature has risen and our muscles and minds have taken a set during the long stopping period. Stomachs now full, we begin the afternoon. Legs abused by the morning schedule fight us as we cross the bridge over the Gadsden River. We head toward landscape that is once again dull and uninviting, making our mental and physical struggles more challenging. It seems as though the short distance we have to walk has doubled in length. We must force ourselves to focus and continue.

Once again, nothing lasts forever, it only seems that way some days. Crossing the bridge back over the Gadsden River, we turn south to the park where we started this morning. Traffic makes one last attempt to intimidate us. We persevere. When we finally near the red van we cannot summon the energy to celebrate with our usual high-five and a kiss. Finally, the walk day is over. The hard-fought miles have been conquered. We ease our aching bodies across a short railing and plop at a picnic table. Paul, sensing our needs, walks to the van and returns with a large watermelon. I am normally not fond of watermelon. After what we have gone through today, I really like this one. Experience tells me that if this is a good one, its inner pulp will be dripping with liquid and, of course, those annoying seeds! It is innocent looking, light and dark green stripes on the outside. However, when he opens it, it is orange inside. Day-Glo orange, I think. Startled by what I see for the moment, I quickly decide I don't care if it's purple or blue. I am going to eat it and like it. While Paul cuts the melon, we take off our socks to air our feet. Dirty doesn't describe what we find. We often end days looking dirty from sweat and road grime. Today we are beyond dirty. We are filthy. We wear socks to protect our feet as we walk, and their pale color is in sharp contrast to our suntanned legs. Our socks and our feet are filthy, especially our toes. Watermelon drippings have run down our shins, leaving sticky, lighter colored streaks along the way, as they continue toward our feet, mixing with the grime and dirt. Paul serves up the slices and we slop and slurp away, watermelon liquid running down our chins and fingers. We eat until we can eat no more.

We offer the rest of the watermelon to a man parked nearby. He, too, seems surprised by the color, and is a bit reluctant. Eventually, he accepts our gift and drives off.

The watermelon repast and the shock of seeing our legs and feet like this amuses us and we can finally muster the energy to laugh. Humor now prevails over the day, evoking new energy, as we load up to return to Steve and Suzanne's home to shower and to get ready for this evening's special event, a softball game, with all proceeds going to Habitat for Humanity in our name.

During this time, we found $3.85.

The Littering of America

The Natchez Trace is an old trade route that passes through northern Alabama onto Nashville, Tennessee. After walking in its serene beauty one morning, Cindy and Jerry reluctantly left the Trace to walk on Alabama Highway 14 into Florence. They were headed for a flurry of weekend activities. As they rounded a corner along the roadway, they came upon the most litter-strewn stretch of roadway they had seen anywhere they had walked. There in front of them were piles of paper, Styrofoam containers, cans, bottles and fast food wrappers. It looked like a tornado of litter had blown in and landed in this one area of this rural road, covering nearly every square inch of earth within a 10-yard area.

Over the first 2,500 miles of this walk, litter strewn along the roadways piqued the curiosities of Jerry and Cindy. While the act of littering remained incomprehensible to them, they did use it study the habits of the people who take part in this activity. There were other uses for litter too.

In areas where road signs were as scarce as snow in Hawaii, litter could tell them how far they were from the next town. Since it took a person less time to drink a small cup of any fast food beverage than a larger cup, they deduced that the smaller the cup size found littering the shoulder, the closer they were to a town. Consequently, the super sized cups littering the roadway could mean the next town was a walk day, or two away.

There were also clues about how far they were from the next restroom, or more likely, what guys did in between restrooms. (They believed only men were capable of leaving this clue, anatomically speaking.) They often walked past remote areas littered with plastic beverage containers filled with urine. The greater the distance between bathroom opportunities, the greater the number of bottles deposited. In areas where the next opportunity was several miles away, there might be a filled bottle every few feet.

When the annual McDonald's Monopoly Promotion was in full swing, Jerry and Cindy rarely kept walking past a large McDonald's drink cup. They just had to flip it over with their toes to see if the game piece had been removed. Often times, it had not. Cindy and Jerry never did find the million-dollar winner even though they dreamed of adding an exclamation mark to their adventure through something a litterbug had tossed out their window.

Jerry's reputation for finding things, wherever they walked in life, became legendary. These 3,000 miles just upped the ante.

While accompanied by John and Roberta Gingerich near Lawrence, Kansas, Jerry found the obvious contents of a man's wallet strewn along a one-mile stretch. When he met up with them for one of Roberta's fabulous catered lunches, it was shocking to discover that the guys name on the license was a friend of theirs. Police had been searching for the contents of his stolen wallet for days. They should have just asked for Jerry's assistance!

Jerry also found (and shipped home) five pairs of pliers, 16 screwdrivers, 29 wrenches, 20 sockets, a Makita Sawzall, a Sony clock radio that still worked and other, miscellaneous items including fishing gear, other tools and toys.

Early in the walk, Jerry's statistically oriented brain began to formulate a list of name-brand preferences of the average American litterbug.

They drink Pepsi most often, although that did change to Mountain Dew in eastern Utah and Coca-Cola when we neared Atlanta. Drinking drivers preferred Budweiser. If they drank the hard stuff, it was usually the little airline sized bottles and schnapps or vodka was a common choice. Smokers toss their cigarette packages a lot and Marlboro was their brand of choice followed closely by unfiltered Camels. Skoal was the favorite smokeless tobacco. Candy bar consumers litter a lot too, although not as much as smokers. Their first choice is Reese's Peanut Butter cups followed closely by Hot Tamales and Snickers. There were also a lot of Bic disposable lighters. Perhaps the lighters should be renamed. Other items that often landed in the ditch were combs, tooth floss "gizzwidgets" and golf tees. While some of these were intended to be disposable by their manufacturers, it is doubtful that they envisioned

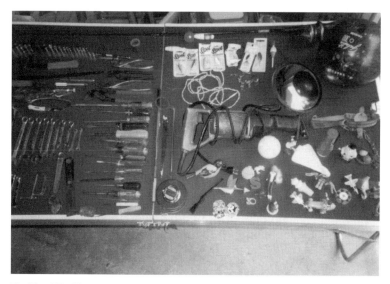

The "Road Find" items Jerry had shipped home.

them being tossed along the highways of America. Pens, audio-tape cassettes and lottery tickets were tossed, perhaps out of frustration, but at the expense of our roadway's beauty. Bungee cords were everywhere, sometimes broken, sometimes still usable. Other items in this general category were broken fan belts, vehicle mirrors, car antennas, car keys and spark plugs, as well as those big Mini-Mart coffee mugs and Styrofoam cooler lids.

Surprisingly, Jerry and Cindy seldom saw disposable diapers. Sadly, they saw more syringes than they cared to.

Many items were obviously not intended for disposal. There are a lot of American children missing binkies, baby bottles, one shoe, toys and clothing. Pajamas were common, but never a complete set. By the time the kiddo got to the top or bottoms, Mom must have discovered her soon-to-be nudist in the back seat and quickly called a halt to the disrobing. Roadside litter became something to be both despised and revered during Habitrek '96. In areas where there was little else, Jerry and Cindy could always watch for an elusive treasure, maybe a tool or a ball to play a road game, or they could add to their growing list of litter survey items as they inched slowly toward Atlanta.

28

Oh Brother, Where Art Thou?

Day 194
Friday, August 21
Piedmont, Alabama

Jerry

We are walking on a narrow paved road named after a Southern folk hero we've not heard of before. John Wisdom was to the Civil War what Paul Revere was to the Revolutionary War. John warned the Confederate army that Union soldiers were on their way. The John Wisdom Trail is scenic and flat with not much traffic. We are happy with the weather today. Temperatures have cooled to the upper 80s. Cindy's blisters are never completely gone. They continue to be much improved since Jamie reupholstered her Birkenstocks and the formaldehyde solution has begun to toughen the soles of her feet. She lost a nail from another big toe last night, the result of a blister that bubbled under it a few weeks ago. She wishes they wouldn't grow back, but they always do.

About 10:30 a.m., we stop at a mom and pop grocery to use the restroom. As we emerge into the glare of another sunny day, we are given a big ol' slobbery southern welcome by a black lab pup. We guess she's about four months old. Paul has some stale popcorn and crackers in the Habimobile. We toss some to her and that's all it takes. She flashes us one of those cute puppy smiles and sets her tail in motion. She intends to walk with us and we cannot bring ourselves to chase her off.

She soon becomes an official mascot of Habitrek '96. We name her Habbie. I find a red bouncy ball, about the size of a jawbreaker. I bounce it towards Habbie and she bounces along with it until she finally catches it in her teeth, not her mouth. She stops, looks up at us with this silly bouncy ball grin and prances on down the road. We laugh like children watching clown antics at a circus. Habbie drops the ball so it will bounce again and then repeats the performance. This continues until we meet up with Paul, two miles down the road.

"You guys ready to have me drive her back to the store?" he asks.

"No way. You've got to see her do the 'bouncy-ball-grin' trick. It's so funny."

Habbie doesn't want to perform for anyone else. Instead she spots a little green frog leaping through the ditch. She prances over toward it. She does a big puppy belly flop where the frog was, but is no more. The frog saw her coming and leaped to safety. The dog pounces. Pounce, sprawl! Pounce, sprawl! The frog never is in any real danger.

Paul heads on down the road to our next meeting point. I retrieve the ball and the game begins again. Unfortunately, this time, Habbie bobbles the ball and it rolls ahead of her into the road. A car comes screeching around the corner and veers onto the shoulder to avoid hitting her as I call to her. Amazingly, she comes immediately. I put the ball into my pocket, not wanting to take another chance like that.

And so it goes, we three, ambling down the John Wisdom Trail with not a care in the world. The three of us stop on a bridge to peer into a lazy creek. Cindy snaps a photo of me with our new friend. Habbie goes down for a drink. We eventually meet up with Paul again.

"Ready to have me take her…?" He looks at us and doesn't even finish his sentence.

"Naw, you're not gonna let me take her are you?"

"Not quite yet. We sure wish we could keep her. She's got the cutest personality we've ever seen in a dog and since there are no houses along here, she must be abandoned."

We keep walking and playing.

At our next meeting, we agree that we must let Paul take her back before it is too far away to be practical. Paul feels like a doggie hit man. He hoists Habbie's rump up into the back seat anyway. I toss the red ball to her. Paul slides the red van door shut. She sits on the seat like a kid and peers out the window with big, sad eyes. We feel like heels. So does Paul. We turn and walk slowly down the road. Paul heads back to where we first met her.

"I bet she was an angel, Jer."

"I bet you are right. Mimi maybe?"

"Maybe."

Down the grassy slope along Highway 278 I've found a full-sized confederate flag. It's in pretty good shape. John Wisdom would be pleased.

After an afternoon of media interviews and a police-escorted walk led by a mayoral candidate into Piedmont, we ride to Debbie and Bayne Smith's home where we will spend the night. Arms loaded down with luggage, we ring the doorbell. A smiling Debbie greets us at the front door. Behind her sit two tail wagging black labs! We tell her about Habbie.

"Oh, you should have brought her here." We like Debbie already, but feel bad for the lost opportunity to stay with Habbie a little longer.

We clean up and head for a special community program at the Baptist church.

Afterward, a guy comes up to speak to me.

"I enjoyed hearing about Habitat and your walk very much. I have to ask you. Though I recognized you, Cindy isn't the same person I saw you with on television, is she?"

I can't resist teasing him.

"Yeah, I pick up women as I walk."

And then I explain this common misunderstanding. "Sometimes people don't recognize us when we're all cleaned up, especially Cindy. She cleans up real good."

Paul had driven over to Jacksonville last night to stay at a motel. We are moving our walk miles off of busy Highway 278 today, so we get our first five miles in on a walking tour of Piedmont with Bayne. Then we walk to the Rails to Trails trailhead and meet Bill Wright, president of the Anniston Habitat affiliate. He has set up this eight-and-a-half-mile portion of the route and will accompany us. The trail is beautiful and it's great to not have to worry about traffic this morning. The bright Alabama sun is bearing down on us like a heat lamp, however.

A television crew is waiting for us on the trail. They ask extensive questions and film us walking. Our water and PowerAde bottles are nearly empty. Bill's cell phone rings. It is Brenda Lindblom asking if there is anything we need. Bill asks us.

"Yes! The biggest Diet Cokes with ice she can find," we blurt.

Thirty minutes later Brenda meets us toting one of those cardboard drink holders. Crammed into it are three, 64-ounce waxed Coca-Cola cups full of ice-cold heaven. We gulp them down, followed by an "in the woods" potty break. Soon on caffeine highs, we finish the trail ahead of schedule. Bill's wife Sally should be waiting for us here as planned. Bill had also talked to Paul and thought he would be meeting us here. They are not there when we arrive, so we wait. Brenda makes a timely arrival for the second time today.

"Hey, Brenda, you really came at the right time with those drinks. Thanks again."

"Glad I could help. What's the plan now?"

Bill tells her we're trying to decide. "Sally was supposed to meet us here. We've waited quite awhile now. Jerry told Paul they would meet him at his motel, we would all go to lunch and then he would take up his job as support driver the rest of the day. It's getting hotter and Cindy and Jerry still have six and one half miles to walk today. The Jacksonville police are scheduled to escort us through town beginning at 1 p.m., and we still need to get lunch."

"Why don't we hop in my car drive over to your brother's motel and go from there," Bill suggests.

We arrive at the motel. The desk clerk tells us that Paul left a message for us. He will be back at 12:30 p.m. We wait until 12:40. No Paul. Brenda borrows Bill's cell phone and then drives us to Hardees for a quick lunch. Bill will call us when Paul returns. The phone never rings. We return to the motel. Still no Paul. We have missed the police escort. It is getting hotter. We feel an urgency to get back out and finish today's miles.

We walk with distraction. How could there have been this much of a communication breakdown? We are worried about Paul. Where is he? Bill drives by to see how we are doing. He has not found Paul or Sally yet, so he will continue looking. We keep walking toward Anniston, still watching for Paul to drive by.

The thermometer dangling from my daypack reads 96 degrees. The humidity is stifling. The heat index must be in the hundreds. Finally, at 3:30 p.m. we finish walking for the day and hurry into the welcome air conditioning of the Habitat Affiliate office housed in the Episcopal Church. Workers there recognize us from the latest media blitz and are very friendly. We try to be cordial, but we are still distracted by Paul's disappearance. Bill meets up with us here. He has finally found Sally. She told Bill that Paul finally gave up trying to find us and followed the old Boy Scout adage to stay in one place when lost. He is back at his motel.

Bill takes us to their house where we will be spending the night. We shower and watch ourselves on the evening news. Sally is leaving and says little. It hasn't been a good day. We encourage Bill to call Paul and suggest that we all meet at Applebees for dinner. At this point we don't know much about the Habitrek missing persons report. We know Paul has been found and that's a relief.

We all rendezvous at the restaurant. Its warm welcoming atmosphere is in sharp contrast to the mood around our oversized booth. We are all a bit disgruntled over the day's events. After a pregnant pause, we begin to compare notes and are finally able to understand all the confusion.

Paul was sitting in the van at the trailhead when Sally arrived. He had changed his plan for where to meet us after talking with Bill the night before. He had not left a message for us at the motel. Paul and Sally introduced themselves and waited a while for us. When we didn't show up, Sally deduced that we were still on the trail, or maybe something had happened to Bill and we had stayed with him. The two of them walked a short distance down the trail, looking for us. After 30 minutes of walking in the oppressive heat, they gave up temporarily and went to McDonald's for lunch and cold drinks. Sally left Paul there and continued her search, thinking she would come upon the police escort and all would be fine. She had planned to go back and tell Paul when she found us. She never went back. Paul waited and paced and tapped his fingers and paced some more. Finally, not knowing what else to do, he went back to the trail. No one was there. That's when he returned to the motel.

He continued to worry about our well-being and was frustrated at not being able to do his "job" for us. The next thing he heard from us was Bill calling to invite him to join us for supper. Still frustrated and upset, he almost declined, but thought better of it.

It was still not completely clear how our communications with Paul had gotten so garbled and he was still understandably miffed. I had told him that Bill would drive us to meet him at his motel after we got done on the trail. Paul said he never heard that. Bayne had told him he would call him after dinner and tell him the next day's plan. That call never came because I thought he knew the plan.

The atmosphere becomes measurably warmer now that the discombobulated day has been explained. With understanding comes laughter and an attitude of gratitude that each of us have come through a stressful day with no real problems. The tall glasses of iced tea go down very smoothly tonight.

During this time we found $3.91.

"It's better to travel well than to arrive."
Tibetan Adage

29

Realizing The Dream

Day 196
Friday, August 23
Near Tallapoosa, Georgia

On this foggy August morning, the deep green leaves overhanging Highway 8 create, for us, a surreal zone of many dimensions. A five-foot-tall statue, shaped like the state of Georgia, welcomes us to our twelfth and final state. We pose for a photo, as we have at every state line. This feels different, however. Each of those occasions was a milestone to be celebrated. This welcome sign represents the culmination of all we have to give. For years, we have been thinking of this day...of realizing that we have actually *walked* to Georgia.

Memorable events of the past months pass quickly through our minds. We reach for each other and embrace, surprised by our rising emotions. Paul recognizes the moment as uniquely ours and walks slowly to the van. We then kiss, a long "we've done it" kind of kiss. Tears of realization trickle down our sweaty faces. The embrace lasts a little longer. We believe nothing can come between the finish line and us now.

Jerry breaks up the emotional moment by hollering to Paul as we walk towards the van.

"Hey, Paul, what are you doin' up there, lookin' for the hour we lost at the state line?"

"I'm not sure what an hour looks like," Paul shoots back.

"Give me 60 minutes and I'll tell you what it looks like," Jerry retorts.

Paul has a volley. "Wait just 360 seconds! Don't get smart with me."

Jerry can't drop it. "*Hour* relationship has gone like *clockwork* until now."

Paul rubs his wooly gray beard and grins, not wanting Jerry to get the last word. He's up against the Master of Quick Retorts.

"See, he's really *ticked* off at us. He won't *tock*," Jerry tells me with a "gotcha" grin.

After pondering unsuccessfully for a few seconds, Paul admits defeat. "Okay, you win. I'm headin' up the road. I'll see you at the van in about 45 minutes.

When we catch up to him, he reaches into a white paper bag and pulls out freshly glazed doughnuts shaped like puffy butterflies.

"Aren't these amazing?" he exclaims. "They reminded me of the beautiful monarchs that have been with us for the last two weeks. Enjoy!" It is a celebratory gesture for this, the last day that Paul will be with us.

There are no paved shoulders on this portion of Highway 8, so we must pass the time walking single file. It is often difficult to talk to each other when we are walking like this and for a while, we find ourselves alone in our thoughts. There is time to let the reality of this morning sink in, to contemplate the past months and the people who have entered our lives. They are a big part of the overall experience. We can never forget their contributions of love, care taking and friendship. At a time in our lives when we could have sat in our living room and let gravity take its toll, we are so glad we didn't.

Though it is early morning, it is 90 degrees already. The humidity reading is 93 percent. We stop for our first break and slurp extra PowerAde. Traffic is light, so we stray onto the road to walk. Although we are still walking single file, the light traffic allows us the opportunity to share what we are thinking. We are both having mixed feelings as we near the end of this chapter in our lives. There's a feeling of melancholy. It's like having a really great vacation come to an end. On the one hand, you look forward to sleeping in your own bed. On the other, you hate to leave that special place in your life where you have created so many wonderful memories.

We agree that this adventure has been good for us. Our relationship couldn't have gotten better. It has remained strong. We have learned a lot about ourselves and about our ability to accomplish anything together. We are pleased that we have been able to observe the goodness of America's people and had the chance to share the good news about our findings. Even the "in search of bad news" press has covered this trek with a spirit of appreciation for the adventure it really is. It has been good to slow down the pace of our lives. We hope we can maintain it but we wonder if it will be possible once we reenter a normal lifestyle. We feel changed. We wonder if we will drift right back into old ways once we return home in mid-September. We are glad we have decided to ride the train home. It will allow us a slow five-day transition back into our lives at home. As we talk, it is clear we have both been thinking similar thoughts.

This afternoon, we encounter a new irritant. Each time we have to avoid traffic by moving into the ankle high grass overhanging the road, little burs stick to our socks. When we try to remove them they stick in our fingertips and it feels like we are grabbing tiny cactus quills.

Jerry asks a lady at the antique store about them after he uses the restroom. She isn't exactly sure what he is referring to. She guesses they are just a common cocklebur.r.

The green road sign we encounter this afternoon is there for motorists heading toward Atlanta. "Atlanta 59 miles," it announces. It shocks us! Can we now be so close to the end of our cross-country journey? It is the first time we have actually seen our destination city written on a road sign. It makes the end suddenly seem so real, our long anticipated goal within reach. The reality seems like 59 miles of frosting on our cake of dreams.

Today is Saturday, August 24. On this rainy Saturday morning, we are having a gift exchange with Paul in our very crowded motel room in Douglasville, Georgia. It is 6:30 a.m. The two coolers, the donated lawn chair, the shrine and all the other road treasures we have absent mindedly tossed into the "Habimobile" during the last three weeks are now stacked all around us. We are amazed at how much stuff we have accumulated.

Paul is packed and ready to drive to the Atlanta airport. We are trying to keep the mood light, but we are all having a hard time with his departure. We must say goodbye. It feels premature. We wish he could stay until our last mile is done, however his next adventure as an exchange teacher in Japan begins in one week. During all these months, goodbyes have never gotten easier. The longer someone has been with us, the more of our souls we share, the harder it is. When it is a blood relative, it is hardest of all.

Paul presents us with a poem he has written describing his observations of the inner walk. It touches us deeply. We give him the reworked keepsake "shrine" and our traditional thank you certificate for support drivers. It seems woefully inadequate. We are grateful for his generous gift of time and love, not to mention the money he has spent to come to the walk route. Bear hugs and choked emotions are exchanged. The three of us have always been close. Now we are closer.

Paul sends a final e-mail back to the family waiting for his return.

"At the risk of seeming proud or anything, I have to add that this trek is really an inspiration when you are up close and personal. The daily-ness of 20 miles in 90/100-degree weather is awesome. They also are spreading the word of Habitat in a really natural and effective way. It is fun to see and get to sneak in around the edges of this epic journey. Today the Emmy Award-winning TV cameraman of all time captured the essence of Habitrek '96 by doing foot close-ups. It was cool to watch. I got to have my tee shirt used to set the F-stop on the camera. So much for my 15 minutes of fame! I did manage to get my name in the paper; however, I had to walk ahead of a Jerry and Cindy to get to the reporter first. God, the things you do for a little attention."

The end of our trek gets ever nearer. We spend the weekend throwing away the items we will no longer need and packing the things we want to send home. We plan to walk in newly soled sandals next week. Our worn-out ones are packed into FedEx mailers in preparation for shipping to the Birkenstock, Inc. headquarters in Walnut Creek, California for a final resole. We had a little contest going to see who was lightest on their feet and wore out the fewest sandal soles. In the end, we have each worn out 13 pairs of soles. It's a draw. Writing our own return address on the package instead of a host family's address, reminds us once again that the end is coming rapidly.

On Monday we move from the motel to settle into our last host family's home. Denise Mims and her mom, Louise, are the perfect people for us during these last three hectic days. Not only do they generously open their home to us, they have the enthusiasm to oversee the onslaught of our family and all the activities that goes with that.

After a soak in Denise's hot tub, Cindy listens to five messages on voice mail. Her Dad is congratulating us on reaching Georgia. Our friend, Kay Harris, is congratulating us too. Then there is a call from a guy named William Petty. He explains that Patrick's letter to NBC New York, telling of our walk, has filtered down to his Atlanta office. He is a producer and would like us to call him as soon as possible. Since it is after hours, Cindy leaves him a voice mail.

Tuesday morning we awake to the realization that we have a much needed day off. We only have 40 miles left to walk and four days before we are due to arrive at the Habitat celebration. We have made it the entire way without having to take any days off for injuries or illness. We believe this to be one more miracle on our walk. Denise loans us her Chevy Blazer so that we can go ship the sandals and mail our road treasures and extra clothes home. Katie will bring our convention and Walt Disney World clothes in an extra piece of luggage Thursday night.

We have not seen any of our kids since Katie left in a flood of tears from Missouri. They begin a three-platoon arrival to walk the final miles with us. Today, we are anxiously awaiting the arrival of Drew, Conner and Kim along with her parents, Larry and Myrna Bowman, around 4 p.m. This will be the third time Myrna, Larry and Kim have met up with us during the walk. Their partnership has been an important part of our success.

We return to Denise's at 1 p.m. William calls soon after to ask a slew of questions. Cindy answers them as honestly as possible. He ends the conversation by saying,

"I would like to do an "In Your Own Words" piece for *NBC*

Nightly News to be shown on Labor Day. I will call New York and the powers that be will make the final decision. I'll call you back soon."

In the meantime, Denise has come home from work early to take us to scout tomorrow's route. She will notify the Douglas County Sheriff's Department of our intended route because they will escort us tomorrow. That accomplished, we return to hear a voice mail from William. It's a go! The camera crew will be at Denise's at 4 p.m., one hour from now.

This will be the "biggest" press we've been interviewed by so we are excited, but not at all nervous. By now, media interviews are part of our life. Denise, on the other hand, would have every right to go into a full-scale panic when we tell her that a news crew will be arriving to shoot a national story in her living room in one hour. Denise does not panic. It appears she is cut out for these kinds of situations.

She goes about vacuuming the blue carpet in her sunken living room while we peruse our luggage for complementary colors to wear on camera. William has given us only one guideline, nothing white by our faces.

Denise gives her dark wood coffee tables a once over with the dust cloth while Cindy applies her makeup. Denise is plumping up the blue couch pillows and turning on the lamps when the doorbell rings. It is 3:30 p.m.

The television crew apologizes for being early, enlists Jerry's help, then immediately begins unloading their van. Dark thunderclouds are gathering overhead.

Cindy emerges from the guest room, as the last of the gear is unloaded. A tremendous roar of thunder announces the coming of a gigantic rainstorm. Lightning strikes nearby and then the downpour begins. Denise's lights flicker, but the power does not go off.

The all-male crew introduces themselves.

William is a tall, slender man in his early 30s with a ready smile and genuine interest in our story. Rob, the cameraman, is a down-to-earth guy, a little older, and as friendly as a golden retriever. Mark, the soundman, is in his twenties and is quieter, but no less interested than the others. We are immediately comfortable with these guys.

William seats us in two of Denise's maple dining room chairs. Rob checks camera angles, adjusts the reflecting umbrella and moves lamps around. Mark puts microphones on us. Rob applies pancake makeup to Jerry's scrunched up and mildly embarrassed face. Just as the guys begin to roll the film, Denise's living room roof begins to leak in several places. The camera stops. Denise retrieves stainless steel cookware from her kitchen and locates one under each drip while we chat with the crew.

Their morning shoot was for the *Today Show*. Richard Jewel's mom was being interviewed about her son's suspected involvement in the bombing at Olympic park last week. We have time to discuss the terrible tragedy of the TWA airline crash over Long Island in July. We like these guys. It would be easy to just sit and talk, but they have an interview to do. We resume at 4:15 p.m. amidst the noise of the storm outside and the "plink, plunk, plinking" of water hitting the metal pans inside.

The phone rings. Denise answers it but does not interrupt us. At 5:30 p.m. the crew says they have enough information on tape. They say we have a natural ability for interviews. They comment on our obvious respect and commitment to each other. They tell us that is unusual in their business. We are concurrently pleased and embarrassed at their compliments. We remind them that we have a lot of experience with reporters and cameras, having been interviewed over 120 times in the last seven months.

The crew would like to spend more time with us tomorrow by getting some walk footage. It is then that Denise tells us that our daughter-in-law, Kim was the person on the phone at 4:15 p.m. They have been at their Douglasville motel room since 3:45 p.m. Once we get that news, it is difficult to concentrate on the details of tomorrow's shoot. Finally, at 5:45 p.m., Denise tosses us her car keys.

"Alright you two go give those grandbabies a big ol' hug. We'll get tomorrow figured out, clean up this mess and I'll see y'all at *Sak's Bar-B-Que* at 7 p.m."

We happily agree to do everything our lovable hostess commands!

Seeing everyone again is like being reunited with a misplaced security blanket. It feels warm and comforting, as if we had just seen each other yesterday. Amidst giggles and hugs and stories galore, we eventually move from the motel to Saks. We feast on authentic dry pit barbecued chicken and ribs, fried apple sticks, deep-fried corn on the cob and the biggest baked potatoes we've ever seen. We wash it all down with huge glasses of sweet tea. All too soon, we must all get to bed in preparation for tomorrow's 20-mile hike into Atlanta. When Drew realizes we are not going to their motel with him, he begins to cry.

"No Poppa and Gramma don't leave again!"

His comment breaks our hearts.

"Oh, sweetheart we are not leaving you for long this time. All of our things are at Denise's house. We will sleep there tonight and see you first thing in the morning, okay? We'll be together for the next two weeks and then we are coming home to Olympia. We promise."

We are mentally and physically exhausted tonight. It seems like we are close enough to the end of our journey to allow our minds to finally convey to our bodies the tiredness that has built up over all these months. We have not allowed ourselves to get too tired, or to give up no matter what we have faced. Each day we looked forward to the journey with little regard for the amount of mental and physical energy we were expending. We often needed to be "up" for media interviews and when staying with host families. Now, our bodies seemed to sense that we didn't need to be "up" much longer. We could be us again. We could soon go to bed on our time, eat when we wanted to eat and go where we wanted to go when we wanted to go.

We decide to watch the news in Denise's rec room before bed. The meteorologist is pointing to the national weather map.

"Jer, does the map look different to you now? All of a sudden it seems like more than a map, it seems like our home! We know the areas we have traveled. We know the people. Some of them have come into our lives for a moment, some will live in our hearts forever," Cindy reflects.

Jerry picks up the thought.

"I wonder if we will ever again be able to look at a map and not think about what is happening to the friends we have made? Before this, we just paid attention to our little corner of the world. Now we have attachments to our diagonal across the country. It's weird to hear forecasts for cold sweeping into Kansas. I wonder how they will cope during the winter? Will their wheat and corn crops survive? How about "Habbie" the dog? I wonder if she found a home?"

We talk about the 82 host families who took care of us and the 34 support vehicle drivers who provided us with companionship and safety. Even the 30 motels we called home on weekends are a part of our memories now.

Day 200
August 28

The week marches on into Wednesday. We want the days to go slowly. We want to enjoy and remember each event, each sweet moment.

Denise drives us through "Mickey D's" for our traditional breakfast then on to the motel where family and the news crew are waiting. At the end of this day we will be in ATLANTA! The destination has only been the name of a distant city until now. Atlanta, the site of the 1996 Summer Olympic Games was a destination for us of great significance. Until today, it was just some place we were headed, nothing tangible. We are anxious to get started.

With the news van and Larry's rental van behind us and the deputy's car ahead, we start walking in the steady drizzle. We cause a few commuter-traffic tie-ups when our group, led by the deputy, blocks part of the roadway. The morning goes quickly, ending at the Lithia Springs City Hall where Mayor Rosa Mary Johnson gives us a warm welcome and then treats us all to lunch.

We are then driven to our scheduled gathering point at a service station on Highway 278, Bankhead Highway. Jerry began the morning filled with a sense of foreboding about the day. Was it the incessant rain, or was it the realization that the journey is almost over? Perhaps it was both coupled with the sudden sense of responsibility for the guidance and safety of the additional family members. Whatever it was, it affected much of his day.

We had received our first warning about Bankhead shortly after entering Georgia on Monday morning. The first folks we talked to reacted with disbelief when we told them of our proposed route into Atlanta. They said we would be walking through "Little Vietnam." At first we didn't understand whether this was a caution from rural folks not comfortable with big cities or an ethnic slur. It was neither. After hearing more from other people along the way, we came to understand that the area of Bankhead we would be traversing was a neighborhood crime zone.

When we arrive at the prearranged spot, the NBC news crew hurries to tell us that we won't have a police escort into Atlanta and that their crew has been called to film another news event. They seem troubled by our circumstances and reluctant to leave us.

Jerry walks over to the passenger side window of the parked police car to talk to the officer inside. The officer, a large man, is brusque and adamant in his statement that we will not have a police escort. If we have a problem with that information, we are welcome to go to the precinct and talk to his supervisor. Nothing Jerry says alters the officer's position and his demeanor remains gruff, rigid and unyielding. He displays no further interest in discussing the issue and appears to loom larger as the conversation continues. Jerry has an increasing feeling that the impatient officer would welcome the opportunity to explode from the vehicle and slam him against the car if he persists with the conversation. Observing a pressure cooker about to blow, Jerry takes his hands off the police car and steps back from the window. Finally, Jerry tries one last cautious attempt to impress on the officer that he is concerned about the safety of the three women he will be leading and his grandkids in the escort van. Their conversation is interrupted when the officer gets a call on his radio. Before driving off, he states that if we are careful and stay on the sidewalk for the next few miles we shouldn't have any problems. As a modest concession, the officer says that police cars patrol Bankhead regularly and they will watch for us. Jerry tells him it should be easy to spot us, since we will probably be the only ones wearing yellow and orange safety vests walking down Bankhead Highway to Atlanta.

Cindy and the rest of our entourage have been waiting nearby. Jerry joins them and tells them about his frustrating conversation. The story shared, the decision comes quickly. The women are impatient and don't understand why the conversation took so long when we could have been walking. We have been safe this far and we have to trust our faith to guide us through this area. Women in front, Jerry walking and watching from behind, the journey goes on. The next 10 miles loom larger than any we have faced so far.

Underlying Jerry's feelings is a sense that vigilance is needed, but there is no need to worry. As the group continues, his brain and heart wrestle for control. Peace of mind comes gradually, but not without him trying to take on the whole issue himself. He finally gives in to the unspoken message that we will be safe. "I believe, help my unbelief!"

Neglected neighborhoods and blight surround the four of us as we walk. It has the look of hopelessness. Yards are barren and brown. The apartment buildings are stark, abused and lack personality. They resemble prisons more than homes. Very little activity is apparent except on the highway and at some businesses. A beat-up car pulls in front of us with four young men inside. It studies us for a moment then whips a U-turn and heads toward Atlanta. Kim's dad has parked the van on the opposite side of the road. A young woman crosses the street and approaches the open window. She makes an offer then notices our two grandsons in the back seat and walks away. About two miles into the walk, we hear a car horn and turn to see our friendly officer go by. It is the only time we will see a police car even though we pass the precinct on our walk into Atlanta. We stop at McDonald's to use the bathrooms. Someone in the restaurant shouts out "Why is whitey here?" We have the same question. We perceive no threat, just amazement from the patrons that the four of us are there. Eventually the miles of despair and starkness give way to single dwellings in neighborhoods with maintained lawns and plants. Psychologically, it is a reprieve from our concerns about the conditions now left behind us. How can there be hope for the future when these people are trapped in the now?

The sun is out and the day is warm as we continue now without the anxiety experienced miles back. Entering Atlanta, we walk past Georgia Tech and Coca-Cola headquarters. We turn south onto Peachtree Boulevard. After a few minutes of confusion, we find Larry parked near a large stone Methodist church. There is no brass band waiting for us. No one inside even knows we are here. It's been a hot, and stressful day tinged with times of gaiety and times of tension, verging on fear. We are tired and hot, but we are elated to be here. In this Olympic city, we don't look like athletes and we sure didn't set any speed records. In the end though, we have accomplished our own Olympic-sized feat. We throw our vests into the air and catch them convincingly. They are faded and dirty and wear the miles like old friends. They symbolize the walk, and us, to some extent. We share congratulatory hugs and smiles big enough to light up the Olympic stadium. We pile our dirty, sweaty bodies into the van and drive to back to Douglasville for one last night. We share the day's experiences with Denise. In all the excitement of having the family arrive, the NBC crew with us, and the walk drawing to an end, no one had remembered to contact the media regarding our arrival in Atlanta. It wasn't truly the end of our journey. We would still be walking another 10 miles to the ultimate finish line. Downtown Atlanta was symbolic in that it represented the eastern most point we would reach. There was more to come.

The family arrival countdown continues as Katie, Curtis and Logan arrive tonight in a second rental van. We are thrilled to have them join the entourage. Their arrival is bittersweet when we realize that an 11½-month-old grandson Logan does not remember his own grandparents. Accomplishing dreams does not come without sacrifice, and we have sacrificed a relationship with the youngest member of our family. He is a beautiful little boy and we interact slowly so as not to frighten him. He shows a little recognition, but no attachment to us. We are glad that will change when we get home. They are not planning to move from our home until December. We look forward to some daily time with him and the kinship that will grow from it.

Thursday morning brings with it the realization that our stay with Denise is ending. Larry brings Drew in the van to load our luggage for the 114th, and final time, as the entire troop moves from Douglasville to the Atlanta Convention Center. Drew and Cindy are descending Denise's front steps when they stop to observe a spider putting the finishing touches on a large web. As with most things these days, we see simple things in a different light. The spider seems to be another symbol of our accomplishment; strand-by-strand we have built our web. Now it is almost complete. It has taken a lot of work, but the finished product is a beautiful specimen of what two people can accomplish when they follow their hearts and dreams.

Today is Katie and Curtis' fourth wedding anniversary. Jerry has planned a just-for-fun 12-mile walk through Stone Mountain Park. We need these miles to make our walk an official 3,000 miles long, Kim and Myrna need them to officially have walked a total of 100 miles with us and the NBC crew wants some more footage. They get it in a setting with little traffic and a lot of natural beauty. We are all relaxed and having more fun than should be legal. It's a party. Conner provides additional entertainment when he walks over to the side of the road pulls his new Spider-Man underwear down to his ankles and pees into the grass. This is not the time for chastising, so we choose to compliment him on his newly honed potty skills! We hope his little tush won't show up on *NBC Nightly News* in a few days!

The crew has what they want for today. They will rejoin us tomorrow. They are becoming part of the family!

We climb the rounded dome of Stone Mountain and enjoy *Slushies* as we sit atop the granite rock Georgians call a mountain. Later, our two vans, loaded down with luggage, head towards the Sheraton Gateway Hotel at the Georgia Convention center where Habitrek '96 will officially end at Habitat For Humanity's 20th anniversary celebration.

Tonight, Pat and Mark complete our family's arrival. They have all come at great expense from carefully watched budgets. Their support and solidarity for their crazy parents is heartwarming. It's hard to imagine this time without them at our side.

As fate would have it, Linda and Millard Fuller are just emerging from their car as we drive up. We jump out to receive hugs of congratulations from two people who never doubted our ability to complete this venture. God has orchestrated this day in a most unusual way. It is a sweet ending to a long year.

We find other Habitat folks and ask where we are to join the walkers from Americus, Georgia. Jerry finds the answer vague both times he asks. The church is "somewhere over there." He knows that folks are busy with the celebration planning, but we need more than that for an answer. No one can pinpoint the church. We will try to find it tomorrow.

Friday, August 30

This day, so far away seven months ago in the lives of two anonymous people from Olympia, Washington, is now a reality. We have not slept much. We believe this will be a great and glorious day. We are psyched. We put on our Habitrek '96 shirts. Each member of the family will wear one today.

The 13 of us have one last symbolic breakfast at McDonald's before driving into town and touring Underground Atlanta followed by a tour of Coca-Cola's Museum. The shirts draw enough attention to get us all free admittance. Employees are enthused about the walk and ask many questions. Their interest in our walk makes us all feel special. The family is getting to feel some of what we have experienced over the past seven months. The news crew rejoins us outside Underground Atlanta at noon and attaches our now-familiar wireless microphones to our clothing. Friends from the Habitat for Humanity regional center in Oregon join us too. We are not quick to leave. This is the last leg; perhaps we want to delay the inevitable. Finally, the energy of the group determines that it is time to go forth. We are as happy as clowns in a circus parade, and just as colorful, people and strollers and the cameras and vehicles serpentine our way along the 10-mile route leading to the Atlanta Convention Center.

Friends and the NBC news crew have all tried, but no one has been able to locate the church near the convention center where we are to join the Habitat walkers from Americus, so we are not sure where we should be headed. We need a rest stop. For the first time in 3,000 miles, we are denied use of the restrooms at the restaurant where we stop. Finally, we find a restaurant that will let us use their restrooms. The manager and his staff are interested in what we are doing, so we share our story with them. Jerry lets the group dally a bit as we all talk to manager. The manager gives us free soft drinks as an acknowledgement of our working with Habitat for Humanity and the miles we have come. Back on the sidewalk, we once again are told that our scouts can't locate the church. It doesn't matter to Jerry anymore. Though Jerry never acknowledges it to himself, or anyone else, he doesn't care. Internally, Jerry is sensing that we really aren't part of that group. He is feeling that it is not right for our family and friends to be absorbed by another group. Subliminally, he has allowed the group to dally at the start and along the way with the latent hope that we will not have to join the other group. He wants us to finish this walk together, to walk in as one Habitrek '96 family.

We are about a mile away from the convention center when someone in the group notes that the other group would have left the church by now. That seals the decision to walk directly into the convention center and join the ceremony in progress.

We hear loud cheering. The other groups that have arrived are sharing cheers for each other's accomplishments. We are 200 yards away from the Atlanta Convention Center. Everyone with us steps back, leaving the two of us in front. It doesn't feel right to us. Someone hands us the road-battered banner that has accompanied us since we walked away from Tumwater City Hall on February

10. Our other two hands are clasped emitting strong feelings of love and respect between us.

It feels like we are living a dream as we slowly walk towards the assembled crowd. Our entourage follows. We want them close. They want us to have the spotlight. In the moment, we forget to hug them, to thank them for all they have done to support and love us. It is too late to turn around. We move slowly towards the throng. 20th Anniversary Celebration speeches have already started. Someone hustles us toward the podium as our family disappears into the crowd. Although we have faced groups and the media for seven months, we are suddenly self-conscious, as if we don't really belong here.

There are other groups in attendance that have gone through physical trials to be here. A group of 175 have walked 140 miles from Americus, Georgia, headquarters town of Habitat for Humanity. One hundred others have ridden bicycles from Louisville, Kentucky and Ontario, Canada. Although our event has taken the longest, it does not make us more special than these groups. Their camaraderie and enthusiasm regarding their accomplishments overwhelm the occasion. Oddly, we feel like interlopers, like parents retrieving their children from summer camp. The group is connected through the experiences they have shared. We are outsiders. Our vision for this day is not the reality.

Addressing the crowd, we both struggle to know what to say. Overwhelmed by what we see before us, we utter a few words about being happy to have finally arrived at our destination. Of the many people assembled, many do not even know what we have done or who we are. We forget to tell them that for the last seven months we have walked 3,000 miles to be here and that each of those miles took 16 minutes to accomplish. We forget to tell them that we have each worn out 13 pairs of Birkenstock soles in our walk through three seasons. Our son Mark, clinging to a lamppost and towering above the crowd, has to yell to remind us to tell the crowd what we have done. His words get jumbled in the humid air and do not reach us.

This is not how we envisioned our emotions at the end of 3,000 miles. Somehow it is appropriate. These folks should celebrate their victories together as they were accomplished. Our emotions say we should celebrate ours alone, just a couple of old "sole mates" who feel incredibly close in their accomplishment. The emcee tells us that our time at the microphone is mercifully over and we slowly ease our way through the crowd to the air-conditioned comfort of the convention center. We are still wearing microphones because the crew is still hoping for a few final words of inspiration. We do not want the new sound guy to hear what we have to say. We want to be alone with our words. We disappear into the dark, cool concrete hotel cavern. While taking long cold drinks from the water fountain, we turn to look at each other. Our confused emotions become crystal clear as we fall into each other's arms. It has taken 15.5 million combined steps to get us to this point. Few words are necessary.

"I love you, Jerry," Cindy whispers. "I love you, too," Jerry whispers in return.

That's all the sound guy gets, and only if he listens very carefully.

During this time we found $3.21 for a grand total of $69.80 during the entire walk.

Fifteen Minutes of Fame

They are rousted out of bed at 4:30 in the morning, dress for a walk day, then make a planned stop at a local television station in Huntsville, Alabama. Cindy and Jerry are to be the guests on a local morning talk show. They have done early morning radio, rush hour radio, noontime TV, stops along the road with multitudes of media and many other media interviews, but this is the first–no one gets up this early in the morning to watch television––interview.

When they arrive, Cindy seems to have it all together. It's not that Jerry feels uncooperative; it's just that he has become a bit lackadaisical about interviews. Al, their local host and president of Huntsville Habitat, is rightfully excited about the interview and what it may mean to the local Habitat affiliate. He seems disconcerted with Jerry's demeanor.

Everyone but Jerry is taking plans for the interview seriously. They properly follow whoever looks like they are leading them somewhere productive (although it seems clear to Jerry that no one is going anywhere immediately). He leaves the group to use the bathroom, taking his time to finish his chore.

Cindy comes hustling down the hall looking for him. Others trail behind her looking quite serious. She mentions quietly, in her "what the heck are you doing" voice, that he should hurry because they are supposed to be in the studio and on the air in seconds.

Jerry, being "Mr. Casual" today, sees no reason for panic and silently dismisses the apprehension on everyone's faces. Jerry thinks about asking what the big deal is all of a sudden, since they have not been in a hurry previously, but he senses he shouldn't do that.

Soon, to everyone's relief, Cindy and Jerry are seated at the elevated, arc-shaped desk with the morning host. There is not a lot of room on the narrow stage. The host is centered at his desk; Cindy is located to his right. Jerry is crowded as close to Cindy as possible, and has barely gotten settled when they go live. The interviewing begins. The host proves to be a great interviewer and Jerry finally musters some genuine enthusiasm and interest, now that the cameras are on. He responds with humor and animation to the questions put before him. While Cindy is answering a question, Jerry peers out toward Al, Paul and some TV crew guys. Is that a look of amazement on their faces now that they realize Jerry is speaking intelligibly?

Still quite relaxed and feeling full of himself, Jerry suddenly notices that one of his four stool legs is not making contact with the stage beneath him. His stool is not stable and, should he relax too much, he will tumble off to his right and disappear from the program. There are probably some folks who would appreciate this after his previous disappearance, but he has no intention of giving them that satisfaction. He forces himself to focus on the interview without relaxing any more and tries not to betray his situation to the viewing audience. He manages to maintain his mental and physical balance until the first commercial break, then he scoots the wayward stool over one inch, about all the room there is to scoot, and settles in for the next round of interviews.

Everyone is having a good time and the people standing around the studio are clearly impressed to see that Jerry continues to talk in full sentences. There's another commercial break, a visit from one of the crewmembers, then back live. Jerry is in a groove! Then, he feels something biting the right side of his bare calf. He briefly glances away from the cameras and sees the little black infidel that has invaded his presence. He has a flea crawling among the hairs on his leg! He obviously can do nothing about it.

Again, forcing himself to concentrate, he ignores the little devil until the next break in action. As a viewer, he does not normally appreciate commercials breaks. This morning, he welcomes every one of them. He whispers to Cindy, and then goes after the little bugger, making sure he doesn't fall off the stool. He gets the flea in a death grip. This TV dinner is the flea's last meal. Jerry drops the corpse to the floor.

Finally, and mercifully, the interview is over. Amidst compliments, Jerry and Cindy climb down from their elevated roost to visit with a much-relieved crew and staff. Al, Paul and the studio staff are looking like they can't believe the interview actually went so well. Jerry and Cindy are invited over to watch the local weatherman stand in front of his blue screen and move his arms about as if he is pointing at a real weather map. Everyone had been concerned about Jerry, but look at what this guy is doing–he's waving at nothing!

Al, Paul, Jerry and Cindy exit the studio. Morning light is just breaking. Paul asks what was going on up there. Jerry explains his two predicaments. Paul is not surprised.

Apparently, not a lot of people watched the telecast. With Paul and Al as support drivers, Jerry and Cindy spend the rest of the day getting their 20 miles in around Huntsville while looking at the 39 houses Habitat has built here. No one ever stops them in recognition or even honks.

Maybe this wasn't Jerry's 15 minutes of fame after all.

The Inner Journey

Crossed into Georgia
The state line crossed
In one human step
Just like so many steps
In this cross-country odyssey.

So many steps
So many state lines
So many emotional lines crossed
Never to be crossed again.

Two people
Moved to walk their talk.
Touching so many lives
Being touched by so many lives.

The inner journey and the outer journey
Which farther?
Which the most perilous?
Like the walk itself,
The inner journey will
Step across many lines
Into the deep south of
These walkers psyche.

Who knows where this
Trip will have taken them?
Atlanta?
I think that was
Just the first step.

Love, Paul
August 24, 1996

Chapter 30

Life After the Dream

The end of the walk was not the end of our life. During the seven days following the Habitat Celebration, we drove to the "most magical place on earth" for a family reunion celebration at Walt Disney World. With this opportunity to reconnect, we added many hours of wonderful memories to our family scrapbook during those seven days. As with any family, though, things did not go perfectly. Jerry caught a nasty cold, Kim, Drew and Conner got the flu, Katie got a kidney infection and Mark experienced long-distance relationship problems. As always we were there to support and help each other through these challenges.

The *NBC Nightly News* piece was never broadcast. Saddam Hussein caused a new brouhaha in the Middle East, hurricane Fran blew up the Atlantic Coast and there were new developments concerning the TWA flight 800 airplane crash. These noteworthy stories effectively "killed" the television piece about Habitrek '96. We did receive a personal copy of the video that would have aired. That 75-second tape was the final result of four days of filming!

While the rest of the family left to fly home from Orlando, our long-time friends, Rusty and Judi Sievers retrieved us from the mouse's house and transported us and our multitude of luggage to the railroad station. The four nights and five days that it took us to travel across America (at an astounding 78 miles an hour) was a wonderful time of rest and reflection. Most days we had a five-hour layover to change trains. During those times, we explored the cities of New Orleans, Chicago and Denver on foot. Our bodies still craved the long distance walking we had recently abandoned.

Word had spread that the well-tanned couple in car number 25 had just completed a walk across America. Each time we had a meal on the train, we shared a table with a different couple. They had many questions about the walk. It was through our answers to them that we were finally able to fully comprehend our accomplishment.

During a summer when over 32 million travelers drove across America, we were the only couple that walked.

We had raised over $50,000 for Habitat for Humanity and the awareness raised about Habitat helped with the formation of new affiliates in some of the towns we had walked through. We also had the pleasure of meeting many of the volunteers who selflessly give of their time to work in partnership with families in need of decent, affordable housing across America. We realized that our accomplishment is nothing compared to the whole of this organization.

On a personal level, we had proven that an ordinary married couple could accomplish anything they set out to do if they worked together for the common dream. We learned that walking across country together was not unlike many of our married years together. There were uptimes and downtimes, struggles and accomplishments, pain and elation, spats and apologies, personal and relational growth and, most of all, proof that we took our marriage vows seriously 32 years before this feat. We learned that by inviting others to share in our dream, through the assistance they could give, we had allowed them to be part of the accomplishment. We were reminded that our struggles during the difficult times were minor compared to those facing much of the world's population. And we always had each other to rely on for moral and physical support.

As we sat in our little berth, we reminisced about the walk, compiled statistics and contemplated our future. Occasionally, the train would travel parallel to roads we had walked on. Vivid memories of our amazing adventure returned, as we romanticized about the life we had led through three seasons and 12 states.

On Saturday, September 14, Amtrak's passenger train, *The Pioneer*, pulled into the Olympia train station and we stepped onto our home turf for the first time in seven and a half months. We were flooded with warm feelings of love for the family members and friends who cheered and waved banners and balloons as we descended the steps. The first hug went to the "retired official worrier" who could not stop smiling! The welcoming continued at a potluck at our home featuring our favorite foods. Kay discovered a stray kitten in our driveway that we immediately adopted and named Habicat. The following week we humbly stood before our church family as they gave us a standing ovation and a special award.

In late September, we walked and completed the Portland Marathon. The formaldehyde treatment on the bottoms of Cindy's feet had made the skin so tough that she did not realize she had developed an egg yolk-sized blister on her heel until she removed her shoes and socks. We had struggled to complete this marathon in 1995, but now, it was just another walk day.

In November, we flew to San Diego, California to be part of a photo shoot for Sun Precaution's clothing catalog.

Cindy had to see her ophthalmologist for the eye infection that had never cleared up.

We unpacked the many boxes we had been shipping home all year and organized gear, supplies and photos. We realized we were unsettled, much like a college student home for the summer. The walk was behind us. What was ahead of us? We had gone from busy to boring, a transition we found difficult. Cindy's final journal entry, on September 27, reads:

"It's a weird time in our life together. We have achieved all of our life's dreams. Now there is a blank canvas. How will we paint it?"

It has been six years since those words were written. During that time, the canvas seems to have painted itself!

Evan Patrick Schultz, the baby we learned was due while we were in Memphis, was born on March 4, 1997. Five months later, his cousin Alyssa Noelle Bryan was born. We also got to know Logan very well while his family continued to live with us until after Christmas. We love grandparenting and now take the five of them on adventures regularly.

We have each had sunspots removed and fortunately, none

have been malignant. Cindy's toenails have never completely grown back because one blister after another has disrupted their normal growth pattern.

The year 1999 tested *us* heavily, but fortunately not our faith. Jerry ruptured a disc in his lower back in January. Three months later, several burglars ravaged our home and cars for five days while we were in the Philippines building houses with Jimmy Carter and 15,000 Habitat volunteers. Besides family keepsakes precious to us, and hundreds of other personal items, they took the moneybag, our daypacks, a suitcase full of Habitat Tee-shirts and most of the road-find items from the walk. Our car and one radio were the only items ever recovered. Only one person involved in the crime was apprehended.

Three months later, we were shocked to learn that Jerry had four occluded arteries in his heart and would undergo quadruple bypass surgery immediately. His surgeon says that the strong heart muscle he developed during training and the walk prevented him from having a fatal heart attack. After a challenging recovery, he is now healthy. We travel in the south frequently, but he can no longer partake of the fried foods he developed a taste for during the walk.

We both feel we are too young to stay retired, so we now work for Habitat for Humanity International out of our home office in Olympia. True to our prayer during the walk, we work and travel together as Conference Specialists while still volunteering as Global Village team leaders, Jimmy Carter Work Project volunteers and as field representatives for Habitat's Regional Center located in Oregon.

As for a new dream, this book is ending one. During the many public presentations we made about the walk, we were asked many times if we would like to do another long walk. The answer is an emphatic yes, we would like to. Will we? It is doubtful. It is hard to imagine taking the time to plan and execute another one. Maybe we will do that walk across the Grand Canyon someday. That is unfinished business. We had plans to do that before our walk across the country, but the rangers canceled that plan due to flooding in the canyon. And that trip across Ireland, just say when!

We also talk about opening a children's restaurant someday. For now, we're happy with our job, our volunteer work, being active in our family's busy lives and tooling around town in our PT Cruiser.

Jerry has landscaped our one-acre lot overlooking Lake Susan and has built a playground and nature trail for the grandchildren. Cindy has completed two quilts and has taken up the old-time art of smocking. We try to make time three to four days a week to walk a three-mile route down the hill and along the shady shores of the Deschutes River in Pioneer Park.

During the walk, we discovered a lot about the goodness of the people of America, one step at a time. As for the dream, we did not follow it blindly. We looked before we leaped, but we leapt with boldness, giving fear no firm place in our plans. We believe that to not try for fear of defeat is really the ultimate defeat. Our lives are richer for the dream and our accomplishment of that dream. Yours can be, too.

Hank from Estes Park

It was September 1999, two months after Jerry's unexpected quadruple bypass surgery. We had finished working at a Habitat conference in Estes Park, Colorado and were riding in a shuttle van to the Denver Airport. With a two-hour ride, no other passengers and Hank, a genuine "people person" driving the van, we fell into easy conversation.

Hank told us that he was retired from his first career and a new resident of this little tourist town nestled in a valley 8,000 feet above sea level in the Rocky Mountains. He was slight of build and wore a cowboy hat over his gray hair. The hat's wide brim shaded his easy smile and deep-set eyes.

As we rode along, Jerry and Cindy began to reminisce about walking through the Rockies and the Denver area three years earlier. Hank's ears perked up. He had never heard of our walk and had many questions to ask. The more he heard, the more amazed he became. His interest pushed Jerry, who was riding in the front seat, to give the highlights of an adventure that didn't get talked about much anymore. It was cathartic at a time shortly after his life had hung in the balance.

When we arrived at the airport, Hank jumped out of the van to unload our luggage. Cindy gathered her carry-ons while Jerry pulled some tip money from his wallet. Jerry disembarked and reached to shake Hank's hand.

"Thanks for a great ride and for your interest in a story that I needed to retell. He then pressed a $10 bill into Hank's hand.

Hank adamantly refused the tip.

"I've never had the honor of meeting someone who has walked across this great country of ours. Your story is all the tip I need." he paused.

"There is one more thing though. Finish that book. I want to read it."

Hank shook our hands and walked away.

Well, Hank, here it is.

To contact the authors, see more photos, read walk e-mails, try favorite recipes from host families or to remind them that you met them during Habitrek '96, visit their Web Site at:

www.solematesbook.com

For further information about
Habitat for Humanity® International
Please phone:
1-800-422-4828
or visit Habitat's website
www.habitat.org

To make a donation, mail to:

Habitat for Humanity® International
121 Habitat Street
Americus, Georgia 31709-3423

To order a book: Amazon.com\inspirationalbooks
or Habitat.org\ourhouse

Support Drivers for Habitrek '96

We would like to acknowledge each of these special folks who patiently supported us in our quest. You are remembered with fondness.

February 10	Kay & Jim Chubbuck, Paul Marshall, Patrick Schultz, Mick Appell, Becky Marvin	Olympia to Centralia, WA
February 12&13	Annie and Larry Wilson	Centralia to Castlerock, WA.
February 14	Pete Anderson	Castlerock to Kalama, WA.
February 15 & 16	Ray Johnson	Kalama to Orchard, WA.
February 19	Larry Bowman	Orchard to Washougal, WA.
February 20	Ray Johnson	Washougal to Carson, WA.
February 21	Linda Roberts-Boca	Carson to White Salmon, WA.
February 22	*No support vehicle*	White Salmon to The Dalles Bridge
February 23	Lucile Torgerson	The Dalles Bridge to Maryhill, WA
February 26-28	Ron Nelson	Maryhill to Paterson, WA
February 29-30	Betty Whittum	Plymouth, WA. to Nolin, OR.
March 4	Laura & Howard White	Nolin to Pendleton, OR.
March 5	Dorothy and Bob Cannon	Pendleton to Mission, OR.
March 6	Terry Warhol	Mission to LaGrande, OR.
March 7 & 8	*No support vehicle*	LaGrande to Haines, OR.
March 11-15	Dotty and Carl Fehring	Haines to Notus, ID.
March 18 & 19	Myrna and Larry Bowman	Notus to Boise, ID.
March 20	Glenn Barker	Boise to Mountain Home, ID.
March 21	Ken Black	Mountain Home to Glenn's Ferry, ID.

March 22	Dick Hagerman	Glenn's Ferry to Bliss, ID.
March 25	Kristy Webb	Bliss past Hagerman, ID.
March 26-28	Dorothy & Glenn Johnson, Ruth & Paul LaRue	Hagerman to Burley, ID.
March 29	*No support vehicle*	Burley to Declo, ID.
April 1-5	Lois and David Halverson	Declo to Brigham City, UT.
April 8	*No support vehicle*	Brigham City to Roy, UT.
April 9	Bernie & Don Mitchell	Roy to Layton, UT.
April 10	*No support vehicle*	Layton to Salt Lake City, UT.
April 11	Marc Miller/Katie Bryan	Salt Lake City to Park City, UT.
April 15-May 17	Janet & Walter Nelson	Park City to Byers, CO.
May 20—June 7	Ruth & Fred Hyde	Byers to Gaylord, KS.
June 10	Loretta & Vernon Kirchoff	Gaylord to Portis, KS.
June 11	Chester Sente	Portis to Glen Elder, KS.
June 12-14	Lela & Gerald Bethke	Glen Elder to Clay Center, KS.
June 17-21	Carol & Tim Bartel	Clay Center to Topeka, KS.
June 24-July 5	Jean & Curtis Wilkeson	Topeka to Vista, MO.
July 5	Pam & Denny Hardesty	Vista to Humansville, MO.
July 8-12	Suzie & Jim Bryan	Near Dunnegan to Bruner, MO.
July 15-24	Norma & Bob Olson	Bruner to Hoxie, AR.
July 25	Catherine Eades	Hoxie to Jonesboro, AR.
July 26	*No support Vehicle*	Jonesboro to Trumann, AR.
July 29-August 2	Al Stokes	Trumann to Slayden, MS.
August 5-24	Paul Marshall	Slayden to Temple, GA
August 26	Virginia & Ed Clay	Temple to Douglasville, GA.
August 28-30	Larry Bowman	Douglasville to Atlanta, GA.

HABITREK '96
TO DO LIST
1995-1996

DATE	DATE	DATE
September 20 1. Ask if we can use Good Shepherd Oct. 25th. 2. Fold Thank-You notes 3. Dr. Scholls	**October 11** 1. Develop pledge sheets and letter to go in. (Rich knows contact at The Olympian.) Names and envelopes home with Suzie Bryan 2. Re-contact AAL 3. Contact various state law enforcement agencies	**October 25** 1. Stuff envelopes and ready to mail personal pledge letter 2. Letters out to 60 affiliates. Routing assistance 3. Letters to each HFH Regional and area director 4. Letters to local churches (Please place in your newsletter) 5. Contact Good Sam Chapters
November 8 1. T-Shirts for walkers 2. Order banner and magnetic signs 3. Print songs and laminate 4. Contact Volksmarchers	**November 22** 1. Brainstorm 2. Gifts for host families, RV support, etc.? 3. Borrow RV for summer? 4. Prizes donated for walkers? By Travel Agency? Most money, etc.?	**December 6** 1. Distribute brochures around town. How? In What? 2. Initial Contact with local media 3. Donors Names computerized 4. Run labels. Office Depot for donations?
December 27 1. Start Planning kick-off walk with local HFHI 2. Figure out something to mark start/stop points along route	**January 3** 1. Mail letters to host families and RV support 2. Letters ready to mail to partnering affiliates along route	**January 17** 1. Kick-off walk work 2. Organize blue file box with maps, etc. for each state 3. Start organizing clothing, etc, by month. Familiarize everyone with list of items and potential needs
January 31 1. Kick-off walk 2. Finalize itinerary for entire walk 3. Delegate unfinished business and other details	**February 7** 1. Final kick-off to do's 2. Distribute itinerary 3. Committee help us pack and organize 4. Don't panic!	**February 10** 1. Start walk: Olympia to Centralia.

Corporate Suppliers to Habitrek '96

We would like to acknowledge these corporations for their donation of supplies and apparel. Their generosity was greatly appreciated.

Birkenstock Corporation .... DeAnn Wiley and Mark Wood
Sun Precautions .... Sean and Lori Hughes, Maria Fredrickson
Patagonia .... Seattle, San Francisco and Salt Lake City staff
Aid Association for Lutherans
Dennis Rhodes and Sue Anderson
Lands End .... Lisa Muller
Treknology Backpacks .... Alex Speer
Schering-Plough/Dr. Scholls .... June Davidson
Colorgraphics .... Fred Gustafson
The Walking Company .... Cherry Hill Mall Store - Denver
KJOY Radio .... Wayne Hagen
New England Over Shoes Company
 Second Wind Corporation/ Shoe Goo
Compeed
Neutrogena
Rapp Capps
Chaco Sandals

HabiTrek '96
ROUTE NOTES
FROM: Centralia TO: South of Toledo, Washington

B.M. MILEAGE	ROAD NAME OR #	APPROX. HWY. MP.	LANDMARK FEATURE	ROADSIDE NOTES	MILES BETWEEN	ACCUM. MILES
20	Pearl St. to Gold St.		**Centralia** Corner of Main and Pearl Streets	Sidewalk. Walk under Gold St. overpass on sidewalk	0	20.0
	Gold St.		SWW Fairgrounds	level	1.6	1.6
	Market St.		**Chehalis**	Train Depot. level	2.2	3.8
	Market St.		Washington Mutual Bank	good shoulders	0.9	4.7
	Jackson Hwy		N. Fk Newaukum River Bridge	Sidewalk on Bridge. level	5.5	10.2
	Jackson Hwy		Trodahl's Market	Nice wide shoulders farmland	0.8	11.0
	Jackson Hwy		Jct Hwy 508 gas station	shoulders narrow to 2'. Uphill, light traffic	1.8	12.8
	Jackson Hwy/ Hwy 12		**Mary's Corner.** Texaco and Mini-Mart	Porta-pots	2.5	15.3
	Jackson Hwy		Lewis & Clark State Park	Shoulder widens good shoulders bathrooms	1.7	17.0
	Jackson Hwy	MP 13	Oak Meadows Road	20 miles from Harrison Ave. I/C	1.6	18.6
	Jackson Hwy		Tucker Road	20 miles from downtown Centralia @ Main & Pearl	1.4	20.0
	Jackson Hwy/ Hwy 505		Cowlitz Prairie Grange Bike Route starts	level to downhill	2.3	22.3
	Hwy 505		Down Town **Toledo** Red Apple Market. BP Station	Cowlitz River Bridge. Narrow shoulder on left	1.1	23.4
	Hwy 505/ Barnes Drive		Intersection to Mt. St. Helens	exit to right towards I-5 wide shoulder-uphill	0.5	23.9
	Barnes Drive at I-5		I-5 Interchange	Cross I-5 on to Barnes Drive. Low traffic volume. Level but substandard gravel shoulder. No bathroom.	5.2	29.1
	Barnes Drive		Dead bus parking lot	No shoulder. Caution. Uphill. Sunset Lodge. Parallel to RR tracks then uphill	4.8	33.9
	Barnes Drive		Cross over I-5. RV Park	Cross over the Cowlitz River. Very poor shoulders.	0.8	34.7
	Dougherty Rd.		**Castle Rock** exit.	Walk alongside on Dougherty Rd. A.M. P.M. with clean restroom. Variety store at this intersection.	2.9	37.6
	Kalmbach Rd.		Intersection with Pacific Ave. North	Top of hill is 20 miles from Cowlitz Grange. Parallels I-5. Good shoulders.	0.8	38.4
	Headquarters Rd.		Cross under I-5.	Poor shoulder. Nice view of River. Cross under RR. Cool trestle.	2.3	40.7
	Headquarters Rd.		Intersection	Outskirts of Kelso	0.9	41.6
	Pacific Ave. No and Kelso Ave.			Stay on Kelso Ave. to Allen Street. Turn left onto Allen until I-5. Turn right onto	4.1	45.7
	Allen St.		Intersection of I-5 and Allen St.	**Kelso**	2.4	48.1
	Kelso Drive		Intersection of I-5 and Kelso Dr.	(Save 0.43 miles by taking Diagonal Rd.)	0.8	48.9

HabiTrek '96 Training Schedule

December 1995

Sunday	Monday	Tuesday	Wednesday	Thursday	Friday	Saturday
					1 Bike 30 Minutes Floor Exercises Weights	2 9.5 Miles
3 OFF	4 9.5 Miles	5 5 Miles	6 17 Miles	7 5 Miles	8 Bike 30 Minutes Floor Exercises Weights	9 12 Miles
10 OFF (2 Months To Go)	11 9.5 Miles	12 7 Miles	13 18 Miles	14 7 Miles	15 Bike 30 Minutes Floor Exercises Weights	16 11.5 Miles
17 OFF	18 12.5 Miles	19 7 Miles	20 19 Miles	21 7 Miles	22 Bike 30 Minutes Floor Exercises Weights	23 13 Miles
24 OFF	25 OFF	26 12.5 Miles	27 7 Miles	28 10 Miles	29 Bike 30 Minutes Floor Exercises Weights	30 14 Miles
31 OFF						